Assessing Allegations of Sexual Abuse in Preschool Children

Interpersonal Violence:
The Practice Series

Jon R. Conte, Series Editor

Sandra K. Hewitt

Assessing Allegations of Sexual Abuse in Preschool Children

Understanding Small Voices

IVPS

Interpersonal Violence:
The Practice Series

SAGE Publications
International Educational and Professional Publisher
Thousand Oaks   London   New Delhi

For information address:

SAGE Publications, Inc.
2455 Teller Road
Thousand Oaks, California 91320
E-mail: order@sagepub.com

SAGE Publications Ltd.
6 Bonhill Street
London EC2A 4PU
United Kingdom

SAGE Publications India Pvt. Ltd.
M-32 Market
Greater Kailash I
New Delhi 110 048 India

Printed in the United States of America

Library of Congress Cataloging-in-Publication Data

Hewitt, Sandra K.
    Assessing allegations of sexual abuse in preschool children:
    Understanding small voices / by Sandra K. Hewitt.
        p. cm.— (Interpersonal violence; v. 22)
    Includes bibliographical references and index.
    ISBN 0-7619-0204-X (cloth: acid-free paper)
    ISBN 0-7619-0205-8 (pbk.: acid-free paper)
        1. Child abuse—Investigation. 2. Interviewing in child abuse.
    3. Communicative competence in children. I. Title. II. Series.
    HV8079.C48 H48 1998
    363.25'9536—ddc21   98-25456

This book is printed on acid-free paper.

99 00 01 02 03 04 05 7 6 5 4 3 2 1

Acquiring Editor:	C. Terry Hendrix
Production Editor:	Wendy Westgate
Production Assistant:	Karen Wiley
Typesetter:	Lynn Miyata

Contents

Preface

We substantiate child sexual abuse by what children are able to tell us about their experiences. Taken alone, young children's words are not strong enough to bear the weight of substantiation for abuse allegations. Yet children are among the most vulnerable to acts of abuse, and their inability to talk about their experiences makes them difficult to protect. This book reconceptualizes the task of assessing young children for abuse. By buttressing small voices with an understanding of developmental contexts, behavioral repertoires, and objective measures, we may be better able to hear what these children have experienced. At the same time, we may be better able to protect them. The following chapters lay a foundation of theory and research based on new ways of viewing assessment. Most important, they integrate clinical practice with practical formats for practitioners to apply to the task of assessment.

I wrote this book with my feet in two separate camps, each with its own very different standards and philosophies:

The first camp is *child development theory and research*. The standards of best practice here involve testing specific hypotheses with different samples, using well-controlled procedures. An important tenet in this domain is the caution not to apply data from one study to an entire population.

The second camp is *clinical practice*. Clinical practice informs us about the interpersonal work with individuals. No one research study can ever encompass all the variables found in a specific child. Current standards for best clinical practice are those techniques that generally "work" in the difficult job of assessing children. Sometimes they are validated with research, but mostly they are not.

Huge chasms exist between these two camps, and often information is not shared across the expanse. The best practice integrates theory and research, but there are almost no road maps for this unchartered territory in regard to the young child. Although I have tried to bridge theory and practice and integrate the result with applied techniques, this is new work and, like any pioneering effort, there will surely be areas to improve as others also join the rethinking of these critical issues.

Recognizing that it can be problematic to present clinical practice ideas along with research and theory, I offer the clinical ideas as just that—ideas that have done their time in clinical settings. Some of these ideas have been subjected to research and they will continue to undergo refinement. It might have been easier to wait to write this book until more information was available, but we can't stem the daily flow of children who need services now.

It is my hope that this volume will lead to better assessment for young children while we continue to build a better understanding of the work we do. The contexts of both research-based information and the richness of clinical experience have validity and deserve respect. It is true that we need more research in order to validate some of these suggestions for new assessment procedures, but we cannot wait for all that to come in. It is important to act now. It is my hope that the informed possibilities in this volume will give the small voices of preschool children a better chance to be heard.

Two audiences will find this book of special value: (a) frontline workers, including police officers, child protection workers, and interview specialists, who are assessing young children for sexual abuse allegations; and (b) mental health professionals who are doing more extended evaluations of children who have allegedly been abused. The material will be useful regardless of one's background or level of expertise.

The first three chapters provide a foundation for the overall topic. Chapter 1 introduces the focus of the book. Chapter 2 is essential child development information that might have most relevance to the first audience above, particularly those lacking foundational course work. Chapter 3 is a collection of information on the research issues that directly affect child abuse assessment and is important for both audiences. Chapters 4 and 5 apply the theory and research to practical assessment strategies. Chapters 6 through 8 deal with applied practice issues: a review of current interview formats, a protocol for interviewing preschool children, and the monitoring of court-ordered re-unification. The book concludes with suggestions for future directions.

Throughout the book, I have integrated practical clinical ideas and applied practice ideas with the content. These ideas are highlighted in the text. For example, *Clinical Practice Notes* are set apart in italics near discussions of theoretical or assessment topics. Second, *Implications for Practice* are located at the end of many sections. These notations are designed to make the material more available for direct application in your day-to-day work. I hope you find them helpful.

Acknowledgments

There are so many thanks that I owe. The children I have seen over the years are the primary influence in creating this book; I have learned so much from them and they have been so tolerant of my mistakes. Colleagues and friends have assisted in many ways: Drs. Chuck Nelson and Pat Bauer, faculty at the University of Minnesota Institute of Child Development, first directed me toward much of the reading in early childhood, and then Chuck agreed to help me on an extended fellowship basis.

The Bush Foundation's award of a Leadership Fellowship for continued study in preschool development directly supported the work in Chapters 3 and 5. Without their generous support, I would not have had the luxury of time to read, to think in a quiet, focused way, and to consult with so many people. The Bush fellowship directly contributed the costs of my contact with Robyn Fivush, Karen Saywitz, and Judy DeLoache, all of whom generously offered me time and advice (and more references to read) as I was constructing this volume. My heartfelt thanks to each of these researchers.

Special thanks to many of my talented colleagues and friends. Betty Carlson helped me better understand the idea of attachment and the research around it, whereas Mark Everson clarified my purpose and expanded the information on children's idiosyncratic accounts of abuse. Bill Friedrich's help in conceptualizing the assessment process was invaluable. Mary Kenning brought her understanding and experience with an offender population to the issue of preschool children's safety, and Marge Steward kindly forwarded her recent research findings and included encouragement when I most needed it. Anne Graffam Walker offered her careful additions to my information on children's language (and on my own language!).

Without Ann West, my Sage developmental copy editor, this book would not have been published; her gifted insights clarified the focus of this book and made it more available to readers.

Colleagues from our monthly Preschool Consultation Group (Vicki Nauschultz, Georganne Farseth, Nancy Lawroski, Deb Clemensen, Linda Bernstein, and Lisa Mages Braverman), all wonderfully competent "frontline" practitioners, took time to read my initial manuscript and offer comments and suggestions. I am indebted to them for their support and encouragement. Ann Ahlquist, Larry Simon, and Judy Wegman have read and commented on this work from their various perspectives in child protection, law enforcement, and forensic interviewer. Lisa Moriarty has waded through the entire process, cheerfully transcribing and efficiently correcting the various drafts, while Dale Rehm and Peggy Nelson assisted in the proofreading. To all of you, thanks.

Finally, and most important, thanks to my family. In the past months, our children, Erri, Anne, and Josh, have periodically told me, "You're not listening to full sentences anymore, Mom," and they have reminded me when I need to get my priorities straight. In doing so, they have kept me in touch with the things that matter most in life. Most of all, however, my indebtedness is to my husband, Tom, without whose help and encouragement I would never have written this book.

❖

For Tom
my husband and anchor

❖

Protecting Our Children
From Sexual Abuse

Across the years of clinical practice there are some cases that stand out more than others. The following evaluation referral was one such case for me.

A 2-year-old child was in shelter with her mother. The mother had been badly beaten by her alcoholic husband. Shelter staff noted when the mother diapered her daughter that the child would become upset, repeatedly grab her vulva, and cry, "Daddy hurt butt! Daddy hurt butt!" Advocates at the shelter pushed the mother to report her daughter's behavior to authorities, and the mother did. Police and child protection personnel collaborated on an investigation, but the child's immature speech and language provided little information. When the child was referred for further evaluation, she did repeat the statements she had made earlier but was unable to give any detail or context. The mother noted she had never observed her husband spank or physically abuse their child, but it was unclear if the child's concern was related

1

to abuse, diapering problems, or spanking. When observed with her father, she was fearful and anxious; afterward, her sleep was disturbed. It was impossible to prove this fear was from abuse and not from witnessing her mother's beating. Despite these signs of distress, no case could be substantiated because the child could not provide enough detail regarding the concerns. At the father's insistence, the child was returned to him for unsupervised visitation, but now there was one important change—the mother no longer accompanied the child.

For a long time I was troubled by this case. I did not want an innocent person accused of abuse, but I also did not want to subject a vulnerable child to a dangerous situation. There seemed so little that could be done in response to this child's signaled distress and fear.

I have often heard these same concerns expressed by police and child protection workers who investigate cases of alleged abuse with very young children. "I think abuse has probably happened, but there's just not enough to substantiate." This concern is echoed in our national statistics. The most recent data (1998) from the National Clearinghouse on Child Abuse and Neglect profiles 1996 statistics. When all rates of child abuse are summed, the highest rates are for the youngest children (0–6), and they taper off as the child grows older. Yet when sexual abuse data are considered, the relationship is inverse; the younger the child, the lower the level of substantiated abuse. Do these data reflect actual incidence of lower levels of sexual abuse with this population, or do they reflect the difficult job of substantiating sexual abuse in children who cannot talk? These data are not broken down into substantiated or unsubstantiated cases, so it is difficult to address this question in this population. Although depicting different populations, data from the Thoennes and Tjaden (1990) study of sexual abuse allegations in the context of custody/visitation disputes are the most available statistics that specifically focus on age and sexual abuse substantiation.

These data clearly reflect lower levels of likely abuse and higher levels of unlikely or indeterminate cases of sexual abuse with a younger age, whereas the inverse is reflected as a child matures.

The younger the child, the lower the substantiation rates. Does this suggest younger children were not abused as often? Probably not; in fact, younger children are more vulnerable than older children as their normal diapering and bathing needs repeatedly expose them to possible abusive situations. Yet without substantiation, there is little hope for protection. Why the disparity between the need for protection of

Table 1.1 Sexual Abuse Allegations in the Context of Custody/Visitation Disputes

Abuse Allegations Perceived As	Age of Victim		
	0–3	4–6	7+
Likely	25%	42%	56%
Unlikely	38%	44%	29%
Indeterminate	38%	14%	15%

the most vulnerable children and the obviously low level of substantiation for the very same children?

The truth lies in this fact: These children could not talk. *We document child sexual abuse by how well children can talk about what has happened to them.* In other words, substantiation rates mirror the ability to talk, not probable abuse. Once children reach age 3, their speech and language reach the level of development where it is understood by most adults, and substantiation rates begin to better reflect their histories.

Random House Webster's College Dictionary (1995) gives one definition of voice as "(noun) the *right* to present and receive consideration of one's desires or opinions" [italics added]. The voice of young children is impeded by immature cognition and language. And our current verbal assessment procedures do not help extend them a voice. Something needs to be changed. But what?

❏ Why Our Current System Is Not Working

Before we consider what to do, we must face the issue of whether this is really an important issue to address. Some say that if these young children cannot talk much, then maybe they don't remember much either. After all, few memories of very early childhood survive into adult memory. This argument is strongly refuted by new research on the importance of development during the early years of life. Instruments like the PET scan can now help us unlock functions of the brain in a way we were not able to before. Feedback from such instruments and data from allied research are offering new information almost daily. The more we learn, the more critical these years are seen to be.

In the press to protect these children, we are called to do a better job of assessment. How can this happen?

First, we need to understand more about such children. What are they like? How do they think? How do they feel? How do they socialize? How do they change over time? Nowhere in life does change occur more rapidly than during the preschool years. In three short years, newborns, who could not talk or walk, can now talk with most adults and move quickly (as any parent will tell you) to explore their new world. The early years are marked by major changes in many areas that affect a child's response to interviewing: language increases, new concepts are understood, memory is put into words, and play is able to reflect a child's experience. All these skills mature during the preschool years. If we are to assess with better methods, we need to understand this rapid change. We need a flexible framework for assessing children with emerging skills, measures that can adapt to rapidly changing status over time.

Next, we need to know how young children store memory, how they express and retrieve it. Young children can and do remember, often for quite lengthy periods of time and with great accuracy. But children do not always express information in words, and their small voices often reflect only a minimal understanding of their experience. Behaviors are precursors to language (Fivush, 1996) and powerful pieces of what preschool children have to disclose about their experiences. We may be overlooking the importance of behavior or nonverbal data in our attempt to get good verbal reports. We need to learn how to "read" these behaviors, developing assessment measures that consider both spoken language and behavioral repertoire. At this time, however, we have no research-based assessment format for evaluating these behaviors.

Another consideration for better assessment is the recognition that not all children develop in exactly the same way, at the same time. Each child progresses within the unique context of his or her environment. For example, children reared in physically or emotionally impoverished environments offer a very different face for assessment. Assessment measures need to take into account not just a child's changing development but also the varying effects caused by environmental interactions such as abuse. Our current assessment process, for instance, rarely uses protocols that explore the various skills required in abuse-focused interviews.

Most important, we need to match assessment strategies—to match the child's needs and status rather than expect the child to match our strategy. Young children are frequently assessed using standard, verbally focused interviews used with older children, but current assessment tools rarely assess the younger child adequately. In addition to stressing good verbalization, they emphasize free recall. However, young children do not provide good free recall. In short, we have no effective standardized framework for assessing minimally verbal children.

We do have some research-based knowledge to help us protect this age group. As mentioned above, there is ample evidence that young children can and do remember early events. Pathology that stems from child abuse is also increasingly documented. It is the one form of psychopathology with implications across the life span that we can really do something to minimize. Young children are among the most vulnerable children for abuse, yet their immaturity makes them one of the most difficult groups to protect when sexual abuse substantiation rests on verbal documentation. Our tools must better capture the needs of the children who are not yet able to tell us what has happened.

New models for abuse assessment are constructed in Chapters 4 and 5, but before turning to direct practice strategies, we need to consider the foundations for these strategies. Meaningful and effective strategies need to be anchored in good theory and research as well as clinical experience. Our consideration of the foundations for new practice approaches will be presented in layers, much like the developmental process in children. Earlier layers provide the base for later, more complex or detailed learning. We will look at three areas:

1. Sexual development (normative and clinical sexual behaviors) (this chapter)
2. Child development theory and how it provides that background against which the symptoms or expressions of child abuse must be understood (Chapter 2)
3. Research on children's memory and the implications for how abuse experiences may be stored and recalled (Chapter 3)

We will conclude by summarizing the implications of this information and proposing a new conceptualization of preschool assessment.

❏ Childhood Sexual Behavior

We commonly look at sexual behavior when we suspect sexual abuse in young children. Research indicates that sexual behaviors are the most frequent sequelae of sexual abuse (Browne & Finkelhor, 1986; Kendell-Tackett, Williams, & Finkelhor, 1993). But before we can argue that such behaviors are evidence of possible sexual abuse, we need to understand what normal sexuality is like in young children, what sexual behaviors are found in sexually abused children, and what behavioral problems are associated with sexual abuse in young children.

NORMAL SEXUAL DEVELOPMENT

Two-year-olds delight in running around naked after baths, and they are eager to lift up their shirts or pull down their pants to show you their belly buttons. Very young children have an unfettered joy in their bodies. How do we know when a behavior is normal or indicative of abuse at early ages? It is difficult to complete effective research on sexuality in young children because parents rarely want a researcher to ask their children sexual questions. Two recent studies used child care facilities to look at the behavior of preschoolers.

Phipps-Yonas, Yonas, Turner, and Kauper (1993) surveyed day care providers about the type of sexual activity they observed with children. Children ages 1 to 3 were seen by the providers as comfortable with their own nudity, both with peers and grown-ups; comfortable touching women's breasts; and comfortable observing each other's genitals. It was found that young children almost never draw genitals on figures (children this age are usually unable to draw representationally), are not seen as acting out sexual activities with dolls or stuffed animals, do not tend to touch the genitals of other children or other adults, and do not tend to hit or hurt private parts. Behaviors with a very low probability, especially with children younger than age 4, are things such as efforts to engage in sexual intercourse; french kissing; requests to have another child suck, lick, or kiss their genitals; and attempts to insert objects into their own or another's buttocks or vaginas.

Children ages 4 to 6 were seen by the providers as having somewhat different sexual behaviors. These children were less comfortable with nudity, much more curious about the mechanics of sexual activity and reproduction, more likely to engage in exploratory sexual games (e.g.,

"I'll show you mine, if you show me yours"), and much less likely to touch women's breasts; they were observed to rarely draw genitals on figures; to interact spontaneously, at least occasionally, in sensual or sexual ways; and to initiate sexual behaviors they had heard about. About a third of the providers said that 4- to 6-year-olds were observed to bribe, trick, or bully children into sexual activities and that they could act out sexual activities with dolls or stuffed animals. Touching other children's genitals was less frequent than with young children, and there was evidence of increasing age-related shame or guilt about sexual areas. The majority of both groups did not masturbate, but about 30% of the providers saw children masturbate occasionally during nap time, although there was less certainty here than in other areas.

Lindblad, Gustafsson, Larsson, and Lundin (1995) had day care staff at Swedish centers complete a questionnaire about preschool children's sexual behaviors. Behaviors such as searching for body contact and responding to body contact were frequent. Fewer than 1% of the children were found to exhibit the following behaviors: touching an adult's genitals, attempting to make the adult touch the child's genitals, using objects against their own or other children's genitals or anus, or masturbating obsessively ("without pleasure or in a way that caused pain"). Fewer than 2% of the children displayed behaviors such as exhibiting their own genitals, playing sexually explorative games, initiating games with a similarity to adult sexual activity, using sexual words, and attempting to touch a woman's breast.

Data from these two studies, although from different cultures, are complementary. These results can help provide a frame of reference for statistically "normal" sexual behaviors in young children. The presence of other sexualized behaviors signals the need for special attention.

NORMATIVE VERSUS SEXUALLY ABUSED CHILDREN'S BEHAVIOR

Clarifying the differences between these two types of behaviors is at the heart of sexual abuse assessment. To establish normative sexual behaviors in children, Friedrich, Grambsch, Broughton, Kuiper, and Bielke (1991) surveyed parents at an outpatient pediatric practice where each case was screened for possible abuse and the parents were asked to identify the child's behaviors from a list of behaviors presented. Normative sexual behaviors were developed from the responses of these parents. The same measure was then used to assess the frequency of these behaviors in a population of children with known abuse, and from this measure, statistical analysis determined levels of significance for the differences in the behaviors of the two groups (Friedrich et al., 1992). Further analysis of these data indicates response differences to items across ages and sexes (Friedrich, 1993).

The newly published measure developed from this research, the Child Sexual Behavior Inventory (CSBI; Friedrich, 1997), is the only research-based measure that provides information on the type and frequency of sexualized behaviors in young children. This parent report measure (see Table 1.2 for a partial list of terms), is for use with children ages 2 to 12. When parent responses are scored, the measure provides three clinical scales: the CSBI Total, Developmentally Related Sexual Behaviors (DRSB), and Sexual Abuse Specific Items (SASI). Separation of developmentally related behaviors from abuse-related behaviors is especially important for younger children. Developmentally related sexual behaviors for children ages 2 to 5 vary slightly for girls and boys, as demonstrated in Tables 1.2 and 1.3. (Note: A full list of the behaviors of sexually abused preschool children can be found in the CSBI manual and score sheet.)

Kendall-Tackett, Williams, and Finkelhor (1993), in their excellent review of the literature about the effect of sexual abuse on children, note that sexual behaviors are the most common sequelae of sexual abuse. Therefore, it is important to understand which behaviors are associated with sexual abuse and which are not. Taken together, the above studies on the CSBI have looked at both normative and clinical sexual behaviors of young children, and these data offer the best information about the differences found in abused and nonabused young children. There is fairly robust evidence that explicit sexualized behaviors (e.g., oral sexual contact, direct genital contact in a sexual way, etc.) are rare in a population of nonabused preschoolers.

BEHAVIOR PROBLEMS IN
SEXUALLY ABUSED CHILDREN

Because sexual abuse is hard to substantiate in young children, it is difficult to find research on the problems in this population. Kendall-Tackett et al. (1993) found that the most common disturbances

Table 1.2 CSBI Clinical/Normative Male and Female Endorsement Contrasts

Item (abbreviated)	Normative Girls Age 2-6 (N=252)	Clinical Girls Age 2-6 (N=74)	Normative Girls Age 7-12 (N=174)	Clinical Girls Age 7-12 (N=113)	Normative Boys Age 2-6 (N=248)	Clinical Boys Age 2-6 (N=41)	Normative Boys Age 7-12 (N=206)	Clinical Boys Age 7-12 (N=48)
Puts mouth on sex parts	.0	12.2	.0	4.4	.4	17.1	.0	16.7
Asks to engage in sex acts	.0	10.8	.6	14.2	1.2	22.0	.0	20.8
Masturbates with object	.8	21.6	1.7	7.1	.8	17.1	.0	4.2
Inserts objects in vagina/anus	2.8	28.4	.6	3.5	.0	19.5	.0	10.4
Imitates intercourse	.4	21.6	1.7	5.3	1.6	19.5	2.4	16.7
Sexual sounds	.8	17.6	.6	8.0	.4	14.6	3.9	25.0
French kisses	4.0	21.6	1.7	5.3	1.6	19.5	2.4	10.4
Undresses other people	4.4	21.6	.0	14.2	4.4	22.0	.5	16.7
Asks to watch explicit TV	1.6	6.8	3.4	15.0	.0	19.5	6.8	18.7
Imitates sexual behavior with dolls	4.0	21.6	7.5	15.0	.8	22.0	1.5	12.5
Wants to be opposite sex	7.5	13.5	1.1	7.1	7.3	17.1	1.9	8.3
Talks about sexual acts	2.8	33.8	10.3	28.3	2.4	31.7	9.2	43.7
Dresses like opposite sex	9.5	5.4	2.9	5.3	6.0	12.2	3.4	8.3
Touches others' sex parts	5.6	36.5	4.0	13.3	8.9	41.5	4.9	27.1
Rubs body against people	8.3	39.2	4.6	17.7	8.5	24.4	4.4	25.0
Hugs strange adults	14.3	45.9	4.0	23.0	6.5	29.3	2.4	8.3
Shows sex parts to children	7.5	31.1	2.3	15.0	15.7	43.9	4.4	29.2

(continued)

Table 1.2 Continued

Item (abbreviated)	Normative Girls Age 2-6 (N = 252)	Clinical Girls Age 2-6 (N = 74)	Normative Girls Age 7-12 (N = 174)	Clinical Girls Age 7-12 (N = 113)	Normative Boys Age 2-6 (N = 248)	Clinical Boys Age 2-6 (N = 41)	Normative Boys Age 7-12 (N = 206)	Clinical Boys Age 7-12 (N = 48)
Uses sexual words	1.2	23.0	12.1	31.9	4.8	43.9	19.9	52.1
Overly aggressive, overly passive	17.5	47.3	8.6	38.9	8.1	29.3	6.3	29.2
Talks flirtatiously	15.9	20.3	14.9	19.5	8.5	14.6	2.9	14.6
Pretends to be opposite sex	20.6	12.2	8.0	11.5	16.9	24.4	2.9	10.4
Masturbates with hand	16.3	41.9	8.6	18.6	22.6	43.9	11.2	43.7
Looks at nude pictures	7.9	14.9	18.4	14.2	11.3	19.5	27.2	41.7
Shows sex parts to adults	17.9	28.4	6.9	9.7	25.8	26.8	9.7	16.7
Touches sex parts in public	19.0	37.8	2.9	10.6	35.5	39.0	15.5	27.1
Interested in opposite sex	20.6	31.1	32.8	46.9	21.0	29.3	19.9	47.9
Tries to look at people undressing	33.3	45.9	14.9	18.6	33.9	48.8	27.7	41.7
Touches breasts	48.4	58.1	9.2	11.5	43.5	48.8	11.7	22.9
Kisses nonfamily children	55.2	45.9	21.3	30.1	41.1	39.0	9.7	20.8
Kisses nonfamily adults	52.4	50.0	26.4	29.2	41.1	34.0	18.9	27.1
Sits with crotch exposed	59.1	60.8	29.9	36.3	35.1	26.5	15.5	27.1
Undresses in front of others	61.9	56.8	23.0	31.0	49.6	61.0	21.4	37.5
Touches sex parts at home	54.4	58.1	18.4	24.8	64.1	73.2	36.4	50.0
Scratches crotch	67.9	63.5	34.5	33.6	58.1	56.1	40.8	50.0
Boy-girl toys	71.4	43.2	42.5	26.5	63.3	56.1	30.6	31.2

Table 1.3   Developmentally Related Sexual Behaviors in Children
2 to 5 Years

Boys and Girls
Stands too close to people
Touches or tries to touch their mother's or other women's breasts
Touches sex (private) parts when at home
Tries to look at people when they are nude or undressing
Add for Boys
Touches sex (private) parts in public places

SOURCE: (Friedrich, 1997).

resulting from sexual abuse were in the sense of self, self and others, and in self-regulation. However, they hypothesize there is no one "syndrome" indicative of sexual abuse, and that abuse may have different forms and effects at various ages. There is a body of research with young children that points toward discernable differences in the behaviors of some sexually abused versus nonabused young children. One aspect of this theorizing might be the frequency of sexualized behaviors with very young versus older children found by Friedrich (1993) on the CSBI. Younger children display more sexualized behaviors, as they are not mature enough to screen out inappropriate behaviors, and their behaviors may more transparently reflect the events they have experienced.

Three preliminary studies conducted by Hewitt and Friedrich (1991) Hewitt, Friedrich, and Allen (1994), and Schirvar (1998) present beginning information on the behaviors of young sexually abused children. When preschoolers who were referred to a specialty child abuse resource were evaluated (Hewitt & Friedrich, 1991), children age 3 and under who were "probably abused" were significantly differentiated from "probably not abused" children by increased levels of sexualized behaviors on the CSBI and by sleep disturbances. (Because none of the younger children in this sample could sufficiently describe their experience, the two groupings of children were considered "probably" abused or not abused.) "Probably abused" children's data included medical findings, or explicit behavioral reenactment accompanied by behavioral repertoire associated with abuse (e.g., sleep disturbance, spontaneous sexualized play, etc.). "Probably not abused" children had no medical evidence of abuse, no behavioral reenactments, little specific verbalized content, and little evidence of behavioral repertoire. Hewitt et al. (1994) found spontaneous sexualized play a significant discriminator between "probably abused" and "probably not abused" children in a sample of 21 two-year-olds. Schirvar (1998) analyzed data from a national sample of 31 possibly sexually abused children, 24 to 36 months of age. He found physical injury and other reliable corroborating information (from child protection, police, day care) to be the most reliable information used to document sexual abuse, but such findings were rare in this sample. Although no one measure of abuse was found to consistently implicate sexual abuse, he found the presence of sexualized behaviors to be the best marker for differentiating sexual abuse. He stressed, however, that they cannot be used in isolation. The CSBI proved helpful in discriminating developmentally related sexual behaviors from abuse-specific behaviors, but scores were subject to parental bias. Overall, clinician's observation, background, and training were important in evaluating the significance of the behavior and weighing it in the context of the child's background and history.

Other important assessment issues were clarified by an analysis of these studies:

1. The importance of careful behavioral charting and behavioral repertoire emerged as a critical factor in assessing abuse at this young age.
2. All studies also highlighted the importance of objective measures, collateral contacts, and interviewer observations in helping evaluate the effects of parental bias in abuse reporting.
3. The context of the child's first allegations is important to assess as it has the potential to influence the child's later statements or an interpretation of the child's behaviors.

---•◆•---

Implications for Child Abuse Assessment

1. The importance of developmental stage knowledge helps us determine which behaviors are truly atypical, and associated with abuse, at different ages. Without this information we cannot successfully argue the uniqueness of certain behaviors as indicators of possible abuse.
2. Research points toward the need to carefully assess behaviors over a period of time and across situations. It is also important to carefully document the environmental context of the child when considering the issue of possible abuse symptoms.

3. Explicit sexualized behaviors in young children have been found to be associated with sexual abuse backgrounds, although there are exceptions. Sleep disturbance and repetitive, compulsive play behaviors have been preliminarily associated with an abuse history.

4. All behaviors of young children must be understood in the context of their backgrounds and experience and the response bias of reporters must be considered.

5. Clusters of behaviors rather than isolated behaviors may be more indicative of an abuse history.

ABUSE IS MORE THAN JUST SEX

To evaluate sexual abuse in young children, we need a focus that goes beyond just sexual behavior. A child's developmental status shapes the way the child perceives, stores, and retrieves information about abuse. It also shapes the way abuse affects the child and dictates how a child must be interviewed. It is virtually impossible to adequately assess young children without a good background in child development. The next two chapters provide this. Chapter 2 covers the material on how children grow, think, socialize, and feel and then adapts this information to the specialized problems of assessment with constantly changing children. Chapter 3 focuses on what children remember, how they remember, and how long and how accurately they can remember. It provides a review of research on the nature, length, and quality of young children's memory and argues that young children can and do remember even very early events. In addition, the influence of early nonverbal experiences on developing feelings and brains is also covered in the sections on attachment and neurobiology in Chapter 3.

You may be tempted to skip these chapters and go straight for the "how to" stuff, but one cannot overestimate the importance of understanding child sexual abuse in its developmental context. Children will often say or do something that throws off an interviewer's entire line of questioning. I think of these times as "right-hand turns with no blinkers." The following chapters supply a framework to understand what children do and why. It is from this framework that the best ideas for improving assessment can be drawn.

2

How Children Express Themselves: Understanding Developmental Context

The way in which young children perceive, store, and express abuse is shaped by their stage of development. It is essential to have a thorough understanding of these shifting stages throughout the preschool years if we are to effectively assess allegations of abuse. The characteristics of various developmental stages also dictate the format for the type of assessment we must do.

This chapter briefly reviews the course of early childhood development, highlighting important concepts and terms and focusing on implications for abuse assessment. The review emphasizes the traditional areas of cognitive, emotional, social, and sexual development throughout childhood: infancy (0–18 months), toddlerhood (18–30 months), early childhood (30 months–4 years), and preschool years (ages 4–5).

For the purpose of this book, however, the ages within these four groupings are slightly different because the information is organized to reflect the changing abilities children have to participate in an abuse assessment. Actually, developmental changes are best considered as broad bands of skills rather than discrete stages. For example, some children's skills will enable them to move into the next grouping whereas other children's skills develop more slowly and are more like those of younger children. Nevertheless, to expedite this discussion we will use here four classifications of children, according to the type of assessment that is appropriate for the abilities of each group.

- *Infancy.* No involvement is expected of the infant. Assessment is through physical signs or eyewitness observation only.
- *Very Young Children* (18–36 months) (Stage 1 Interview). Very young children's actions and their few words give cues to possible abuse, but there is heavy emphasis on the assessor to anchor and structure this information within the child's status and history.
- *Young Children* (3–4 years) (Stage 2 Interview). These young children can participate in abuse assessment, but this is a period of transitioning skills. The emergence of several new skills across this time requires that the assessor carefully evaluate the current status of these children's capabilities to ensure that the best match between interview style and the skills of the child is offered.
- *Early Elementary School-Aged Children* (5–6 years) (Stage 3 Interview). Most of these children are able to respond to standardized interview formats; however, there are still important interview abilities they do not possess.

The following are the *basic tenets* of child development theory:

- Human development is not a random process.
- Early, simpler skills are the basis for later, more complex skills.
- Development unfolds in an organized manner.
- Basic biology contributes certain levels of potential.
- Development of potential is affected by interactions with the environment.

An environment that is attuned to the needs and capacities of the child, and presents new learning at a time when the child is ready for mastery, results in a child with richer growth.

Nowhere across the life span does development move more quickly, or involve such dramatic change, as it does in the preschool years. Let's start with the beginnings of life.

❏ Infancy (0–18 Months)

We do not think of sexual abuse happening to children at this age, but it does. Infants and toddlers cannot talk about their experiences so sexual abuse is rarely documented, and then only under certain circumstances such as (a) a confession by the perpetrator, (b) an eyewitness to sexually abusive acts, (c) the presence of sperm or semen that can be assigned to a specific body, or (d) the presence of sexually transmitted diseases or medical damage.

We often think of children this young as being in a stage of growth that is basically physical, with little going on in their emotional or psychological development. However, this is not the case. Infancy, in fact, is a surprisingly critical stage of development.

OVERVIEW OF CHARACTERISTICS

The first 18 months of life involve incredible change across several areas of growth: social and emotional growth (including attachment), thinking (also called cognition), sexuality, and memory.

Social and Emotional Growth

Children are born with a capacity for relatedness:

[The] response to others as "co-beings" and not as objects is present early in life. Evidence for this can be found in the early sociability of infants . . . . At birth, hearing is most responsive to the human voice, and newborns are capable of remarkable discriminations in human speech. . . . The visual system is also structured to attend to those stimulus features that characterize the human eyes and face . . . and within the first weeks of life the infant develops a strong preference for them. Nursing in close physical contact with caregivers is the primary functions of the sucking and grasping reflexes. Research has revealed a number of other remarkable social capacities of newborns: they have a highly developed sense of smell that enables them to identify the unique odors of their mothers, they are capable of complex imitations, they engage in reactive empathetic crying, and they are able to coordinate their limbs to the rhythm of adult speech.

    These rather remarkable social sensitivities of infants and newborns reveal a strongly developed sense of relationship with others that is present from birth. The infant is biologically anchored and oriented in the social world; . . . [A] special relationship with others . . . is something that is elaborated from these primitive forms of attunement with others. (Vandenberg, 1991, pp. 1281-1282)

"A baby cannot exist alone, but is essentially part of a relationship" (Winnicott, 1960/1965). The idea of a self *emerging* through the interactions with a caretaker is essential to understand. The organizational framework for the emerging self is in the quality of the early infant-caretaker relationship; the infant is embedded in the caretaking process. The caregiver's response to the infant's signals shapes the signals' meaning and organizes them as a part of a meaningful system. From the regulation found in this early dyadic interaction, the child moves to later self-regulation. In this framework, the child is not just presenting a series of developmental stages that emerge biologically, the self is also shaped by the quality of the caregiving and the organization in this relationship. From early sensory experiences, the child begins to be organized and, as language gets incorporated into this existing system, it integrates the sensory experiences. Essential movement during these early months involves a subordination and integration of existing skills into newer, more complex levels of organization (Sroufe, 1989).

> *The abuse of young children is a violation of the bonds of healthy attachment and a betrayal of the trust children must have in adults to provide adequately for their needs, but it is even more than a simple violation or betrayal. The aberrant patterns of relationship that are laid down in the process of abuse alter or replace positive behaviors. By laying down unhealthy patterns, the child is shaped to be vulnerable in future relationships as well.*

Thinking

Infants can't use language to store their experiences. So what do they do with what happens to them? Zeanah, Anders, Seifer, and Stern (1989) suggest the following:

> The infant lives a particular experience, and, when it is over, the experience is instantaneously transformed into a memory. After the infant has lived a number of similar experiences, each of which has been transformed into a particular memory, the infant abstracts an average

version of the experience. This abstract average of related memories of experiences is an *internal representation* [italics added]. . . . There is increasing consensus that internal representations are organized hierarchically from small units reflecting subjective experience to increasingly larger networks reflecting more global appraisals. These large networks, termed "working models" by Bowlby, not only represent lived experience, but also are presumed to perceive and interpret incoming information selectively, to generate anticipations, and to guide behavior in relationships. (p. 663)

Thus the child is shaped by repeated interactions with the environment. Because young children have very little capacity to leave their environment and are so dependent on it, we think of them as being more *embedded in their context*. If the environment is a healthy one, children are shaped in healthy ways. If it is not, children become vulnerable to later problems.

> *Because children cannot remove themselves from a damaging environment, it is the job of others to monitor their early environment and initiate intervention when needed. Such embeddedness is also a critical reason why the behavior of young children must be investigated and understood in the context of their current environment.*

The infant engages the world through sensory motor experiences (how the world feels, smells, tastes, sounds, and looks) and maybe through memory. Infants move from simple responses, such as sucking and grasping, to more awareness of people in their environment. By 9 months of age, infants show recall for objects that are hidden while they are watching, an ability called object permanence. The emergence of this ability marks a new stage in memory capability. The infant is learning things about the world, and this learning is demonstrated by showing familiarity with various routines rather than by verbal expression.

Piaget (1970) has called this the *sensorimotor* stage. Note that the word *stage* is commonly used in describing early developmental periods. This term does not imply a strict or abrupt transition from one point to another; rather, it suggests a broader band of competence, with some children mastering age-specific tasks more rapidly than their peers.

By 12 months of age, the use of symbols—which includes language—begins to develop. Language progresses from one or two words at

1 year to dozens of words by the second year of life. Using language, the child starts to create an additional mechanism for storing experiences, and—even more important—for expressing them.

As children mature, they learn to imitate, play, and respond with different feelings. By about 1 year of age, they show recall for events and varying sequences. Even after the onset of language, however, early experiences still remain deeply embedded in the sensory realm.

An excellent review of the astounding growth that happens in infants is found in the *Time* magazine cover story, "How a Child's Brain Develops" (Nash, 1997). As research continues in this area, the critical nature of early development will be further elaborated.

> *We need to anticipate the needs of even very young children because they cannot talk. It is very difficult to determine abuse without concrete physical findings or an eyewitness, so these two types of substantiation become most common. But as the infant matures, his or her behaviors and emerging language help communicate his experiences, then other ways of assessing abuse can be used (see Chapter 3).*

Sexuality

Even infants are sexual beings. Sexual development in infants and toddlers begins in utero, where males are clearly observed to have erections. Although it is difficult to measure lubrication in an intrauterine state, newborn infant females do lubricate. Clearly the capacity for sexual arousal is present in a child at the time of birth. Sexual development does not, however, mean the capacity for sexual relatedness as some abusers argue. Adult sexuality is a complex interplay of emotions and physiology. Infants and toddlers present the primitive beginnings of what is later an interpersonal matter. During the first 18 months of life, children's sexual development may include exploring the body and beginning to learn the names of various body parts.

> *Prevention efforts for child sexual abuse should begin as a child learns language. The naming of genitals and the demonstration of respect for them is important. If a young child is abused, having the correct names for body parts is an important aid in the assessment of possible abuse.*

Memory

It is important to know that even when young children cannot express their learning in words, this does not mean that they are not learning or they will not remember experiences (see Chapter 2).

The above areas of development are not isolated areas, they all act together and influence each other. An example of this is reflected in the development of attachment. Attachment is one of the critical aspects of development during these early months of life. In fact this concept is so important I am going to donate a special section to detail its meaning and process.

CONCEPTS OF ATTACHMENT THEORY

I must hear a dozen times a year, "She's very attached." This expression comes from social workers, police, foster parents, and so forth. It usually means "she gets upset when her mom is gone." That is not attachment. That is anxiety about leave taking. Though this statement reflects the mother-child relationship at this stage, it does not necessarily mean it's a good thing. Because the formation of early relationships is so critical, the following information is given to help you be precise when you say that a child is attached.

Bonding

Bonding refers to the initial parent-child relationship during the time just after birth and somewhat beyond. It occurs when the parent comes to feel that the child belongs to him or her and commits to love and protect this new being.

Attachment

Attachment refers to a longer-term process, although it can grow out of this early bonding, and it is reflective of the quality of the early parent-child interactions that the child internalizes. Virtually all children are attached, but some attachments promote adaptive long-term functioning whereas some do not. By 12 months of age, a clearly established pattern of interaction can be reliably measured, as seen in Ainsworth's "strange situation" (Ainsworth, Blehar, Waters, & Wall, 1978). In this research format, a caretaker and child are presented with an increasingly stressful series of separations and reunions. The strange situation begins with a child playing in a room with the caretaker. A stranger enters, later plays with the child, then the parent leaves, followed by the stranger. The child is alone briefly and then the stranger returns, followed shortly thereafter by the parent. It is the child's response to the return of the parent that is coded to indicate the form of attachment. What is read in the infant's reaction to the separation and reunion with the caretaker is the sum quality of the interactions that have been laid down between the caretaker and child. Bowlby argues it is this early internalized pattern of expectations and attitudes that will shape responses to future interactions with other caretakers. Although this procedure is primarily a research tool, the patterns seen are applicable to clinical work.

There are four patterns of attachment, each of which is described briefly below.

Secure attachment. If a caretaker is reliable, sensitive, nurturing, and responsive, the child develops a secure attachment to this person. The caretaker comes to represent a reliable place where the child can reanchor and calm him- or herself, a safe place to reorganize before going back out into the world to explore. Through smoothly regulated dyadic experience children internalize patterns of self-regulation. Securely attached children have a balance between attachment and exploration. Children learn that the world is a responsive place and that their needs are important. Thus, they begin to experience a good sense of self. About 65% of American babies show this form of attachment. There are two forms of insecure attachment; anxious resistant and anxious avoidant.

1. *Anxious resistant attachment.* Some caretakers are inconsistent in their relationships with children; they may not coordinate their behaviors to the child's needs, they may be ineffective at soothing the child, or they may overstimulate when the child needs calming. Research has indicated a relationship between inconsistent care and anxious resistant attachment patterns. Children with the latter pattern of attachment seek

comfort but have trouble using the caretaker as a secure base. Researchers noted that "one moment they were raising their arms and
asking to be picked up, the next moment they were twisting and squirm-
ing, pushing away, or kicking their feet in anger. Their approach to the
mother was clearly ambivalent, which greatly interfered with their
ability to settle down and begin exploring the environment again. They
behaved as though they could not get what they needed from the
caregiver" (Sroufe, Cooper, & DeHart, 1992, p. 210). Anxious resistant
attachment children are caught up in a reluctance to separate from their
caregiver at the expense of exploring the world around them. These
children may also display a hypervigilance due to uncertainty about the
availability or consistent responsiveness of their caregiver. About 10%
to 15% of American infants show this form of attachment.

2. *Anxious avoidant attachment.* Caregivers who are "either indifferent and
   emotionally unavailable, or who actively rejected the baby when the
   child sought physical closeness" (Sroufe et al., 1992, p. 210) are associated with anxious avoidant attachment. In this pattern of attachment,
   the infant may separate from the caretaker to play but may not appear
   afraid when a stranger enters the room. "Yet what was striking about
   these children was their response when the mother returned. They
   actively avoided her, turning away, increasing their distance, or unscru-
   pulously ignoring her" (Sroufe et al., 1992, p. 210). Rather than using
   the caretaker as a secure base in a time of stress, these infants actively
   avoided their caretaker. As stress increased the infants became more
   avoidant. Such avoidance interferes with the ability to settle down and
   return to active exploration. For these children, exploration is at the
   expense of attachment. About 20% of American babies show this
   pattern.

Disorganized or disoriented attachment. Caretakers who are overtly or
indirectly threatening from unresolved experiences of trauma in their
life, who are actively abusive or "emotionally absent," or who have no
consistent way of relating to the infant in times of stress are associated
with disorganized or disoriented attachment. This attachment style
may contain pieces of both anxious and avoidant attachment, but it is
most characterized by a variety of confused, contradictory behaviors.
"Infants may appear dazed or disoriented, they may move very slowly
or become motionless, they may seem depressed" (Sroufe et al., 1992,
p. 210). It is as if they have learned no consistent pattern for relating to
their caretaker when they are stressed. Carlson, Cicchetti, Barnett,
and Brainwald (1989) found links between abuse and disorganized

attachment, and Carlson (1997) indicated that disorganized attachment has a relationship to later dissociative disorders in school-age children, up to age 17. About 5% to 10% of American infants show this pattern.

The presence of a secure base in these early months of life is critical because it forms a pattern for the quality of subsequent relationships, and it is critical in developing self-regulation skills. Sensitive care and attention communicate to the infant that their needs are important, a major component in good self-esteem.

In all cultures, children form attachments, but there are differences in the frequency of the various patterns of attachment. Asian cultures, which stress minimizing anxiety for the young child, show fewer anxiously attached children. They also stress more communal ways of relating, as do Hispanic cultures. These cultures may have greater incidence of emotionally enmeshed relationships. Northern European cultures that stress early independence, such as the German culture, have higher levels of insecure avoidant attachment (Grossmann, Grossmann, Spangler, Suess, & Unzer, 1985). Every culture has some level of problematic attachment, but secure attachment is still the most common form of attachment.

Early attachment styles can have long-ranging effects for later emotional and interpersonal development. One would think to respond reliably to a baby's crying would just reinforce the crying and make the child more dependent; but reliable, responsive, nurturing caretaking actually creates more independent, secure children. Waters, Wippman, and Sroufe (1979) found that later childhood social competence was predicted by secure attachment in infancy. In a sample of high-risk preschool children, Erickson, Egeland, and Sroufe (1985) noted that among all forms of abuse and neglect (physical abuse, sexual abuse, physical neglect, emotional neglect), the children who had "emotionally absent" caregivers suffered the most long-term negative effects. Children with secure attachments had higher self-esteem, were more popular with peers, and showed less negative emotion. Children with anxious attachment had poorer social skills, were less flexible, more dependent, and had lower self-esteem (Sroufe, 1983).

What shapes the parent's ability to create healthy attachments? One of the most amazing findings about the later effects of early attachment is found in the work of Mary Main (1991). Adult caregivers repeated, with their children, the type of attachment style they experienced with their own parent! The implications of this are profound. Without intervention and change, damaged parents often repeat their history of damaged attachment. Attempts at intervention with high-risk parents and their infants have shown that attachment styles can be improved, but results are not immediate and these parents need multiple levels of support to shift problematic attachment styles.

Empathy

Empathy is also formed during the early years. By about age one, children begin to show empathetic reactions (e.g., the capacity to recognize others in distress and then reach out to help them). Pancake (1988) and Park and Waters (1989) have demonstrated that securely attached children are more empathic toward their peers and have a greater ability to form friendships. The experience of being treated empathetically is reflected in empathy toward others.

Most longitudinal studies have not yet followed children into adulthood, but there is some evidence that effects of early attachment are apparent even into adolescence (Sroufe, personal communication, 1996).

SUMMARY

In sum, attachment patterns that can be reliably measured as early as 12 months appear to have a significant relationship to the long-term nature and quality of emotional responsiveness.

We all carry our early histories with us—for better or for worse. It is interesting to think that for many adults the capacity to become intimate in later life has its genesis at this stage of life. The ability to be vulnerable, to share, to nurture, and to empathize—all critical interactions between adult partners—have their origins early in life. In similar fashion, the capacity to inhibit closeness, to relate without empathy, or to be caught up in anxiety about the continuity of relationships also has origins early in life. Knowing this, we need to observe and strongly advocate for intervention when we encounter young children who are developing poor early attachments. Our advocacy is important because such children cannot speak for themselves, nor can they seek their own interventions for problematic situations.

What relevance does attachment theory have to child abuse investigation? Understanding attachment is important because young children's attachment history is reflected in the way they interact with an interviewer. Securely attached children are used to having good relationships so they may trust more readily, whereas the anxious or avoidant child may be less able to create relationships. The ability of adults to create a good relationship with a young child is one of the most essential elements in the child's ability to interview well.

Implications for Practice

The responsibility for attending to abuse issues is with the adult because the child cannot talk or find resources for reporting. In a system with dwindling resources and increasing needs, the responsibility to be proactive is an uneasy one. Our challenge to protect this young population is best met by programs that involve extended home visitation (e.g., Hawaii's Healthy Start, a support program for parents and infants that begins at birth and continues through early childhood years). Trained visitors can provide a critical link to needed services and interventions, as well as act as a frontline sentinel on the alert for abuse.

❏ Children 18 to 36 Months

Between 1½ and 3 years of age, there are marked changes in developing language, in new motor skill capacity, and in the child's capacity to explore a new world. In this exploration, the child keeps the primary caretaker and close family nearby as a resource and guide. When these very young children are pressed to talk about abuse, they have insufficient language to fully express what they have experienced. Their small statements must be understood in the context of their overall capabilities, their environment, and their history. Children move from being toddlers with little language ability to talkative young children whose language can finally be understood by most adults. Because of the rapid improvement in language skills, the incidence of child sexual abuse begins to be measured in documented cases toward the end of this period.

CHARACTERISTICS OF THIS AGE

Thinking

Very young children think in ways quite different from adults. As young children learn more language, their thinking and memory become coded in language. New possibilities for communicating open up, but this very early communication has its own special characteristics.

Some theorize that children's skills emerge in a stage-by-stage fashion (Piaget, 1970), with biology shaping the timing of certain new skills. Other theorists argue that development is shaped by social and environmental interactions (Vygotsky, 1978). Both of these ideas have validity. From 18 to 36 months, a child is moving from a sensorimotor understanding of the world to a worldview that is more verbally encoded and understood in terms of relationships, sequences, and procedures, with interactions shaping the quality of the child's learning.

There are several special characteristics of thinking at this stage that are relevant to abuse assessment issues. One of the most important is *egocentrism*. Children are very self-centered and assume others see, think, and feel the same way they do. Because they see the world primarily from their own point of view, the idea that others may not have the same knowledge of their experiences does not occur to them. They do not understand that they must work to convey their own thoughts and feelings.

A second characteristic of this age is thinking that is *concrete*, or tied to the way things look or act, the immediate appearance of the object. Limited language and experience circumscribe the ability to fully describe an experience and lead to concrete thinking. A bright and verbal child (toward the end of this stage) told her mother, "He had a penis under a penis, he took it off and threw it away. It had a rubber band on it." She was probably referring to a condom she had seen. At this age, a child's unusual ideas stem from their incomplete knowledge about the world, not faulty thinking.

> *To truly understand what very young children are saying, we need to know how they view the world. Understanding egocentrism means that we work to understand what the child says and does, as it has been shaped by their environment. Very young children do not have a clear perspective of the separate nature of the self, so they don't know that you don't know all their experiences. It never occurs to them to explain their actions to you and the relationship of these actions to their history. Without a good history from the caretaker, you may not understand who or what the child is talking about.*

A third characteristic of very young children's thinking is that only *one central aspect of a situation* (which may not be the same one you would choose) is usually the focus; thus, other important features of the experience may be neglected. Because early childhood utterances are short and simple, abuse may be described as "hurts my butt," the salient feature of the child's experience. The child typically may not talk about the context of the situation or the unique specifics of an action.

A fourth characteristic of thinking is that young children report only *the state of things at the moment*. Their concrete form of thinking does not take into account that things may change over time. They cannot go easily backward or forward in their thinking, and they cannot yet classify by hierarchies (e.g., What was stronger? Which was first?).

> *Children with a simpler cognitive state and limited language experience will say puzzling, idiosyncratic things to make sense of an atypical experience such as abuse. This does not mean their information lacks validity. Their statements must be understood in the context of their life experiences.*

When children can talk, they can interact with a wider circle of people. This wider socialization expands knowledge, increases cognitive growth, and develops socialization skills. Developmental tasks at this age involve creating a clear and concrete sense of self (e.g., " I am Sarah," "This is my mom," "I am strong"). The idea of sexual identity is also formed, and by age 2, most children are clear about their gender.

As children socialize with more people, they move away from the initial, almost exclusive relationship with a primary caretaker. New boundaries and a new sense of autonomy are explored. A secure base from the early months of life gives the child firm ground from which to move out on her own, and then return when feeling anxious or afraid.

Children continue to *internalize,* or incorporate into their own repertoire, the regulatory and soothing functions initially provided by the parent. In this way, children expand their *self-regulatory skills* (e.g., controlling their temper, following directions, adapting to schedules). The areas of self-identity, self-regulation, and social relatedness show remarkable growth in these very early years. Repeated patterns of interaction become templates for expectations in future interactions.

> *This period of socialization is when children may express their abuse in patterns of behavior. As one of the windows into a child's history, behavioral expression is a significant marker for sexual abuse.*

Play

Children 18 months to 3 years old show a clear progression in their play development. Whereas infants are busy learning the sensory qualities of items in their world, the child with emerging language capabilities is beginning to use *objects as symbols.* Suddenly a little girl begins to feed her dolly, put it to sleep, or pretend it is going potty. This symbolic use of play has several stages and affects how we interview (for the best results, see also Chapter 3).

The play of very young children may mirror abuse experiences. For example, I saw a 2-year-old boy with medical findings of sodomy. His mother related that he took his Cabbage Patch doll everywhere he went and pointed to the doll's bottom while saying, "Owie bottom! Owie bottom!" Very young children will play out experiences using toys, but when they are specifically asked to show what happened to them, children 18 to 36 months old will use their own bodies to demonstrate.

Play moves from being a self-focused exploration of objects to the beginnings of shared experience. The earliest pattern is called *parallel play*—the child plays by, but not with, another child. There is no real give and take, and superficial cooperation belies the lack of true social skills. Children have not learned to negotiate their needs verbally and commonly yank toys away or solve conflicts by biting or hitting. Size and determination often decide who plays with what. Parents who expect children of this age to share or cooperate have developmentally inappropriate expectations. Young children are usually too self-centered to cooperate and share. Better techniques for management are distraction or adult mediation to reassign toys or playthings.

Emotional Growth

Erik Erikson (1950), a major theorist in emotional development, describes very young children as moving from the infant's task of developing basic trust into an emergence of more autonomy and the beginnings of will. As children begin to walk, they can determine the distance between themselves and their primary caretaker. Suddenly they can control something! If they have a good sense of *basic trust*, they have an internalized, secure base so they are freed to move away and explore and then move back and re-anchor as needed. This process reflects a basic tenet of developmental psychology: The success of later skills rests on the resolution of earlier, more basic skills. One skill is followed by a second as the skills increase in complexity. This growth does not appear in the form of fixed or rigid stages but rather follows a course that is influenced by social and environmental interactions.

"Terrible twos" are created by the child's new sense of autonomy and will. When a child learns the little but very powerful word *no*, suddenly he has some effect on the things that happen. This two-letter word helps the child control his proximity to the parent. He can move out and explore and, in so doing, individuate, or acquire a distinct and unique individuality. Mahler, Pine and Bergman (1975) write about the process of *separation* and *individuation*. Mahler describes birth as a specific point in time with a clear emergence of the child as a being but the psychological birth as something formed over time. As children move from an undifferentiated relationship with the parent to a beginning sense of a self, they begin their psychological birth. Growth and development is all about separation and individuation.

A 16-month-old with a secure attachment acts like this: Sarah has been playing quietly by her mother's feet. She gets up. First she turns over and puts her feet and hands on the floor, then raises her bottom followed by her torso, and finally lifts her head, with arms following, to an erect stance. She moves away from her mother to another room and explores a new toy or situation there. As she plays, she may talk or call to her mother as a way to remain linked to her, or her mother may periodically poke her head around the corner to check on her child, and they may have brief eye contact. When the doorbell rings, Sarah hears her mother move, followed by the sound of a stranger's voice. Sarah leaves the exploration and comes to her mother, hiding her face in her mother's legs as mother and the stranger talk. If the stranger stays and is friendly toward Sarah, she may leave the security of her mother's presence to move toward the stranger and get acquainted. When frightened, she will return to her mother to renew her sense of safety and security.

If a child has not developed a secure base, then her freedom to explore (and carry with her the belief that someone will be available to help) can be in jeopardy. Thus, the chance for growth and development is compromised. When a child is securely attached, she has the freedom to explore. Confidence with autonomy leads to more initiative, and growth speeds forward.

> *Despite the need to do interviewing in a way that minimizes contamination, interviewers of this age group should recognize the importance of letting children be seen in their caretaker's presence. Separation of a young child from their primary caretaker, in order to interview, creates additional stress. The level of stress is increased if the child has been frightened by abuse. Despite the need to do interviewing in way that minimizes any contamination, these children have a very real need for caretaker closeness. On the other hand, some children readily come to any stranger and initiate intimate contact. They appear fearless, having no need for their caretaker. Often these children are pseudo independent and poorly attached. Part of the assessment means looking at such a child's emotional needs as well.*

Empathy is present in toddlers, emerging at about age 1 along with self-awareness. Gains in language and understanding support an increase in empathetic reactions. By the end of the second year, emotions such as shame, embarrassment, and pride emerge. Children also must learn strategies for emotional self-regulation. As children grow older, they begin to transfer or internalize the soothing and regulating behavior previously done for them. This is evident as a 2-year-old moves away from a conflict situation and quietly tells herself, "No hit, no hit."

Language

Children have two forms of language: (a) what they can produce or express, called *expressive language,* and (b) what they can understand, called *receptive language.* Children understand much more language than they can express. Expressive language begins at age 1 with one- or two-word expressions and increases to two- or three-word sentences by age 2. Finally, by age 3, language blossoms into full sentences that can be understood by most adults. This bridging time, from nonverbal to verbal expression, presents an interesting challenge for the assessment of sexual abuse, which requires verbal interaction. As language moves from primitive to more advanced constructions, so do cognitive functions. Receptively, these young children often understand the simple questions put to them, but their expressive language skills may not yet allow full disclosure of their knowledge.

Implications for Practice

Immature cognitive skills, and a language skill that is only beginning to emerge, combine to produce short, sketchy, concrete, and often "out of the blue" incidents of disclosure. Children aged 18 to 36 months cannot give good spontaneous verbal narrative to an account of abuse. Neither can very young children provide a beginning, middle, and end to their accounts. Instead they tell about their experiences in the context of their own idiosyncratic and limited backgrounds. They often have no names or labels to express what they have experienced. Frequently, they lack the necessary concepts even to reply reliably to an interviewer's questions (see also Chapter 3).

❏ Children 3 to 5 Years of Age

By 3 years of age most children are understandable to adults. A sharp rise in the documentation of child sexual abuse cases begins at age 3.

Young children can now talk about their experiences, but they still think and understand in a way that is quite different from adults. They have a wider association with people and other children beyond their primary caregivers, and many new skills emerge. They bring unique skills and perspectives to the task of reporting their own abuse.

Some of the qualities of 3- to 5-year-olds make for great fun in interviewing preschoolers. The book, *A Monster Is Bigger Than 9,* by Claire and Mary Ericksen (1988), captures the wonderful thinking children do during these years. For example:

- "My dad can fix anything because he has a work shirt."
- "I'm never ascared of anything, but my tummy is."
- "When something is sour, you have to eat it with one eye closed."
- "I can't see you because you don't have your glasses on."
- "The polka dots on my arm means they are shivering."
- "What happens at the end of the year? Does time stop?"
- Pointing to a paper clip: "Please pass the trombone."

In these delightful examples, we can see how preschool children attribute causality on a superficial level (if you have a work shirt you can fix anything), have trouble seeing things from different perspectives (I can't see you because you don't have your glasses on), and add meaning to new experiences from the limited language they know (polka dots on my arm mean shivering, a paper clip is a trombone). Let's look at the changes that produce this fun perspective.

CHARACTERISTICS OF THIS AGE

Thinking

As a child moves from 2 into 3 years of age, she moves from thought that is tied to concrete objects to the beginning of abstract thinking. Language is a symbol, and with words children can think in new way. However, there are limitations in the child's thinking (Piaget, 1970). Seeing mostly the physical appearance of things, children do not notice intent or change well. Yet, this limitation is also what allows them to see "magic" in their world (Fraiberg, 1959). For these young children, the Easter Bunny is real. They do not ponder the physical impossibilities of a waistcoated bunny hopping on two rear legs while carrying a basket of eggs with its front legs.

Some other characteristics of preschool thinking are as follows:

- Complex relationships between two or more objects are not well comprehended. The idea of rank ordering is minimal—understanding the "biggest" or "strongest" is common, but discussing gradations of ranking is not.

- Children judge the severity of an act by the magnitude of the consequence, not the motive or underlying aim (e.g., it is worse to break five cups accidentally than to break one cup intentionally).

- Perceptions are dominated by subjective experience and personal vantage points (e.g., "My Mom and Daddy fighted because I spilled my milk," when in fact the parents were fighting over issues that were not related to the child).

- Absent is the ability to self-reflect (e.g., "I think I hit my brother because I was angry because I didn't get a popsicle first") or to evaluate others' actions by comparing them with a societal standard (e.g., "My sister can't cross on red because she could get hit by a car and it is illegal").

- Two opposing ideas cannot be held simultaneously (e.g., people are either good or bad; they cannot be both good and bad at the same time). Young children focus on parts and have a hard time entertaining the idea of a complex whole.

- Children do not understand temporal relationships. When a 4-year-old is told she will go to a party "tomorrow," she awakens and asks, "Is it tomorrow yet, Dad?" Relationships of time (e.g., yesterday, today, before, after) are all difficult concepts until the early elementary years.

- Young children are unable to enumerate various episodes of action (e.g., the first is number one, the second number is two). This capacity also emerges during the early elementary school years.

When you ask a young child where his dreams come from, he may describe dreams as a sort of TV camera that goes on in the night. Understanding the origins of internal processes such as dreams is a challenge. The capacity of younger children to distinguish such differences increases as they become able to see their world from different perspectives (see also Chapter 3).

Emotional Growth and Socialization

Three- to five-year-old children understand a lot more about themselves than do children 18 to 36 months. They are also a lot more interested in social interaction. With increased social interaction comes the work of emotional self-regulation and conformity to societal rules and regulations. Now that children are using language more, they can also use language to make statements to themselves that help keep them in control (e.g., "I don't have to be afraid," "My mom says this is safe," or "My dad says I can't cross the street all alone"). Signs of emotions, both facial cues and behavioral acts, are better understood. There is also a better understanding of causes and consequences of different feelings. Three-year-olds are able to label feelings of being happy, sad, and mad, but feelings of fear or worry are not well recognized until age 4.

The psychosocial theorist Erik Erikson (1950) identifies a drive toward *initiative,* incorporating ambition and responsibility, as a major emotional focus during this time. With parents creating the organizational framework, children learn to master new skills and gain new information about their world.

Temperamental differences in children (e.g., shy and reticent or bold and outgoing) are more apparent and show consistency over time, but they are also affected by the characteristics of different ages. Three-year-olds don't seem to mind cooperating in various tasks and doing as their parents ask, whereas 4-year-olds frequently challenge rules and limits, pressing their parents to determine "who's in charge here." Patience, understanding, and clear and consistent boundaries are needed to deal with a 4-year-old's struggle for autonomy.

Increased language ability allows children to socialize in a broader context, which in turn helps them to grow intellectually and learn about other people's points of view. As more emotions are understood, the ability to empathize increases.

Play

The play of 3- and 4-year-olds is much more interactive than 2-year-old play. Other children are actively sought for pretend play, and children begin to learn how to take turns with toys and to share varying roles. Even with this advancement, they still have a hard time recognizing or dealing with other people's perspectives.

By age 3, play is well beyond just exploring the physical properties or functions of objects. One new function of play is to promote mastery, allowing a child to practice or rehearse various scenarios and to explore a response to them. Another function is to reflect and expand the child's experiences. Thus, play increases in complexity—a 2-year-old repeats the experiences she has known with her dolly (e.g., go to sleep, go potty) whereas a 3-year-old begins to use objects more independently (e.g., a parent doll now feeds a child doll). True fantasy play emerges at this time, and play becomes less self-focused and more abstract. By ages 4 to 5, children can make-believe with each other and can create and coordinate elaborate play scenarios (see also Chapter 4).

It is not unusual to see children this age play out sexual abuse scenarios with each other. Often they play out abuse with the very same words or affect they experienced because their history lacks other experiences to modify this presentation. See Implications for Practice below for more information.

Language

By age 3, most children can be understood by adults. They have good articulation, use well-formed sentences, and are able to express their observations and needs. Preschoolers can tell about who, what, where, and often how; but they cannot give good responses to when or how many. These children will often give accounts of their abuse that include location and participants, but they are not yet skilled in giving extensive contextual information or detail, and they have great difficulty with temporal order. Young children do not have the organizational strategies available to adults; for example, they still do not usually structure their information with a beginning, middle, and end sequence. They tend to tell only what is most important to them. Children aged 4 to 5 may be better able to use language than children aged 2, but their explanation of abuse is usually very concrete (e.g., "He peed in my mouth," "He hurted my butt") because they don't have adult words for sexuality.

Memory

Words now anchor memory as well as call up memory. Almost every parent I talk with can tell a story of the amazing things his child has remembered. As children's language abilities increase and their experience broadens, memory expands. Because preschoolers can now verbalize their memory, we become much more aware of the extent of their memory capabilities. However, there are still limitations. Young children have less experience and a smaller vocabulary than do adults, so they encode and store less information. The whole idea of remembering (i.e., recalling something from the past) is what children can now begin to think about. Memory and its retrieval is a critical area to understand for any child abuse investigator. (A very detailed description of what children can remember, for how long and how well, is found in Chapter 3.)

> Wherever there are therapists treating preschool children for abuse, I have found about 30% to 40% who are treating 4- or 5-year-olds for abuse-related problems that have their origin in an earlier, less verbal time. I have been intrigued with this little-discussed element of therapeutic life with abused kids. I have seen several such children myself during the last 10 years, and I have written a detailed therapy case history (Hewitt, 1991a). In this example, the child was abused somewhere between 18 and 35 months of age, but the abuse was never discussed or reported because she had significant speech and language impairment. When the child was 3½ years old, she began acting out sexual behavior at her day care, and her behaviors were traced back to experiences with an adolescent male babysitter. The acting out of an earlier stored experience is not uncommon in children whose abuse has been during a time of little language ability.
>
> Why does this behavior come out later? At age 4, there is adequate language ability for experiences to be put into words. In addition, normal developmental cycling at age 4 resonates to sexual issues, and the memory of stored experiences comes to the fore when triggered by new interests. (See Hewitt, 1994, for two case studies of children abused at age 2 who report at later ages.)

Sexuality

Where 2-year-olds will gleefully streak from the bath, running stark naked through various rooms of the house, 4-year-olds will talk about their private parts, their pooping, or their peeing but are more cautious in the exposure of their genitals. Freud (1920) theorized that very young children move into an *oedipal* stage of development at about age 4, and the awakening of their sexual feelings becomes directed toward one parent or the other. (Freud's *Oedipus complex* is drawn from an ancient Greek play in which the son inadvertently marries his mother and suffers for his mistake. Girls who fall in love with their fathers are considered to have an *Electra* complex.) When Freud saw pathology around sexual issues in his clients that was related to incest or other forms of sexual abuse, he initially thought he had found the root of much psychopathology. Then he proposed his findings to his colleagues. They strongly refuted his ideas and so Freud capitulated. He reframed his first interpretations, theorizing that the pathology was instead a result of the child's unconscious wishes for sexual contact with the parent, and he ascribed this wish a central place in the emotional development of preschool children. Fortunately, things have now righted themselves, and Freud's initial hypothesis has been reaffirmed.

Although Freud may have been equivocal about childhood sexuality, it is quite clear to any preschool teacher that 4-year-olds are interested in sexual parts and functions. This interest is seen as developmentally appropriate and not viewed with alarm. It stems from increasing cognitive complexity and a new awareness of sexual differences between boys and girls. Sexual play at this age is not uncommon, and it is frequently expressed as "you show me yours and I'll show you mine" or "doctor" or "house." However, research has not shown nonabused children to exhibit graphic sexualized actions or play (see also Chapter 1).

Parents often find their preschooler in the bathroom with the rest of the young kids in the neighborhood milling around in there, too. Modesty is not a priority until about age 6 or 7. For now, there is little self-consciousness with group experiences around toileting, but parents and teachers work to establish culturally appropriate norms and behaviors around genital display. Between the ages of 3 and 5, children are instructed to develop a greater sense of privacy for their private parts.

Role of the Environment

A child's environment has a tremendous role in shaping the child, for better or worse. When environments are safe, secure, predictable, and nurturing, a child reflects this environment. But children can also reflect chaotic environments, and these environments can cause significant lags or problems in the development of some skills. When an environment is secure and predictable, a child is freed up to turn his or her energies toward learning about new things. When the environment is not safe, energies are diverted elsewhere. I often think of the effect on young children's learning when I see a child who has been relocated four or five times in 2 years or has been bounced around to several caretakers. These children bring an entirely different approach to the organization and understanding of their world and their experiences, and this of course affects my job of trying to understand what has happened to them.

-----------------------------------•◆•-----------------------------------

Implications for Practice

Because interactive play emerges during this age, it is not unusual for young children to express sexual abuse experiences in their play. In fact, many cases of sexual abuse are first discovered from inappropriate sexualized play. Questions may arise about the origin of such play: Is this the normal sexual exploration that children may engage in? A thorough review of children's normative and clinical sexual behavior is found in Chapter 1. The next largest key to distinguishing play as abuse is the use of power. Normal sexualized play interactions have a mutuality about them; one child is not forced or coerced into an activity. When there is the use of force, threat, domination, or other forms of violence and intrusion, a history of abuse is more suspect. It is recognized that preschoolers will faithfully play very graphic reproductions of their own or witnessed abuse precisely because they do not have extensive life experiences from which to draw other scenarios.

The incomplete and often idiosyncratic understanding young children have of bodies and their functions leads to unusual understandings of abusive acts. A young child explained to my colleague that his penis had been "buggatised." When asked what he was referring to, he indicated that, because the abuser had put the boy's penis in his mouth, it meant there were bugs growing on it and it was thus contaminated. In this case, simply explaining the function of washing off germs and restoring the penis's wholeness was important for regaining body integrity. Young children will not tell you they misunderstand basic information; it is up to the adult to carefully check out the interpretations children have made from their abuse so misunderstandings can be corrected.

Fantasy is a common occurrence in children ages 3 to 5. This fact prompts the often used defense against allegations of sexual abuse: the child made up the allegations. However, the capacity to fantasize does not include the capability to create explicit sexual scenarios. This is a period when children are learning to distinguish which thoughts are generated by reality and which are generated internally. Unless they have experienced abuse, they do not have the life experience to provide graphic sexual information. The origins of children's accounts of detailed and specific sexual abuse need to be investigated because there is no substantiation in experience or research for such material to come from fantasy alone.

Self-regulation is impacted by abuse. Kendall-Tackett et al. (1993) found self-regulation problems to be one of the main sequelae to abuse. One of the jobs of being a kid is to learn to keep feelings and actions within limits. The experience of abuse adds stress and disrupts the homeostasis of normal development; stress and sexual molestation disrupt self-control. Often a hypervigilance, or a hyperactivity that is not neurologically induced, marks the child who has had repeated exposure to abuse. Abused children need to be watchful as part of their survival, but when this vigilance is practiced repeatedly and becomes a part of ongoing coping, then it can be damaging to the capacity to regulate. About two thirds of sexually abused children show behavioral adjustment problems; some are anxious and fearful whereas others are aggressive and angry. These characteristics can affect the ability to interview effectively.

Can abuse from an earlier time be distinguished from recent abuse? We may not be able to make such a distinction. Expressions of early sexual abuse are typically much more concrete and simple in presentation than abuse that is ongoing at the current time. Children often cannot place their abuse in a strong context or give much detail, in a manner that would be contrasted with their capacity to relate details at their current age. Furthermore, the resurfacing of this old abuse may appear in unusual contexts; it may come with exposure to some form of sensory motor trigger (e.g., a certain smell, a sound, a visit to the location of the previous abuse, or contact with the person associated with the abuse).

When required to recall experiences that are retrieved from very early years, adults must traverse backward to a more primitive style of thinking and remembering. Material from this time frame is more primitive and often fragmented; without language to anchor memory, early fragments frequently feel like part of a dream. This is a normal form of early childhood memory encoding and storage, but it can have important implications for later life.

❏ Children 5 Years of Age and Older

By the time most children are 5 years of age, they can respond well to standardized interview formats. This is because they have a good attention span, they have sufficient mastery of language and concepts, they have a clearer sense of self, their thinking is less concrete and egocentric, they have a clearer sense of truth and lie, and they can better understand the reasons for interviewing. However, they still lack some important interview abilities. Preschool children

- have difficulty with temporal concepts. Dates, times, and the relationships between times are still difficult to handle. This ability does not fully mature until about age 7.
- have difficulty with abstract reasoning. These children reason on a more concrete level, keeping a focus on concrete objects and actions rather than concepts and ideas.
- don't know when they don't know.
- need permission to correct you.
- try to give you what you ask.
- assume adults are correct in telling them things.
- are not good at evaluating their own information, or taking multiple perspectives on a specific piece of information.
- may still need adult permission to voice discomfort, signal need to go to the bathroom, or express a level of emotional upset with difficult material.
- may have difficulty fully evaluating other people's motives or perspectives.
- cannot draw detailed maps or use elaborate symbolic representations. Good map drawing skills are present by age 7.
- cannot anticipate a line of questioning that is leading and suggestive.
- have great difficulty with negations.
- do not have the capacity to create elaborate fabrications.
- cannot go forward and then backward in time to discuss their allegations.
- cannot hold opposing concepts simultaneously (someone is both good and bad).

❏ Summary

Developmental stages shape the manner in which a child perceives, stores, recalls, and discloses abuse experience. Skills change dramatically during the early years of life. This chapter has identified young children's changing capacities and the importance they have for the way we assess abuse. Without a good understanding of early child development—how it shapes disclosure and how it affects the way we interview—we cannot do an adequate job of assessing these young children. Children in the first 5 years of life are more vulnerable and less able to report; they are at higher risk for abuse. The responsibility for good assessment lies with the evaluator, and good evaluation demands broad knowledge and careful technique.

The next chapter is about memory. It is a review of the research on the nature, length, and quality of young children's memory and it argues that young children can and do remember even very early events. In addition, research about trauma, suggestibility, attachment, and the neurobiological effects of stress on young children is integrated into arguments for the importance of assessment and protection of very young children.

3

Knowing More
Than They Can Tell

In the case described in Chapter 1, I felt I was not able to argue strongly enough for the child's protection, because I had few facts from which to argue. Researchers still don't have all the pieces to understanding how young children recall what has happened to them. Could this very young child remember early trauma? If she could, then how long would the memory last? Would it be accurate? If she had been abused but could not talk very well, would she register the abuse in ways other than by talking?

I found some facts in the literature on memory, trauma, behavior problems, and sexuality in young children. I learned that researchers are clear that even very young children have memories that can be stored for long periods and later retrieved with surprising accuracy. I discovered that children with abuse can display atypical sexual behavior and have accompanying behavior problems. I encountered new research that indicates that very early experiences can have a long-term influence on later relationship styles, and early trauma or prolonged stress may powerfully shape the development of neurological pathways—thus predisposing us to later ways of reacting.

I was profoundly moved by the importance of experiences during these earliest years in creating the foundations of our lifetime. The strength of my findings stood in sharp contrast to the substantiation rates of abuse with very young children; the younger the child, the less likely substantiation—and protection. There was a chasm between the understanding of research about early experience and the way in which children are protected.

I concluded that our assessment procedures are not tailored to match the young child's capacities for disclosure. The literature also hinted at things that might create a better assessment format. Effective assessment must be broader than just an interview; it must consider a child's statements along with his or her developmental context, past history, and behavioral presentation. New ways to approach the assessment of child abuse in young children were needed.

The first part of this chapter reviews early child development related to memory, and examines potentially interfacing topics such as suggestibility, trauma, attachment, and neurological development. Each issue is tied to child abuse assessment practice. Next is a research review of young children's sexual behavior and behavior problems as they may affect behavioral presentation in cases of sexual abuse. The concluding section integrates the extent of these findings into a new conceptual framework for the assessment of preschool abuse.

❏ **How Early, How Long, and How Accurately Can Children Remember?**

There is evidence that memory begins at the very youngest of ages. Children as young as 33 hours old can recognize auditory stimuli presented during the last trimester of pregnancy, a learning that could not have occurred after birth (DeCasper & Spence, 1986; Spence & DeCasper, 1987).

Rovee-Collier and colleagues (Hayne, Greco, Early, Greisler, & Rovee-Collier, 1986; Ohr, Fagen, Rovee-Collier, Hayne, & Vanderlinde, 1989; VanderLinde, Morrongiello, & Rovee-Collier, 1985) tied a ribbon to both a mobile and a 2-month-old infant's ankle and found that the infant could learn and later remember the relationship between his kicking and the mobile movement. In trials from 2 months of age through 6 months, the infants retained more information and retained it over longer periods of time. This learning was, however, "context dependent" (i.e., tied to the specific context in which it was laid down) and not easily generalized to other situations. When surroundings changed, the learning was often not evidenced, but it could be reactivated by a return to the original environment. As children matured, their capacity to generalize increased.

Some of the most surprising and interesting research I reviewed focused on memory in the first year of life. The brain develops myelin sheathing around nerve fibers in phases, with one phase (motor roots, peripheral nerves, etc.) occurring prenatally, a second phase in the first 1 to 2 postnatal years, and the last (prefrontal cortex, association cortex) occurring through late childhood. The areas that have to do with memory pertain to the second and third phase. At about 9 months, the brain begins to increase the process of myelinization and the relevant neocortical areas become sufficiently mature to support long-term memory. It is the cortex that stores the type of memory we use as long-term memory. Prior to this time, the hippocampus (a portion of the brain located deep in the temporal lobes and below the cortex) is the part of the brain that has to do with encoding new information and then consolidating this information; it then transfers all this to long-term memory (in the cortex). Monitoring electrical activity in the brain can give us an idea of what's going on inside, even when young children can't tell us what they are doing. Using a special cap with electrical receptors, the ERPs ("event-related potential," an electrical measure of brain activity somewhat similar to an EEG) of children about 9 months of age were measured as they reviewed a series of pictures (Carver, Bauer, & Nelson, 1996). For those infants who demonstrated evidence of recall memory 4 weeks after initial exposure to the sequence, the ERPs (when evaluated 1 week after initial exposure) revealed a stronger response to novel stimuli than to the familiar stimuli. In other words, for those infants who showed ERP evidence of discrimination, there was a difference in reaction to the old stimulus and the new material. There were no ERP differences for infants who could not recall (reproduce) the sequence. This form of memory is called *implicit memory* and refers to memory that is not consciously recalled. (This term will be defined in more detail after the next study.)

Myers, Perris, and Clarkson (1987) found memory in children first exposed to an experimental situation at 6 to 40 weeks of age. As infants, these children were involved in 15 to 19 trials of an experiment that paired tones with visual stimuli. All trials were stopped before the children were 12 months old. When the children were just about 3, they were returned to the original laboratory situation. Their reactions to the old experimental situation were different from another group of children who had not experienced the earlier trials. The experimental group of children were not afraid of the darkened room, and they showed evidence of anticipating the trial procedures. By their actions rather than words, they gave evidence of memory for the procedures they experienced 2 years ago. One boy, when asked to guess the identity of a hidden picture, correctly guessed the identity of the decal as a "whale." Does this mean that all these young children could give an explicit autobiographical narrative account of their early experiences? No. With the exception of the boy who talked about the whale sticker, there was little evidence of explicit, verbal recall of the early experiences (called *explicit memory*), but there was evidence of recognition memory in these children, now almost three years old. Subsequent experiments by Perris, Myers, and Clifton (1990) and Myers, Clifton, and Speaker (1994) also found evidence for nonverbal recognition memory of an unusual activity learned in a unique location during infancy. In all these experiments, children with previous exposure behaved differently from nonexposed children when reexposed to the original situation. Exposed children had faster relearning of the original tasks than the nonexposed children, and they exhibited more interaction time with objects from the earlier experimental situation (reaching for toys in the dark, patting puppets). However, there was little evidence of explicit or verbal recall from these early exposures.

The above study illustrates two important forms of memory: *implicit* and *explicit* memory (see Squire, 1987, for a more detailed description of this taxonomy).

Implicit memory refers to a nonconscious, nonverbal form of memory. It is sometimes called procedural or nondeclarative memory. The anticipation responses of the exposed children in the Myers et al. (1987) study are an example of this learning. This behavior is composed of habits and skills, learning thought of as classically conditioned. Implicit memory is defined by a change in performance or behavior.

Explicit memory refers to the ability to consciously recall a past event; it is often called declarative or episodic memory. It is event specific in terms of names, places, events, and dates. Verbal expression of this type of memory is the statement of the child who identifies the whale decal in the Myers et al. (1987) study cited above. Explicit memory is defined as those things we commonly think of as "memory." This is the memory we tap when we are asked to recall and tell about a past event. It can be either nonverbally or verbally expressed.

NONVERBAL EXPLICIT
MEMORY RESEARCH

If memory is measured by verbal recall alone, very young children's memory is seen as inadequate. When we develop measures that tap memory without requiring verbal recall, a rich and amazing store of memory is revealed. Bauer (1996) and her colleagues developed the concept of "elicited imitation" tasks. These tasks require "the same cognitive processes as those involved in verbal recall by older children and adults, yet [they] do not require. . . . a verbal response" (p. 31). (They are measures of nonverbal, explicit memory.) The elicited imitation tasks are composed of a variety of novel events with multiple components and a final function (e.g., sequentially assembling a goalpost-shaped base, bar, hooked metal plate, and mallet, to make a gong). After the initial exposure, there is a delay of a varying number of weeks or months and the child is again presented with the original materials and asked to reproduce the target action and sequence. Recall is determined from the child's demonstration at this second exposure.

What can children remember, for how long, and how well can they remember it? Children as young as 13 months were able to remember event sequences during a period of 8 months (Bauer, Hertsgaard, & Dow, 1994). By 20 months of age, Bauer and Dow (1994) and Bauer and Hertsgaard (1993) found that children can reproduce almost perfect three-step sequences; at 30 months, they can immediately reproduce as many as eight-step sequences (Bauer & Fivush, 1992). These findings indicate that as early as 13 months, the capacity to construct and store memories of specific events is sufficiently developed to allow recall over extended times.

Factors That Affect Recall

Young children's memories are not internally cued; they rely on external cues or "triggers" to elicit recall. Early studies of memory used mothers' journals of their children's experiences. Todd and Perlmutter (1980) found that toddlers' memories were precipitated by trigger events (i.e., events that evoked some component of the original experience). The child's recall was dependent on these external cues; it was not spontaneously generated or elicited by verbal command.

In an interesting experiment to explore what increased recall, Bauer and Wewerka (1995) found that when a child was told to remember something, the simple demand to remember also increased memory. (It is interesting to wonder if an offender's frequent injunction of "and don't you tell anyone" might act as a memory tag. Could it possibly result in *improving* a child's memory of an abusive event?)

Factors That Encourage the Retention of Memory

The nature of the material to be remembered, the number of experiences with the event sequence, and the availability of cues or reminders influenced better recall (Bauer, 1996). Very young children are cued to sequential events, but these events need to be meaningfully related and not appear just randomly. Event sequences, such as the gong sequence mentioned above, were easily recalled, whereas recall of events that were random, or disconnected actions, were not (Bauer, 1996). Even very young children can discern the meaningfulness of events.

Factors That Influence a Translation to Verbal Expression

Can this nonverbal recall survive a transition into verbal expression? Bauer and Wewerka (1995) found that it could; they document evidence of verbal memory for specific events by 1- to 2-year-olds. Interestingly, they also found that children's sequence recall was not determined by the level of their language development, for they could recall without language. Later, verbal expression of memory was correlated with the level of language development at the time of the exposure; children who had more language at the time of exposure were better able to talk about it later. This is important, for it appears that the verbal encoding of an event is what allows its retrieval into language expression at a later time, and it is this type of memory that is carried forward into later years.

Early Memory and Adult Memory

Can this early memory last into adulthood? Some research conducted with adults shows memories from age 2 and occasionally from age 1, although questions can always be raised about whether this is an actual memory or part of a history one has been told. Sheingold and Tenny (1982) document memories from ages 3 and 4 that are carried on into adulthood. Nevertheless, most adult memory research shows little recall under 3½ years (Howe & Courage, 1993), a phenomenon called *infantile amnesia*. Several reasons have been suggested for this: lack of language to encode, lack of a language-based retrieval system by which to store and later retrieve early experiences, and lack of sufficient cortical maturation to allow long-term verbal storage, among others (Howe & Courage, 1993; Nelson, 1993; Newcombe & Fox, 1994).

Implications for Practice
(Nonverbal Explicit Memory)

1. Basic capacities for memory skills are present and active very early in life, although the infant's skills are modified by immature neurophysiology (Howe & Courage, 1993). The same mechanisms operating in adult memory are present here. Very early memory is more context dependent, but as children mature and language begins to form, information is stored.

2. Early memory is not fully demonstrated if recall is only verbal. Behavioral manifestations of early experiences are important vehicles for the expression of early experiences.

3. Does this mean that we can all remember bits and pieces of information from 6 or 12 months of age? No, it does not. The phenomenon of infantile amnesia is sometimes cited as a reason for not pursuing abuse investigation with a 2-year-old (i.e., "If I can't remember it as an adult, then what difference does it make?") This does not mean, however, that there is no recall of these early memories at younger ages and that early memories cannot influence later responses to similar situations.

EXPLICIT VERBAL MEMORY RESEARCH

Research on early explicit verbal memory, or verbalized memory for specific situations and experiences, shows that experiences at age 2 can be reliably carried into later preschool years and verbally expressed. Such early memories are capable of creating effects into the future. But first, some cautions about how to interpret the findings:

1. The research in early memory has been conducted primarily with white, middle-class children. There is little research on children of color or with children who have abuse or neglect backgrounds. Some initial research by Saywitz and Lyon (1997), and research with preschoolers by Dorado (1996), found delays in

skill acquisition for children from lower socioeconomic backgrounds. Wellman (personal communication, 1995) suggests that the acquisition of skills may be along the same sequence, but for children with early developmental interference, the timing of the skill emergence may be delayed. Therefore, extrapolation of the data in this chapter needs caution as it is applied to any specific case. The closer the case matches the research sample, the stronger the associations can be.

2. It is important to note that not all children perform in the same way, even though they are the same age; there is individual variability that needs attention. Some children show more or earlier memory than other children. Not all the children in the Myers et al. (1987) study cited above remembered specific details as did the one boy cited. In the following research, remember the data given are for a particular group. Individual cases may vary.

Young Children's Ability to Remember

What can children remember and express verbally? For how long? With what level of accuracy? With the onset of language, memory can be measured verbally, as explicit verbal memory. Despite the difficulties of measuring early memory in a verbal format, research with children as young as 2 and 3 years of age has found that they could give intelligible and organized accounts of daily activities they had experienced (see Nelson, 1989, for a review), and they could also give accurate and detailed reports for novel, or one time events (Ashmead & Perlmutter, 1980; Fivush, Gray, & Fromhoff, 1987; Fivush & Hamond, 1990; Fivush, Hudson, & Nelson, 1984; Hamond & Fivush, 1991; Hudson & Nelson, 1986; Todd & Pearlmutter, 1980).

One of Hamond and Fivush's studies (1991) clearly demonstrates very young children's capabilities to remember. Two groups of children who had visited Disney World were asked to recall their experiences. The younger group was between 33 and 42 months of age ($M = 37$ months) and the older group was between 43 and 54 months of age ($M = 49$ months). Half of each age group was interviewed 6 months after the trip, the other half was interviewed after 18 months. All the children, regardless of age or time of interview, recalled a great deal of accurate information. Even the children who were now 4 years old accurately reported information from their experience at 2½ years of age.

Although verbal reports of event memory can be gathered from young children (Fivush, Kuebli, & Clubb, 1992; Price & Goodman, 1990), researchers tend to underestimate the memory competence of young children because these children cannot talk very well. The research on early memory is very clear and widely replicated. (See Howe & Courage, 1993, for an excellent review. It concludes that young children can remember, and for long periods of time.) Some of the studies in this area are specifically relevant to child abuse assessment, and these are detailed in the following section.

*Differences in Event Characteristics
at Different Ages*

Two-year-olds and 4-year-olds focus their recall on different things. Fivush and Hamond (1990) interviewed two groups of children about several past events. One group was interviewed twice, once at age 2½ (by their mother) and again at age 4. The second group was interviewed three times: first at age 2½ when they were first interviewed by their mother; second, 6 weeks later, when they were interviewed by an unknown interviewer; and third, at age 4, when they were interviewed by another stranger interviewer. There were clear differences in the children's recall during the different interviews, over time and across ages.

In the second interview, by the unknown interviewer, the 2½-year-olds gave a surprising 76% new and different information (verified as correct by the mother). The children seemed to know the interviewer did not know about the past event, and they gave different material than they had given to their mother. It could also be that the mother asked more specifically detailed questions, or that her questions focused on the things she featured in her memory. The information reported in this second interview was about events that could be considered *routine, mundane, or typical.*

When the children were interviewed again, at 4 years of age, there was a second surprise. The children now gave 74% new information (verified by the parent as accurate). This information was of a different nature than the information given at age 2. At 4 years of age, the children gave more information about the *unique or distinguishing events* they had experienced. This is in line with theory that purports additional complexity in memory as children mature, but it also suggests that there is a different memory focus at age 2 versus age 4.

This focus on routine, mundane events by 2-year-olds is echoed in other research. Nelson (1989) first detailed this focus in the bedtime monologues of 21-month-old Emily, which she collected over time. Emily's spontaneous recounting of her experiences did not dwell on special occasions like the birth of her baby brother, but she recounted routine events, such as going to her babysitter, over and over again. She seemed to focus especially on the deviations from routines, like the time she had to go to the babysitter in a different car because the family car was broken.

Why would 2-year-olds be more focused on routine events? Nelson (1989) hypothesized that very young children are tuned into routine events because this is what makes the world predictable. Fivush and Hamond (1990) also suggest the purpose of this focus is " . . . to be able to anticipate and predict what is going to happen . . . because it is these aspects that give the world predictability" (p. 241). Once routines are established and predictability is anchored, the child's increasing cognitive developmental capabilities allow focus on "deviations or distinctions from routines." Additional cognitive capacity permits greater skill in recognizing and comparing differences.

Differences in event category focus at different ages. Two-year-olds also report different types of information than do 4-year-olds. Fivush and Hamond (1990) noted that children at 2 and at 4 gave more information about activities and descriptions versus explanations or statements about affect. Fivush (1996) expands this finding to discuss the different kinds of information reported during the early preschool years. Two-year-olds report in the following ways:

- They report on activities that occurred, objects that were present, and who was present.
- They do not report on location.
- They have conceptual and cognitive limitations that interfere with the reporting of time.

- They have difficulty with temporal concepts such as before and after. Temporal questioning must be in the context of a concrete activity (e.g., was this at bedtime?).
- They do not spontaneously report emotions or thoughts, but if asked they may be able to report some feelings.
- They regard "yesterday" as generic for any past event. It is only when children are about 6 years old that they fully understand temporal order.

Prior to 3½ years, children do not understand location questions very well, but by 3½, they can begin to provide some concrete information on location (e.g., where did it happen? at my home? at my school?).

By age 4, children can give some temporal order to events if the events are in a concrete or relational format (e.g., after Halloween and before Christmas), but they cannot specify the amount of time between the two holidays. They give little information about emotion, mainly reporting that they felt good or felt bad. They are also unable to hold two opposing feelings at the same time (e.g., I love my dad, but I was mad at him). At about age 7, children are able to recognize that they can feel both positive and negative emotions together.

Older children's reports are more detailed than younger children's, and they recall more information spontaneously than do younger children (Hamond & Fivush, 1991). The authors note that the amount of information does not increase during preschool years, rather,

> the *way* in which information is recalled does. Children seem to be gaining more control over the retrieval process and are thus able to retrieve more information without adult guidance in the form of questions and prompts. . . . The present results indicate a developmental continuity in the memory system; even quite young preschoolers can recall a great deal of information if given appropriate cues and prompts. (p. 445)

Young children do not recall all the information they know in a single interview. Children may focus on different aspects of the event at different times, and this may make them appear inconsistent or unreliable. Children may give brief and incomplete reports to open-ended questions, even though they can give more detailed memory when asked specific questions.

———————————————— •◆• ————————————————

Implications for Practice
(Explicit Verbal Memory)

1. Young children's early abuse concerns should not be ignored; it is clear that even 2-year-olds can understand and remember events in their lives. They can also recall this information with good accuracy at a later time.

2. Differences in the information recalled at earlier and later questioning should not be seen as a demonstration of inaccuracy. The change in the type of information recalled, from the routine sequential event focus of 2-year-olds to the more complex assessment of unique and distinguishing detailed account of 4-year-olds, is a normal developmental phenomenon.

3. Assuming that all children can report equally on various types of information can lead to young children's responses being seen as less valid than the reports of older children. Different types of information are reported at different ages. Children mature in their ability to describe events, feelings, locations, and temporal information. Young children's reports would be less likely to be seen as invalid if professionals recognized that young children may not spontaneously report feelings and may report only one aspect of their feelings (e.g., the love and not the mad). Recognizing developmental differences in the content of recall is important in shaping the kind of recall we ask for, and the kind we expect.

Very young children's memory has been demonstrated by the repetition of multistep sequential events. Why don't they act out well-developed, multiple-step, clear behavioral sequences as evidence of their abuse?

(a) *Early learning is often tied to the situation in which it was first learned (i.e., situation-specific learning). In child abuse assessment, children are not usually returned to the original situation in which they were abused, so specific learning may not be exhibited.*

(b) *In nonverbal analogue research (Bauer's work), someone does something for the child (i.e., novel event sequences are presented visually, the child has a chance to observe and then interact with the sequence toward the completed result— ring the gong, for example); actions are demonstrated and explained. This is not always the case in child abuse. In abuse, someone does something to the child and the action sequences may not be fully observed, only felt. The action sequences may not have the same* order on each repetition and there may be no verbal description of the process.

(c) Material presented in the research cited is not threatening or invasive; it is not necessarily painful to recall or reenact; therefore, recall is not resisted or avoided as it may be in abuse assessments.

Any combination of these issues may explain why in abuse interviewing we do not see the same form of memory recall (Bauer, personal communication, 1996; Sroufe, personal communication, 1996).

FACTORS THAT AFFECT RECALL REPORTING

Scaffolding or Cuing

A significant difference in the number of questions needed to elicit recall was found between younger and older children (Fivush & Hamond, 1990). Two-year-olds were able to report a good amount of accurate information—as much information as the 4-year-olds, but they had to rely on the adults to provide a framework or *scaffold*. This was provided in the form of questions about details, such as, "Did you eat anything there?" "What did you eat?" or "Who went with you?" versus more open-ended questions, such as, "Tell me about your trip." The different retrieval cues the adult offered may also explain why recall was inconsistent between the above-mentioned mother interview and the stranger interview. The researchers conclude, "Younger children need more questions and prompts from the adult in order to recall as much information as the older children . . . [as they] are more dependent on adults questions to guide their recall" (p. 244). This also implies "that young children will tend to recall information only when it is asked for" (p. 243).

Nelson (1993) echoes Hamond and Fivush's (1991) findings: "Children often require extensive cuing to elicit any information about events that they have experienced. Asking children to report on events they have experienced is not always fruitful; it often seems that the adult's memory is not matched by the child's, although children may report elements that adults have not noticed or have forgotten" (p. 4).

There is a difference between *recognition memory* and *recall memory*. Generating a memory for yourself and verbalizing it is more difficult than recognizing something that is cued or offered as a choice. Recognizing certain information does not mean a child can spontaneously recall that same information. Again, the importance of interviewer structure and cuing to elicit early memory is underscored.

Spontaneous Comments

On the whole, older children gave more spontaneous information, but "across age groups and retention intervals only 21.65% of all children's narrative was spontaneously generated, indicating that the majority of all children's responding was directed and a much smaller proportion was spontaneous" (Fivush & Hamond, 1990, p. 422). Younger children need more assistance in disclosing their memories. Hamond and Fivush found that both younger and older children gave more spontaneous comments when the event was more recent.

Repeated Exposure

Memory is strengthened by repeated exposure to the material to be recalled. Fivush and Hamond (1989) had children 24 to 26 months of age participate in an unusual laboratory event. Half of them were returned after a 2-week delay and again after a 3-month delay, and the other half of the children returned after only a 3-month delay. The children who had reexperienced the event remembered more information than the single-experience children. Reexposure to elements of the original event can strengthen recognition memory, and this can aid recall.

Repeated Interview

Fivush and Hamond (1989) found repeating memory to different interviewers did not result in more false memories, but it did result in longer storage. In fact, the children were very reliable in providing accurate information across time to different interviewers; the only change was in the form of the information as it shifted with maturation.

When Fivush and Hamond (1990) looked at the differences between
2- and 4-year-old recall, they also looked at children's reports of an event
across time. (Remember, they had mothers interview their 2½-year-old
children after they had experienced an event, then 6 weeks later the
children were interviewed by a stranger interviewer, and then interviewed again by another stranger when they were 14 months older, or
not quite 4 years.) In this repeated recall situation, the children produced different recall material at different ages, but at both ages, the
content accurately reflected the events experienced. Three main reasons were offered for these inconsistencies:

1. The amount of distinctive or unusual versus typical information increased as the children got older. With maturation, children could give
   more information about what was distinctive, that is, unique and different. Younger children focused on generalized patterns, whereas older
   children could focus on things that were different from the generalized
   script.
2. The interviewer's questioning influenced the children's responses. The
   2-year-olds were very dependent on their mother's questions to elicit
   recall, but in response to her queries they gave accurate information. In
   this experiment, however, there were different interviewers for all three
   interviews. The children gave different responses to other interviewers
   simply because other interviewers asked different questions. As noted
   above, children are dependent on adult organization and cuing to facilitate their recall, and varying adult cues can prompt differing accounts.
3. The structure of a child's narrative influenced the type of reporting they
   did over time. Older children have learned more of the framework for
   narrating memories whereas younger children simply do not have these
   structures, thus the same content may not emerge. It is one thing to have
   a memory for an event, it is another thing to be able to tell about it.

Narrative Capacities

Children's emerging capacity for telling their stories reflects the
quality of the caretaker's interactions with them (Fivush & Hayden, in
press). Culturally, we tell stories with a focus (there is a beginning,
middle, and end), and the narrative moves toward a conclusion. A *high
elaborative* mother helps frame her child's recall into a narrative form.
She encourages reminiscing about past events, and in so doing she helps
her child to focus on what happened, what it meant, how the child felt,

and so on. A *low elaborative* mother focuses more on recall of specific items, or specific details. She may repeat her questions and offer little elaboration or detail. Children of high elaborative mothers have richer narrative that is retained longer (Pipe, Dean, Canning, & Murachver, 1996), and they come better prepared to deliver memory in a narrative framework (Fivush, Pipe, Murachver, & Reese, 1997).

A child's narrative skill, her "story telling capacity," also becomes the basis for her earliest ideas about herself (i.e., the stories that we carry about how we were when we were young). These memories mark the beginning of a separate sense of self, and they are called *autobiographical memory.* This is the term used to refer to the memories that go forward in time to become adult memories of childhood. These memories are verbally retrievable and include a sense of self (i.e., "this is what *I* did," and "this is what happened when *I* was small"). Autobiographical memory emerges with the increased use of language and symbols at age 3, but it is dependent on more than language and symbol facility. It is in conjunction with these skills that a separate sense of self begins to emerge (i.e., "I begin to know that I am *me*"). Our autobiographical memory is a compilation of the stories we know about ourselves, delivered in a narrative format (a story with specific elements, a developing progression, and an ending), with sufficient language to relate it. It may be composed of memories that are based on fragments of old experiences, of things our families have told us about our early history, or from pictures of events that occurred when we were small. This form of memory is the focus of the new narrative style therapy that seeks to encourage people to heal by recreating new stories out of old information (Freedman & Combs, 1996; Rosen & Kuehlwein, 1996).

Children's Motivation

The various research studies cited above offer detailed accounts of children's recall, even at young ages. This is not often the case in child abuse interviewing. When asked how researchers got very young children to talk about their experiences, Robyn Fivush (personal communication, 1994) said that one of the best indicators of whether the 2-year-olds would give information was the child's motivation or their willingness to cooperate.

Verbalized Memories

Events that are spoken are retained longer than events that are not talked about, and "events unspoken are more prone to error than events spoken." (Fivush et al., 1997). Things children talk about are more likely to be remembered and they are less prone to error. As noted above, Fivush and Hamond (1989) also found that repeating memory to different interviewers did not result in more false memories but it did result in longer storage.

------------------------------•◆•------------------------------

Implications for Practice

1. Open-ended questions alone will not effectively measure very young children's memory. Interviews with very young children should not be held to the standard of affording validity only to information gathered in free recall. To apply this standard to young children's recall is to discriminate against their normal, developmental capacities. Minimal response to open-ended questions does not mean invalid report capabilities in young children.

2. Younger children need more adult questions and prompts to guide their recall. Recognizing this greater reliance on adult structuring and cuing should not invalidate a more directed interview; however, care should be taken that follow-up questioning is not done in a leading and suggestive manner. Older children are able to report more information without adult guidance. For young children, knowing does not mean telling.

   It is important to remember that even the most experienced and well-trained interviewer may ask a leading or suggestive question during an interview, or such questions may be asked as a last resort. Asking such a question does not invalidate an entire interview, and its use and outcome must be considered within the content of the entire case. Contamination concerns arise when problematic interview techniques become frequent or an established pattern. For more discussion of this important issue see Myers, Saywitz, and Goodman (1996).

3. Young children give less spontaneous information than older children. Spontaneous utterances of young children must be explored with additional directed questioning.

4. Repeated interviewing, carefully done, does not result in false recall. Multiple interviews may help tap young children's full knowledge of

an event. Because different interviewers provide different structure and focus to their inquiry, different memories may be cued. If a child is first interviewed by a parent, then by a child protection worker, and later by a mental health professional, they will probably give different responses. If the interviews are carefully done, this normal developmental fact does not lessen the validity of different types of information given to different interviewers. Multiple interviews can have the effect of increasing detail of information recalled.

Of course, this is dependent on the quality of the interview. Care must be taken that the interviews are not leading or suggestive and that cross-contamination (presenting information gathered from one child in an earlier interview in a new interview with another child) does not occur. The idea of multiple interviews for young children challenges current recommendations for the field. If multiple interviews are to be considered, it is imperative that interviewers have a clear knowledge of the factors creating suggestibility in young children and take precautions that their interviews avoid such practices. Once this is understood, then the dangers of repeated interviewing can be minimized.

5. Repeated interviewing, if carefully done, may help strengthen a child's memory.

6. Different forms of interviewing are needed across different age groups. Failure to adapt to younger children's needs can lead to failure in fully assessing their history. One interview format will not work for all children.

7. Young children's ability to give good narrative for their experience is shaped at home. Children with high elaborative caretakers are better rehearsed in a format that is useful for the disclosure of abuse; therefore, children with low elaborative caretakers may appear less able to disclose information. This should not mean that their disclosures should be considered less valid. Such children should be screened for narrative abilities prior to target interviewing and the interview adjusted to their capabilities (see also Chapter 4).

8. Children's willingness to talk about their experiences increases the amount of information they offer. Children with abuse backgrounds may not want to discuss their experience, or they may have been directly censured. Child abuse inquiry may encounter a different environment than does research interviewing.

Children who have come from a secure and nurturing home, whose environment has been organized and explained, and who have experienced one incident of abuse often present that abuse as clear and specific. Their abuse stands in stark contrast to other experiences they have had. This disclosure background is markedly different from the child who was raised in a home where he was the fifth out of seven children, had a depressed or chemically dependent parent, had multiple caretakers and may, in fact, have had primary parenting from siblings who were only slightly older. Such at-risk children may also have been subjected to more episodes of abuse over longer periods of time. Disclosure of their abuse may have a markedly different format because they may not give good narrative accounts, and they may blend and mix information from the multiple experiences they have had. Behavior may be their most telling witness. These children are the most vulnerable, and yet their disclosure skills render their recall the most difficult to validate.

The above-cited research findings come from carefully constructed laboratory procedures. Child abuse interviews do not occur in laboratory situations. Interviewers with widely varying backgrounds in child development or interview experience are conducting interviews. Children may resist talking about their experiences because of threats or censures, and interviewers do not have knowledge of the original situation in which the memory was laid down to guide their interview or to validate the responses received. When the statements of young children enter a court of law, issues of memory and accuracy are subjected to a new arena. Defense experts argue that leading and suggestive questioning alters children's recall, resulting in false memories and creating accusations against innocent victims. Suddenly all the optimism and excitement found in the literature on children's early memory is cast into doubt. When it comes to child abuse, can children still recall with good ability and accuracy, after a period of time? Can young children's recall be manipulated by leading and suggestive interviews? Are young children's memories susceptible to bias or alteration from leading and suggestive interviewing? If they are, under what circumstances? Last, and most important, what are the implications for child abuse assessment; that is, how do we craft our assessments to avoid these pitfalls?

❏ Suggestibility in Young Children

Repeated research studies find that preschool children are more susceptible to leading and suggestive questioning than older children or adults (Bruck, Ceci, Francoeur, & Renick, 1995; Ceci, Crotteau, Smith, & Loftus, 1994; Ceci, Loftus, Leichtman, & Bruck, 1994; Eisen, Goodman, Qin, & Davis, 1998; Goodman & Aman, 1990; Leichtman &

Ceci, 1995; Oates & Shrimpton, 1991; Ornstein, Gordon, & Lazarus, 1992). This is a robust finding and not to be denied or minimized. Does this mean children are now inaccurate? No. This finding means that we need to understand the dynamics that underlie this susceptibility, which conditions heighten its occurrence, and how we might minimize the probability of such factors in our assessments.

The following section will (a) review the hypothesis of why young children are more susceptible to suggestion; (b) highlight the literature on children's suggestibility, emphasizing the specific conditions that heighten and create suggestibility; and (c) discuss the accuracy of children's recall for events, and apply this information to practice.

WHY ARE CHILDREN MORE SUGGESTIBLE?

There are several factors in young children's development that make them more suggestible. Some of the reasons that have been hypothesized for this susceptibility to suggestion are as follows:

1. Young children are dependent on adult retrieval cues to access their memories. If adult cues are inaccurate or misleading, children may have difficulty with memory retrieval. With additional knowledge and age, there is a greater ability to organize in a more meaningful way, and children are less dependent on the validity of external cuing.

2. Children do not correct adults. If an adult's questioning is leading and suggestive, especially if this is a repeated process, children's information is vulnerable to distortion.

3. The strength of a memory depends on the amount of language and number of experiential associations one has; the more language and experience, the richer the encoding. Young children have limited language and limited encoding, therefore their memory store may be weaker. Weaker memory store is more vulnerable to suggestion.

4. The level of children's language development also determines the kind of questions they can respond to (i.e., length, complexity; Faller, 1996). Adults' more complex language use may make their questions not understandable to young children.

5. Very young children have difficulty understanding the source of their knowledge, and they have difficulty analyzing their own thinking. Therefore, they may be more prone to misattribute sources of their information.

6. Adults are more powerful than young children—they know more, have more experience, and a kid's job is to learn from them. Young children assume adults are accurate informers, and they do not question their veracity.
7. Because young children are so dependent on their caretakers, they are sensitive to their status. If a child is questioned, and after giving an answer is questioned again, the child may feel his initial response has been inadequate and offer another response.
8. Accuracy of recall may vary across different categories. As noted above, young children attend to and store different types of information at different ages. Recall abilities may be weaker or stronger depending on the areas searched.

CONDITIONS THAT HEIGHTEN SUGGESTIBILITY

The next portion of this section highlights some of the literature on suggestibility that deals with preschoolers. Note that age 4 is used in many of these studies because it marks a transition time in the suggestibility of memory (Goodman, Aman, & Hirschman, 1987). At age 4, children begin to have an understanding of false beliefs and they recognize intentional deceit (Bussey, 1992). The important question to be addressed in this review is this: Under what circumstances and what conditions are young children more suggestible? When this is clearly in mind, then we will go on to consider how to craft our assessment procedures to minimize the possibility of contamination by suggestion.

Prompting

Repeated questioning using leading and suggestive questions has found increased levels of suggestibility, especially in younger preschool children. Two of the studies in this area require additional elaboration, especially in light of the publicity they have received (Stossolt, 1993) and the negative effect they have created in the public's view of young children's credibility as reporters.

Pre-event stereotyping and post event misleading suggestions. In the "Sam Stone" study (Leichtman & Ceci, 1995; N = 176, ages 3–6), children were exposed to both pre-event stereotyping and postevent misleading suggestions to look at the effects of this type of questioning.

A stranger named Sam Stone paid a 2-minute visit to the children's day care. Once a week for 4 weeks, prior to his visit, half of the group was provided stereotyped information about Sam Stone's visit. He was portrayed as a clumsy person who always got into trouble and broke things. Over a 10-week period, following his visit, four groups of children were interviewed four times. In the stereotype information group, children were divided into two groups. One group received stereotyped information and no postevent suggestive questioning. A second group received both stereotyped information before the visit and postevent suggestive questioning. A third group was presented with no preevent stereotyping but with postevent suggestive questioning, and a fourth group received neither the stereotyping nor suggestive questioning. Following the fourth interview, children were interviewed by a new interviewer using forensic procedures (e.g., free narrative, followed by probes encouraging children to say if they did not remember, etc.). This interviewer also asked the children if they remembered two fictitious events in which Sam Stone allegedly soiled a teddy bear and ripped a book.

The control group of children (i.e., no pre- or postsuggestive or misleading information) were very accurate in their account of the past events. The majority of these children did not give false information when suggested by the interviewer. In the rest of the conditions, the error rates of the younger children were significantly higher than the rates of the older children. With gentle challenging by the last interviewer, error percentages in the three groups decreased; however, important other concerns remained. In the combined stereotyped information and suggestive interview group, 21% of the 3- and 4-year-old children continued to maintain that they saw Sam Stone do the misdeeds, even after being challenged (conversely, 79% did not maintain the incorrect information). In contrast, the older children—5- and 6-year-olds—maintained the misdeeds at an 11% rate when challenged (89% did not). A number of the children gave convincing false perceptual details.

Repeated suggestive interviewing and visualization encouragement. In the "Mouse Trap Study" (Ceci, Crotteau, et al., 1994; $N = 122$, ages 3–6), once a week for 10 consecutive weeks, children were individually interviewed by an adult who encouraged them to "think hard" about whether they had ever experienced a series of real or fictitious events. The children were asked to consider questions such as whether they had ever gotten their finger caught in a mousetrap and had to go to the hospital to get it off. They were also encouraged to visualize the scene. At the end of 10 weeks, a stranger interviewer interviewed the children. Again the children were asked the real and fictitious questions they had been asked for the previous 10 weeks. The interviewer prompted with statements like "Think real hard, and tell me if this ever happened to you. Can you remember going to the hospital with the mousetrap on your finger?" The interviewer would follow up on the child's reply and ask for additional details, based on the child's answer.

True events were almost always recalled correctly. False events were reported by 44% of the 3- and 4-year-old children during the first interview. By the seventh interview, 36% of the group reported false events. The 5- and 6-year-olds had lower rates of false narratives; 25% were reported falsely after the first interview, and 32% were reported by the seventh interview. Many of the children gave detailed and convincing narratives of the false experiences.

This study was replicated by Ceci, Loftus, Leichtman, and Bruck (1994), with forty-eight 3- to 6-year-olds. This time, the interviewer informed the children each week, for 12 weeks, that they had actually experienced fictional events. With this type of interviewing, there was an increase in the children's endorsement of the fictional experience. Different suggested events were endorsed at different levels; however, neutral nonparticipant events received the most false endorsement and negative events the fewest.

After the 12 interviews, the children were interviewed by a new stranger interviewer. They were told that the previous interviewer had make mistakes about what they experienced and what they had not experienced. The children were then asked if they had actually experienced the false event. The majority of the children rescinded their previous endorsement. Slightly more than 50% of the neutral nonparticipant events and positive events continued to be endorsed, however.

Because very young children have difficulty distinguishing the sources of their thought, the request to imagine something, to visualize it, or to "think real hard" about something can easily tap the developing status of source attribution skills. Particularly when young children have been asked to visualize something, they will have difficulty distinguishing this visualization from actual experience. Both the Sam Stone study and the Mousetrap study are constructed to show evidence of some of the developmental phenomena that are specific to early childhood years but that also make the area of interviewing children problematic.

Another study on suggestive interviewing, one of the first such studies done (Thompson, Clarke-Stewart, & Lepore, 1997), had eighty-eight 5- and 6-year-old children interact with a janitor. The janitor used two scripts, acting as if he were either cleaning or playing. One hour after the interview, the children were interviewed again with the interviewer using neutral, accusatory, or exculpatory statements. The children were then reinterviewed by a second interviewer, and finally interviewed again by their parents. Clarke-Stewart et al., found that children gave brief and accurate statements in response to the interviewer's neutral statements. Under the misleading conditions, two thirds of the children gave information that contradicted what they had witnessed when they agreed with the misleading interviewer. They did give accurate answers to factual questions. When the second interviewer contradicted the first interviewer, the children again changed to agree with the first interviewer, and on the third interview, with the parents, the children retained their agreement with the misleading interviewers rather than remain consistent with what they had seen.

The Sam Stone and Mousetrap studies have both been used as demonstrations of conditions that may be simulated in actual leading and suggestive interviewing or in therapy. As mentioned in the previous section, young children have difficulty distinguishing internally generated and externally generated thinking. This ability is specifically in transition with children $3\frac{1}{2}$ to 4 years old.

This research highlights specific developmental transitions, and it demonstrates the problems that can occur during these changes. The encouragement to "think real hard" or to visualize a scene both capture the essence of change points in this skill. It is not surprising that such results were obtained; in fact, their outcome could easily have been anticipated by understanding developmental changes. These results should not be generalized to preschool children of all ages. Saywitz and Goodman (1996) also argue that the events in this study do not match actual abuse case experience, and the results are not generalizable. What does this all mean? Don't do interviews with children in transitional change periods in a way that incorporates problematic procedures!

Despite concerns about the generalizability of these studies, they do define a particular set of factors that can influence false reports. But it is inaccurate, and a misrepresentation of the total findings in the studies, to leave the impression that all children are prone to high rates of suggestibility. This is simply not the case.

At the time of these studies, there was no systematic evaluation of a series of actual child abuse interviews, so there was no data-based argument that interviewing of the form cited by Ceci and colleagues was not commonly done. Recent data, however, exist to substantiate that fact. A systematic analysis of actual child protective interviews in Tennessee (Boat & Everson, 1996) has not found evidence among professionals of the frequency and severity of errors depicted in this research.

There are two messages for child abuse interviewers in this data. First, interviewers of preschool children must be careful not to duplicate this problematic format in actual interviews. Second, it can be argued that interviews conducted in an appropriate manner produce results that are now supported by the findings in the overall studies of children's credibility: children are credible witnesses.

Parental Influence

Children are more susceptible to giving false information if they have been told incorrect information by their parents. Poole and Lindsay (1995) found that when parents read a book to their preschool children and told their children that Mr. Science had put something yucky in their mouth, 59% of the children reported false information. Ceci and Leichtman (1992) reported preliminary research by Ceci and colleagues that showed 3- and 4-year-olds could be manipulated into lying to protect their parent. Parents kissed their children while giving them a bath and dressing them. The following day the children were interviewed and told it was very bad to let someone kiss them when they had no clothing on. With this censure, the majority of the children denied being touched, but when told it was not bad to be kissed by a parent when they were naked, the same children correctly revealed they had been kissed when nude.

Effects of Age Alone

The younger the preschool child (i.e., 2- to 3-year-olds), the more prone to errors with leading and suggestive questioning (Bruck, Ceci, Francoeur, & Renick, 1995; Goodman & Aman, 1991).

Individual Differences

One of the newest studies of children's memory and suggestibility (Eisen, Goodman, Qin & Davis, 1998; Eisen, Goodman, Qin, & Davis, in press-a; Eisen, Goodman, Qin, & Davis, in press-b) was designed to assess the reliability of abused and neglected children's memory and resistance to misleading information. The ecological validity of this study—that is, the degree to which the study measures the same types of variables as are measured in actual abuse cases—is striking. A research context was constructed to encompass many of the specific issues in actual abuse cases. As part of an in-patient evaluation at Mt. Sinai Hospital in Chicago, 108 children, ages 3 to 15, who had been determined as maltreated (53% were either physically or sexually abused or both, 15% were neglected) were subjected to an anogenital exam. During their stay at the hospital, the children received a physical exam on day one, and on day two they received an anogenital exam that involved taking a sample of secretions from the child's genitals and rectum and digitally penetrating the rectum of the child to assess muscle tone. Heart rates plus doctors' and nurses' judgments of stress were also collected during the interview. In addition to medical data, a forensic interview and psychological consultation (involving assessment of mental status, emotional functioning, and psychological sequelae to abuse or neglect or both) were also coordinated. All parents and caretakers available were interviewed and social service system files were reviewed. All children ages 6 and under were screened for developmental delays. On the fifth and last day of the hospitalization, each child was administered a structured interview, composed of a series of specific leading and misleading questions, to assess his or her memory and resistance to misleading information for the details of the anogenital exam given 3 days earlier. Each child was thoroughly debriefed immediately after this interview.

For data analysis, the children were divided into groups by the type of abuse, and later they were assessed on their recollection of the exam. Inquiry about memory of the anogenital exam paralleled many of the elements found in actual abuse exams, because all the children in the study had experienced some form of maltreatment. The study found that younger children performed more poorly than older children on a measure of memory for the anogenital exam. The 3- to 5-year-old group made significantly more errors on misleading questions than the 6- to 10-year-old group. This is consistent with earlier research by Goodman and Aman (1990). Despite a poorer performance than the older children, the 3- to 5-year-olds still showed good resistance to misleading information in answering the abuse-related questions. Children with lower income levels evidenced significant lags in test scores for basic skills. This is in concert with other findings of achievement or skill lags associated with lower SES by Dorado (1996) and Lyon (1996).

As in many other studies, this study also found important individual variation. Some children were more suggestible than others. Variability in response to suggestion clustered in specific children and was not spread across the group. Forty percent of the errors made by the 3- to 5-year-old group were produced by only 4 of the 26 children in the group. Again, the importance of variability in suggestibility in different children is apparent.

A second study of this population (Eisen, Goodman, Qin, & Davis, 1997) confirmed the differences cited above and also found that dissociation was related to memory and resistance to misleading information. In both studies, global adaptive functioning was significantly related to children's memory and resistance to misleading information.

ACCURACY OF CHILDREN'S RECALL

Despite findings that young children are more suggestible, and despite the fact that many elements in their immature development can predispose them to a vulnerability for leading and suggestive questioning, the research on suggestibility in child witnesses supports children's overall abilities for accurate recall.

Ceci and Bruck (1993), in an exhaustive review of the literature on suggestibility in child witnesses, conclude their study as follows:

> In light of the full corpus of data that we have reviewed . . . this research shows that children are able to encode and retrieve large amounts of

information, especially when it is personally experienced and highly meaningful. (p. 434)

They also conclude that

> there do appear to be significant age differences in suggestibility with preschool-age children being disproportionately more vulnerable to suggestion than either school-age children or adults. (p. 431)

Neither is there substantiation in the research that children will provide detailed lies about abuse (Goldman & Goldman, 1982; Goodman & Hegelson, 1985; Gordon, Schroeder, & Abrams, 1990). The following indicate areas of research that support the general reliability of children's memory—a memory that is nevertheless quite vulnerable to a number of circumstantial influences.

Underreporting

Some children underreport their experiences. Ornstein et al. (1992) assessed 3- and 6-year-olds' memories after a pediatric examination. Results showed high rates of omission with both groups of children when interviewed with open-ended questions. Younger children had poorer results to open-ended questions than older children and younger children were more susceptible to suggestive questioning. Recall decreased with delays in the time of recall assessment.

Steward (1993) and Steward et al. (1996) report on children's reports of painful medical procedures. In general, children were quite reliable in their reports of their medical procedures, but a subgroup of children refused information about a painful medical procedure, despite having good recall for other aspects of the procedure. Steward (1993) had previously labeled such a subgroup as "he didn't touch me, and it didn't hurt." Careful examination of the children in the Steward et al. work found that such children had significantly greater endorsement of shame and embarrassment items. Although the research measures used did not clarify exactly how the shame and blame dynamic influenced the disclosure, the researchers offered several hypotheses for the impact:

1. The child's sense of powerlessness and helplessness may have left him or her with a feeling of shame, much like victims of abuse. Exposing this helplessness to a strange interviewer may be "more than the child could handle and thus the denial of pain in the subsequent interview might be interpreted as a coping strategy on the part of a child—negating the experience " (Steward et al., 1996, p. 151).

2. Feelings of embarrassment or shame might block access to the child's internal feelings of pain and thus interfere with the focus on pain. Coping is done by blocking the pain.

3. Children's socialization experiences in the family may be some of the most significant influences on the child's experience, and expression of pain as attachment history, communication patterns, and disciplinary practices may all interact to affect the child's reactions to interview.

Steward et al. (1996) underscore the need to "relate interaction dynamics during medical procedures to the overall history and quality of the parent-child relationship. It seems likely that how parents organize their caretaking behavior around a distressing or traumatic event reflects important aspects of the parent-child attachment history" (p. 152). It is quite possible that these same factors may also be at work affecting children's willingness to disclose information about painful abuse.

Saywitz, Goodman, Nicholas, and Moan (1991) investigated the memories of girls, ages 5 and 7, for medical exams. Children who were given genital exams (vs. children whose exams included a scoliosis exam) were more likely to have omission errors unless asked specifically about genital examination.

Young Children Are Not Highly Suggestible

Rudy and Goodman (1991) interviewed pairs of children, ages 4 and 7, who were left with an adult stranger. This stranger asked one of the children to dress in a clown's costume, lifted up the child, photographed the child, and asked the child to touch his nose and also tickle him. The other child was an observer. Ten days after this experience, the children were interviewed and asked misleading and nonmisleading questions. The 4- and 7-year-olds did not perform differently on their resistance to misleading abuse-related questions, and only one false report of abuse was given, that by a 4-year-old. The 7-year-old children gave more correct information to nonmisleading questions, and to misleading questions that were not abuse related, than did the 4-year-olds.

In the Saywitz et al. (1991) study of 5- and 7-year-old girls' recall of a pediatric exam, omission errors were more common than commission errors, and only a few children made commission errors. Seven-year-old children never made a false report of abuse and only three of the total sample of 5-year-olds ($N = 215$) made a false report.

Supportive Interviewers Get More Information and More Accurate Information

Children interviewed by supportive interviewers not only gave more information but the information they gave was also more accurate (Goodman, Bottoms, Schwartz-Kenney, & Rudy, 1991). Children questioned in an intimidating atmosphere were more susceptible to suggestibility in abuse-related questions.

Younger Children Can Be Accurate, Even With Adult Censure

Younger preschool children gave accurate information, despite being told not to, whereas older preschoolers colluded with the adult censure to not disclose (Bottoms, Goodman, Schwartz-Kenney, Sachsenmaier, & Thomas, 1990).

Repeated Exposure Yields Less Suggestibility

Pezdek and Roe (1994) wanted to find out if memory for a more frequently occurring event had a greater resistance to suggestibility than memory for less frequently occurring events. One hundred and twenty children (sixty 4-year-olds and sixty 10-year-olds) were presented with a series of slides. On recall interviewing, it was suggested that certain items in the pictures were in fact of something else. Findings showed that 4- and 10-year-old children were less vulnerable to suggestibility about more frequently presented information.

Planted or Erased Memories Are
Difficult to Create

A second study by Pezdek and Roe (1997) addressed the question of whether it is possible to suggestively plant false memories in children by comparing their vulnerability to the suggestibility of changed, planted, or erased memories. Eighty 4-year-olds and eighty 10-year-olds were either touched in a specific way (on their head or shoulder when the examiner moved to focus the projector) or were not touched at all during the viewing of some slides. After the slides, it was suggested to them that a different form of touch happened (the changed condition), or that there was no touch (erased), or that a completely new touch (planted) occurred. Findings were that suggestibility occurred only in the changed memory condition. In the planted and erased memory conditions, no suggestibility effect occurred. The findings were obtained with both the 4-year-olds and the 10-year-olds.

The authors conclude that—although it is relatively easy to suggest to a child a change in an event that was experienced, it is less likely that an event can be planted in or erased from memory. Thus, the concept that child witnesses are greatly subject to suggestibility based on the classic research showing the probability of planting false memories in children through suggestion, is inappropriate. In other words, many researchers agree that by age 10, children are no more suggestible than adults (Cole & Loftus, 1987).

"Yes" or "No" Questioning Alone Is
Insufficient With Preschoolers

Conditions that enhance or diminish the suggestibility of young children are critical for interviewers to understand. It may not be appropriate to decide an abuse case involving a preschooler with only the "yes" or "no" response to a directed interview question. Preschool interviews need to be much broader. Ceci and Bruck (1993) recommend that interview material be buttressed by broad-based information:

Therefore it is of the utmost importance to examine the conditions prevalent at the time of a child's original report about a criminal event. . . . It seems particularly important to know the circumstances under which the initial report of concern was made, how many times the child was questioned, the hypotheses of the interviewers who questioned the child, the kinds of questions the child was asked, and the consistency of the child's report over time. If the child's disclosure was made in a nonthreatening, nonsuggestible atmosphere, if the disclosure was not made after repeated interviews, if the adults who had access to the child prior to his or her testimony are not motivated to distort the child's recollections through relentless and potent suggestions and outright coaching, and if the child's original report remains highly consistent over a period of time, then the young child would be judged to be capable of providing much that is forensically relevant. The absence of any of these conditions would not in and of itself invalidate a child's testimony, but it ought to raise cautions. . . . (p. 433)

Implications for Practice

1. Assessment of young children's allegations needs careful attention to control for their vulnerability to leading and suggestive questioning.
2. Young children are credible reporters when there is an absence of leading and suggestive questioning.
3. Construction of assessment procedures to avoid pre-event stereotyping, post-event leading and suggestive questioning, and repeated suggestive interviewing (accompanied by visualization encouragement) for a nonexperienced event is important.
4. Check for parental influence as a source of contamination.
5. Recognize that in several research studies, much of the variability in vulnerability to suggestion was centered in a few children, not distributed across the group.
6. Some children are more susceptible to leading and suggestive questions than others; for these children, careful documentation of history, current status, and collateral information is critical.
7. Some children may deliberately underreport their recall for emotionally expensive experiences.
8. Employ a supportive versus intimidating presence in conducting interviews to maximize amount and accuracy of recall.
9. Recognize that children are more suggestible when changes in a memory event are suggested versus having a memory event erased or a new memory planted.
10. Children's resistance to suggestibility matures with age and cognitive maturation.
11. Broad-based information is needed for adequate assessment of young children (see also Chapter 3).

❏ **Fantasy**

Sometimes young children say bizarre or unusual things in the course of a child abuse investigation. When bizarre or fantasy-like elements intrude into an otherwise credible interview, doubt may be cast on the entire account. What about fantasy in the world of the young child?

Young children have active fantasy lives. By about age 3, words are no longer tied only to the objects they represent, they can be thought of independently in the child's mind. The young child must learn how to understand this new capability (DiLalla & Watson, 1988; Welch-Ross, 1995; Wooley & Wellman, 1993). Between the ages of 3 and 4, there is a major developmental transition in the mastery of real and pretend. Young 3-year-olds do not know that their thoughts can come from their head alone; these young children do not analyze their own thinking. By about $3\frac{1}{2}$, young children are beginning to be aware of multiple sources for thought origination, and by age 4 most children (at least in the population of white, middle-class children who come to university research centers) are able to distinguish the origin of their thoughts. This transition time, which may be longer in children with poorly stimulating environments, may cause some problems in interviewing.

What about fantasy in child abuse assessments? Interviewers have long seen children respond to the emotionally stressful experiences of abuse by ending a credible line of questioning with, "And then I kicked him, and I hitted him, and I killed him." This elaboration often comes to buffer the child's sense of vulnerability and fear. To admit to a devastating experience of abuse would be to sacrifice too much sense of self and personal integrity, and to admit the world is too unpredictable to be safe. Young children do not have a wide array of coping skills to deal with stress, and this "rewriting" of an ending to an abuse situation is often done in the service of the ego. As mentioned above, there is no research that has found children fabricating detailed histories of sexual abuse, but interviewers often consider a report with fantastical elements as generally less credible. Dahlenberg (1996) has found fantasy elements in accounts that have been clearly proven, "gold standard" cases (i.e., cases with perpetrator confessions, medical evidence consistent with the alleged crime, and, in the majority of the cases, at least one piece of persuasive external evidence [e.g., eyewitness, sibling with similar statement]).

A review of more than 5,700 interviews of children ages 3 to 17, with allegations of sexual abuse, were cross-referenced with data banks for medical records and criminal outcomes to determine a gold standard group. The videotaped interviews of these children were then analyzed for evidence of fantasy elements. Two classes of fantastic elements were examined—highly implausible or impossible events, and gross exaggeration of a plausible event. Dahlenberg (1996) summarizes, "the most compelling result of this investigation is that fantastic elements occurred most frequently in the accounts of children known to have been abused, and indeed were most common among children *known* to have suffered severe abuse" (p. 8). These findings directly counter the hypothesis that fantastic elements in children's accounts of abuse give reason to discredit the entire account. Of the 12 fantastical stories evaluated on the videotapes, 10 came from children in the 3- to 9-year-old group. Findings here are even more dramatic: "Subjects were more likely to disclose fantastic elements within their accounts of abuse if they were in the gold standard group; most important, they also were more likely to produce fantastic elements when abuse was severe" (p. 7). The assumption that fantasy elements should lead to suspicion of the entire allegation is not supported by this research.

Why would children incorporate fantasy into their accounts of abuse? Child abuse literature is virtually silent on this issue, except for the work of Everson (1997). Everson has extensively detailed the mechanisms that might underlie bizarre, improbable, and fantasy-like elements in children's accounts of abuse. Twenty-four explanatory mechanisms are grouped into descriptive categories on the basis of an interactive framework between the child and elements in the environment. The child's characteristics interact with three groupings of potential sources of fantasy-like material: (a) the abusive event itself, (b) the assessment process, and (c) "extrinsic influences," such as cultural influences, cross-contamination, dream incorporation and psychotic delusions. Proposed explanations for the incorporation of fantasy into an interview are summarized in the clusters below:

1. Interaction of the abusive event with the child's characteristics:
   - The account may be a true account of reality;

- The account may be a deliberate attempt by the perpetrator to confuse or discredit the child or a misperception due to drug effects;
- Trauma or stress may induce the misperception that a threat has been fulfilled when it has not, or it may act to cause selective misunderstanding or contamination of event material;
- Coping mechanisms to deal with abuse may involve fantasy to master anxiety, overstatement to adequately convey the intensity of the experience, or misreports to avoid blame or deny victimization;
- Cognitive immaturity may lead to misperception or miscommunication, or distortion may result from attempts to assimilate new information into old frameworks.

2. Interaction of the child's characteristics with elements in the assessment process:

- Error may be due to miscommunication between the interviewer and child, or there is distortion from multiple reporting of an account;
- The interview process may present leading or suggestive questioning; different media used to interview may introduce errors; error may come from confabulation—filling the gaps in memory with information that is not true—or error can result from interview fatigue;
- Children may exaggerate for attention or approval, an innocent lie may snowball, there may be deliberate exaggeration or lying, or there may be fantasy lying.

3. Interaction of other "extrinsic influences" with the child's characteristics:

- Cultural influences may be a source of bizarre or unusual accounts;
- Cross-contamination may result from exchange of information with various sources;
- A dream can be incorporated into an account;
- Delusions may occur due to psychotic processes.

Implications for Practice

The presence of fantasy in a young child's account of abuse should not in and of itself be seen as a cause for considering the allegation false.

❑ Trauma

VERY EARLY TRAUMA

Can very early trauma or abuse be remembered for recall later? Fivush and Hamond's (1990) work showed that 2-year-old children can accurately retain early memories over the course of about 18 months. However, in the research reviewed, the events recalled were interesting, personally meaningful events. What about recall of events that are traumatic or frightening?

Terr (1988) found behavioral and some verbal memories in the 20 children she interviewed who all had experienced severe trauma prior to age 5. She compared the later verbal and behavioral remembrances of these children with documentation of the original events. Verbal memories of the events were fragmentary or absent for children who were 28 to 36 months or younger at the time of the trauma. Girls were better than boys at being able to verbalize parts of traumas from before ages 28 to 36 months; and single, short events were more often remembered in words. Most interesting, she found that all children who had directly experienced the traumatic event displayed behavioral enactments that were accurate when compared with the events that stimulated them. Terr theorized that "behavioral memory appears to operate by different rules from those governing verbal remembrance. . . . Verbal recollections require conscious awareness, but behavioral memories do not" (p. 103).

Sugar (1992) documented three case studies of memories for events from 16 months of age and up. He found that the earlier the trauma occurs, the less the child is able to organize the material into narrative form. He argues that the age at which memories can be verbalized depends on the age of onset for speech phrases and on cognitive ability. The memory of these early experiences may persist for 30 years.

Terr (1991) later wrote about two types of trauma and the varying effect on memory related to the type of trauma. Type I trauma refers to single episode trauma and Terr predicts clearer memory for this type of event. Type II trauma refers to repeated events, often over time. This repetition is seen as blurring the individual details of the events and leading to a more sketchy recall account. This theorizing would appear to be in contrast with some of the above-reported information (i.e., repetition enhances memory); additional research reported later sheds some light on this seemingly contradictory aspect of memory and trauma.

Hewitt (1994) detailed two case studies of preverbal abuse in which children later gave detailed accounts of their abuse, indicating that their memories were still intact despite insufficient language to report the abuse when it occurred. Both of these incidents are one time occurrences in the context of otherwise healthy development, and they may offer an example of the clear recall cited by Terr as Type I experiences. Both of the children were also female, and Terr (1991) found that girls had better recall of earlier experiences than did boys.

Very young children's expression of their traumatic experience may differ from the expression of trauma found in older children or adults. Scheerings, Zeanah, Drell, and Larrieu (1995) documented reactions in 20 cases of severely traumatized infants and young children. They noted that a developmentally sensitive and behaviorally anchored symptom checklist was better at diagnosing Post Traumatic Stress Disorder (PTSD) in infants than the standard *Diagnostic and Statistical Manual of Mental Disorders, Fourth Edition* (*DSM-IV*) criteria. The young children did not evidence verbalizations of flashbacks, frightening dream content, and so forth, as specified in *DSM-IV* criteria because they obviously lacked verbal skills. They did, however, have several behavioral reactions indicating fears or anxiety (e.g., trouble falling asleep, nightmares, reenactment of trauma through play rather than verbalizations, avoidance, hypervigilance, aggression).

As Scheerings et al. (1995) noted, "criteria for diagnosing these disorders in standard nosologies may need revision for use with children younger than 48 months of age" (p. 191). When assessment with more behaviorally anchored and developmentally sensitive criteria was applied, cases of traumatized infants were more consistently diagnosed. They conclude that

> the clinical importance of these findings is that a post traumatic syndrome does appear to exist in infants and children exposed to traumatic events. The sequelae can be severely debilitating . . . . We hope these findings encourage clinicians to think backwards when they see a disturbed infant, particularly one who exhibits new onset of fearful and aggressive behaviors, and to probe for traumatic events in the past. (p. 199)

Knowledge of the special characteristics of very young children, both behavioral and developmental, is critical to understanding their history.

CHILDREN'S RESPONSES TO
MEDICAL PROCEDURES

Some research supports the presence of traumatic or stressful events as facilitating children's memory. Goodman, Hirschman, Hepps, and Rudy (1991) reported recall of blood drawing and experiences of immunization. After varying delay intervals, children were asked for free recall and prompted recall. Highly distressed children recalled significantly more correct information and they were more resistant to suggestion than children rated as less stressed. In general, there were few age differences in recall of the events, with little deterioration over time, and accuracy was maintained.

The severity of the event may also influence recall. A simple understanding of event recall and distress would be to assume that the more distressful the event, the more recall there would be. In practice, however, this has not been found. Easterbrook (1959) demonstrated that intense emotional experiences limit the range of perceptual cues that the individual is able to process, thus making very stressful events less well remembered. Steward (1993), while studying memory and stress with children in medical situations, noted that no one model explained the effects of trauma on memory. Steward et al. (1996) found that family variables may have an impact on a child's disclosure of painful medical procedures.

The children in the Steward et al. (1996) study were rated by staff on their level of distress during a medical procedure, and the children also related their own recording of distress. Steward et al. conclude that memory and emotion may have a "U-shaped" relationship. Children who have routine, uneventful visits report less information about the visit, those with mid-range stressful experiences remember more, and some children who experience very stressful events appear overwhelmed and report less recall. This finding supports some of Terr's (1991) contention that repeated, stressful experiences may overwhelm the child's coping mechanisms and thus narrow the perceptual field, resulting in less recall.

Steward et al. (1996) stress the importance of children's self-report data. The children's own judgments of pain contributed to the predictions of both completeness and accuracy, though adult eyewitness estimates of child trauma should be viewed with caution. Remembering and reporting are not the same thing. The best understanding of the effects of trauma and memory on a child appears to be related to the child's judgment of the meaning of the event.

In addition to looking at the effects of stress on memory, Steward et al. (1996) also considered the use of stimulus materials (anatomical dolls, pictures, props and cues) in facilitating a child's disclosure of a medical procedure. When anatomically detailed materials were provided to enhance verbal interviewing, reports by children after the procedure and after a 6-month delay allowed them to give more complete and consistent reports of their experiences. In their study, when children 3 to 10 years of age were provided with anatomically detailed dolls, no child made a spontaneous commission error and reported genital touch at the initial or the 1-month interview, and only one child did so at 6 months. The dolls did, however, elicit spontaneous erroneous reports of anal touch at all three interviews. Line drawings elicited no spontaneous anal touching but did elicit spontaneous erroneous genital touch. When directly questioned about genital touch, Steward et al. did not find error rates comparable to those found by Bruck et al. (1995), even with the youngest children. But interviewers in the Steward et al. study did not ask leading or suggestive questions during their interviews. Computer drawings were also used as cues, and they elicited spontaneous reports of body touch as well. All three formats were effective in eliciting reports of body touch, and all three could be used across an age range of 3- to 6-year-olds, but none was error free. Props were also used in the enhanced interview, and they were more accurately used by older children. Younger children, with subsequent interviewing, enjoyed handling the props, but they also demonstrated a marked drop in the accuracy of correct touch reporting. Playing with the props may refocus the interview more on current uses than on past recall of a specific event under question.

Uniting findings across several studies, Steward et al. (1996) state that children's memories are affected by all three factors found in an interviewing situation: (a) the status of the child, (b) the nature of the material to be remembered, and (c) the nature of the interview. This finding nicely summarizes what much of the above review has shown in a piecemeal fashion. Interviewing children is not a simple matter of attending to the interview protocol alone. It is a much more complex mix of events and people and emotions.

STARTLE RESPONSE

One more area of emotional processing with the very young is the fascinating work on nonverbal responses to emotional signals. The eye-blink reflex could be an informative measure of understanding about the development of responsiveness to emotional signals. In rats, the startle reflex is exaggerated in a conditioned fear situation. In adults, reflex blinks are facilitated while viewing unpleasant arousing scenes and inhibited when viewing pleasant scenes. This affective modula-tion of the startle response has been found in 5-month-old infants. Balaban (1995) found significant blink magnitude to auditory stimuli presented during the viewing of angry expressions compared to audi-tory stimuli presented during the viewing of happy expressions. This early indication of emotional responsivity to different emotional states is an interesting peek into the beginnings of emotional development. It also alerts us to the possible beginnings of emotional storage. These early memories are not explicit verbal memories, but they may become part of the fabric of expectations that a child builds about the world. This very early responsiveness gives pause to the argument that in-fants are not affected by their emotional environment and it should also begin to raise concerns about the possible effects on young chil-dren who have repeated exposure to violent or traumatic situations.

Implications for Practice

1. Nonverbal behaviors are expressions of early traumatic event experi-ence. Young children can recall early trauma, but it is not always expressed in words.

2. Not all children will express traumatic histories in the same way. Trauma can facilitate memory in some cases, or inhibit it in others.

3. Children's reports of earlier trauma offered at a later age should not be discounted.

❏ **Neurobiology**

Prolonged or repeated stress or trauma has an effect on the body, even in young children. Three areas of biological response to stress will be considered here: (a) cortisol research, (b) sleep disruption, and (c) neurological development.

CORTISOL RESEARCH

When an organism is in a stressful situation, the body reacts by secreting several hormones that help the body respond. One such hormone is cortisol, a focusing and orienting chemical secreted by the adrenal glands. In its arousal, it helps prepare the body for flight or fight, and in so doing it shuts down other responses that are operating during nonstress times. One of these responses is the immune system. Cortisol is also toxic to brain tissue, and the body acts to suppress prolonged elevation of cortisol levels. Hart, Gunnar, and Cicchetti (1995) found maltreated children failed to show elevations in cortisol on days of high versus low social conflict in the classroom, whereas the control group of nonmaltreated preschoolers showed elevated cortisol levels in the face of school stress. Reduced cortisol reactivity in maltreated children related to reduced social competence. Early responses to stress can shape patterns of responding that can affect later ways of reacting.

SLEEP DISRUPTION

When adults are anxious or upset they often find it difficult to sleep. It is the same with young children. Sleep is a regulatory function and it helps restore and maintain the body's homeostasis. There is a period of time in the process of sleep when the sleeper must "let go" of the day's concerns and allow the sleep process to override thinking. Many young children, when subjected to trauma or prolonged stress, are unable to fully relax and let go. They evidence difficulty falling asleep and may also evidence repeated awakening and sleep disruption. When very young children cannot tell you about their level of fear or anxiety, careful monitoring of their sleep patterns in the wake of abuse allegations is a powerful, nonverbal indicator of the child's stress levels. One other word about sleep and young children. We are programmed as a species for "flight or fight" in the face of danger. Very young children are unable to fight very well, and their limited locomotion also inhibits their ability to flee. But they are able to dissociate or space out in the face of intense stress. When infants are subjected to extreme stress they may simply fall into a very deep sleep. This sleep is different from their normal sleep: it is much deeper and the child is less easily aroused. Common naps of about an hour may extend far longer and the child may be less oriented on arousal. Repetitive exposure to stress can create a well-developed pattern of dissociative responding to extremely stressful situations, and this pattern may persist over time. Hewitt and Friedrich (1991) found sleep disturbance to be a significantly differentiating factor between abused and nonabused children.

NEUROLOGICAL DEVELOPMENT

A new and exciting area of research and theory on the relationship of memory and trauma involves the role of neurological functioning. The work of Bruce Perry and his colleagues (Perry, Pollard, Blakley, Baker, & Vigilante, 1995) traces the impact of various stimuli on the development of the brain and the role that early abuse or trauma can play. "Experience literally provides the organizing framework for an infant and child. Because the brain is most plastic (receptive to environmental input) in early childhood, the child is most vulnerable to variance of experience during this time. . . . The traumatized child experiences overactivation of important neural systems during sensitive periods of development" (pp. 276-277). Adult hyperarousal reactions to stress, the "flight or fight" stance in the face of danger, may not always fit children. Children begin responding to a threatening situation by attempting to contact their caregiver for protection (e.g., crying, fussing), but if they are unsuccessful, they begin a process of quieting, reorienting, and turning inward. This process, at its most intense, is a dissociative reaction. Behaviors developed in response to a threatening situation, especially if repeatedly practiced, can become firmly developed traits, and their neurological activation pathway can be elicited by less and less subtle cuing of the original threatening situation. In this manner an original adaptive response to trauma can become a long-term maladaptive pattern of behavior. Perry et al. argue for a neurodevelopmental conceptualization of childhood trauma and a view of children not as "resilient" but rather as malleable. Very young children are affected even by early trauma, and this trauma can sensitize neural systems to result in either persisting hyperarousal or dissociative symptoms, or both. There are different maturational trajectories for different areas of the brain and different capacities. Trauma at various times in early childhood can result in differing effects. Intervening in the case of suspected child abuse with very young children, although difficult because we continue to demand verbal disclosures, can have important, long-term neurological consequences.

Perry et al. also note that one of the most important factors in a child's response to trauma is the presence of a healthy caretaker. "This presence can dramatically diminish the alarm response of the dissociative response in the young child" (p. 285). This is one of the reasons I discussed attachment in Chapter 1.

If the parent is also sufficiently traumatized by the child's experience, or if the parent's own history is reactivated by the child's trauma, then the parent can communicate a sense of fear to the child, and the child's continued hyperarousal may go unmediated. This is interesting thinking when we consider the cases with allegations of sexual abuse that appear to be driven by an anxious and hypervigilant caretaker. If the child witnesses the parent's upset before a visitation and resonates to that discomfort, and also feels the anxiety and discomfort after a visit, then visitation contact may be paired with the primary caretaker's fears. Because the child is closely tied to the primary caretaker, the fears of the caretaker are transmitted to the child as well. These ideas need additional research and follow-up over time.

Implications for Practice

1. Early experiences of abuse or trauma can have significant effects on the long-term development of the young child; early abuse should not be overlooked.

2. New information on the neurological basis of emotion also highlights the importance of assessing abuse with very young children.

3. Early experiences have an affect on emotional development and the organization of behavior and personality. Experience shapes brain functions, and early experiences shape the foundations of life's behavioral responses. It can affect the development of the emotions that make us human.

4. Just because children cannot talk about their experiences does not mean that they cannot remember. Early intervention in trauma is not just for the child, or the parent; it is for the future too.

❏ Attachment

It is difficult to determine damage to an area of human development that is not physical or palpable, yet this new area of research is quickly finding links between early experiences and later emotional reactions, such as self-regulation, responsiveness to others, overdependency on preschool caretakers, antisocial behavior, and depression. Attachment research points toward important links in interpersonal styles and later school and social behaviors.

As I reviewed the above areas in early development, I was more and more convinced of the importance of early experiences and early memory. Researchers on attachment and memory do not often inter- face, but the information I found on attachment seemed to be one of the most compelling examples of the long-term influence of very early experience. By 12 to 18 months, very young children have internalized a relationship pattern with their primary caretaker that becomes the prototype for later relationships. Longitudinal research on attachment types points toward a long-term effect from these early relationships. Early attachment styles can affect things such as interpersonal relation- ships, school learning behaviors, and emotional adjustment.

Attachment, as defined in Chapter 1, refers to the pattern of relation- ship between a child and the caregiver, and it can be measured. Mary Ainsworth, a pioneer in the field of attachment, developed a laboratory procedure she called the "strange situation" (Ainsworth et al., 1978) to assess attachment. The reaction of a 12- to 18-month-old child to the return of his or her mother, after the child had been left alone or with a stranger, could be reliably used as a measure of the child's form of attachment. This finding gave new importance to the early life experi- ences of infants and toddlers. Repeated, often nonverbal interaction sequences between caretaker and child were well enough internalized, even at this young age, so the child had in place a clear expectation of the nature and quality of human interactions (see Bowlby's description of an "internal working model," 1982). Even more amazing is the persistence of the effect of this early attachment history, extending into adolescent and early adult years (Carlson, 1997; Warren, Huston, Egeland, & Sroufe, 1997). The long-term effect of early attachment style on later behavior has been demonstrated in several studies. The devel- opment of hyperactivity and inattentiveness in middle childhood was predicted more strongly by early childhood quality of caregiving than by early biological or temperament factors (Carlson, Jacobvitz, & Sroufe, 1995). Caregiving and contextual factors, along with early distractibility, best predicted hyperactivity in the middle childhood years. Additional analysis of attachment relationships and the nature, frequency, and severity of mental heath problems at 17, show a relationship with attachment style (Sroufe, 1996).

Egeland, Sroufe, and Erickson (1983) linked early attachment styles to later behavioral problems and styles in preschool. Especially detrimental were the effects of psychologically unavailable mothers, as their children showed marked increases in maladaptive patterns of functioning from infancy through preschool. These children were avoidant of their mother, angry, noncompliant, and highly dependent. Neglected children had the most difficulty organizing themselves to deal with various tasks. One of the significant findings of this research was the tremendous effect that neglect and psychologically unavailable caretakers exerted on the later behaviors of their children. Emotionally neglected children *fared even less well* than the children who were physically abused! Additional work in the area of attachment and later development has supported these findings. The relationship of aggression and passive-withdrawal in early elementary ages (Renken, Egeland, Marvinney, Mangelsdorf, & Sroufe, 1989) was predicted by a history of insecure attachment and poor adjustment, inadequate or hostile parental care, and stressful or chaotic life circumstances. The effect was stronger for aggression in males but less strong for passive-withdrawal in females. Children showing positive adaptation in the infant or toddler period showed greater rebound in elementary school years, despite poor functioning in the preschool period (Sroufe, Egeland, & Kreutzer, 1990).

Some would argue that what is being reflected is not the recall of early child-caregiver relationships at 12 and 18 months but rather the reflection of a long-standing pattern of child care. Newer research addresses this issue, however, and it supports the important role of attachment. For those who would continue to argue the long-term salience of early experience on later life, one need look no farther than the work of Mary Main and her adult attachment interview. Main and colleagues noted that a mother's early attachment history was often duplicated in the style of attachment with her children (Main, Kaplan,

& Cassidy, 1985). Robert Karen, in his book *On Becoming Attached* (1994), carefully traces the relationship between early attachment styles and later adult relationships. Although statistically these relationships are not without error, there is a sufficient body of work to support the lasting effect of early relationships on later adjustment styles.

There is also mounting evidence about the physiological effect of good attachment and its relationship to stress in young children. If a child has a secure attachment, the impact of later stressful events is buffered: "The secure children seemed to be saying, 'This is scary, but I feel safe'" (Gunnar, 1995). What happens when there is no warm, individually responsive care? Research with Rumanian children reared in orphanages provides important clues. Cortisol, a hormone that is released with stress (see Neurobiology above) can be measured in the saliva of infants. Gunnar (1997) found major differences in cortisol levels between children who were reared with good primary caretakers and Rumanian children who were reared in orphanages. Children with good attachment had lower baseline cortisol levels that peaked in the morning and then dropped or moderated during the course of a day. They evidenced an ability to moderate their levels of arousal and stress as their caretakers helped them respond to their environment. Orphanage-reared children evidenced abnormal cortisol levels; they had overall higher levels of cortisol that rose during the morning and peaked by noon, then decreased slightly by evening. These children gave evidence of difficulty in moderating their levels of stress and arousal. Gunnar found a major negative effect on emotional development in the orphanage-reared children. The presence of a nurturing, responsive caretaker helped the children self-regulate or moderate their stress levels. It would appear that early stimulation, with a variety of emotional responses, excites the brain and helps develop a range of affect.

Schore (1996) approaches the issue of attachment and neurological maturation in another way. He proposes that "the maturation of corticolimbic systems that neurobiologically mediate essential affective and social regulatory functions is experience dependent" (p. 59). During the first years of life the combination of problematic attachment patterns with the primary caretaker and the exposure to "prolonged episodes of intense and unregulated interactive stress" result in impairments of this important regulatory processing and can create impairments in the circuitries of this prefrontal system which is then implicated to "later forming psychiatric disorders" (p. 59). This underscores, again, the importance of the early years of life and attention to children's situations and needs during this time.

Parent-child attachment may be affected by a young child's abuse although there is little research on this topic. Clinical experience suggests several ways the relationship might be affected. For example,

1. *Parent response. Some parents may reject their children after abuse, feeling they are damaged or in some way "soiled." Consequently, at a time when a child needs support and approval most, they may instead find rejection. A second type of parental response can occur when the "ghosts" of a long-repressed abuse experience trigger depression, and a mother may become overwhelmed by having to deal with a traumatic past she has tried to forget. When this coincides with the child's increased needs for contact, the child may experience the parent as emotionally unavailable. A third parent response may be in reaction to a child's sexualization. We do not think of our children as being sexual, but the abuse experience destroys the natural naivete about sexual matters and distorts the boundaries against sexual touching. For young children, this aberrant behavior may mistakenly now become the norm for sexualized touching practices. Children acting in a sexualized manner may be very disturbing to a parent, and this may lead to harsh discipline, distancing, or rejection.*

2. *Child responses can shape the forms of adult interactions. In addition to the parental effects, there may be other effects on the child. When deviant sexual practices are normalized by abuse, it may prompt abused children to respond to others in a sexualized way and thus unwittingly make themselves more vulnerable to further abuse. Consequently, when a potential abuser approaches a child and the child does not display the usual negative reactions that would push abusers away, then this lack of resistance or hesitancy may be read as permission or even approval. "But she didn't stop me," one teenage abuser said; abnormal sexual behavior has been normalized for the abused child.*

Implications for Practice

1. This research shows that simple, repeated interactions with nonverbal infants are indeed stored, and the memory of these interactions go on to become the framework for later relationship expectations (i.e., attachment style).

2. Our adult ability to be intimate, to give, to receive, to share, and to empathize has its roots in this very early relationship and the patterns it sets up for human interaction expectations.

3. The finding that emotional neglect or "psychologically absent" caretakers have a greater effect on a child's later adjustment than either physical or sexual abuse is very significant.

4. It is even *more* significant because we intervene for children's well-being when there are observable and medically documented signs of abuse, but we find it virtually impossible to have children removed from an emotionally abusive, much less emotionally neglectful situation!

5. Protecting early emotional development is virtually impossible given our current laws, decreasing funding, and the prospect of even greater funding cuts for child welfare. New legislation passed by Congress in 1996 raises the threshold for responding to child abuse. These guidelines changed the level of child abuse that must be responded to from "potential harm" to "imminent danger." Thus, more minor concerns about child abuse will now receive less attention.

6. These findings and their implications represent a major schism between the research on children's welfare and the actual practice found in day-to-day child protection work.

7. The mere idea of embracing the notion that we should be about protecting young children's emotional growth and development is mind-boggling, especially when considering the current overworked caseloads of those mandated to protect our children.

8. Current child abuse staffing demands that only the most severe cases of abuse get service (*most severe* is usually defined by physical findings, death of a sibling, failure to thrive, and dangerous acting out); this practice exists despite the research showing the significant effects of all early experiences of abuse and neglect.

The benefits of good attachments are clear, and the long-term consequences for poor attachment relationships are also clear. Monitoring attachment quality in the lives of young children and helping provide adequate caretakers can be one of the best prevention efforts we can make on behalf of children and the adults they will become.

There is little we can do to control the abuse that has happened with a child, but when a child comes into the protection system, there is much we can do to help ensure safety and guard the right to healthy emotional relationships and good attachments.

❑ Early Memory and the Unconscious

The research we have just reviewed is very clear. Even before words can carry our memories forward, there is good evidence that experiences are already shaping our first expectations of the world. Verbal recall of specific events and interactions may come later, but the effects of early experiences may have already laid the foundation for the way we make meaning of later experiences.

An intriguing exercise is the consideration of the active nature of these old memories. Maybe the lingering effect of early, nonverbal, but shaping experiences is what Freud meant in his idea of the unconscious (Bowlby, 1983; Loevinger, 1976; Sroufe, 1996)—a collection of very early experience, linked-event sequences that shape our brains and our expectations. If this is the case, then it is significant to recognize that early abusive or traumatic experiences may be difficult to alter or reconstruct given our current therapy format. The primary way we now mediate or reorganize the trauma of past fearful or damaging experiences is through verbal interventions. Therapy is for verbal, or at least play-proficient, children. Yet very young children possess neither capacity! These powerful nonverbal experiences that shape our expectations may be very hard to alter. It is precisely this potential, if this hypothesizing is true, that could make very early experiences so powerful. This hypothesizing, along with other research reviewed here, underscores why early abuse is so important to address.

* * *

❑ Reconceptualizing Preschool Abuse Assessment

This section will integrate the above research and theory into a proposed foundation for practice. You will find a summary of major research findings, implications from the research, and new assessment strategies for preschool children.

SUMMARY OF MAJOR RESEARCH FINDINGS

1. Even very young children can store memories of early experiences.
2. Many young children can accurately retrieve early memories over time.
3. Young children's experiences may be expressed behaviorally rather than verbally.
4. Young children do not spontaneously give detailed and complete accounts of their experiences.
5. Young children need help from interviewers to retrieve memories through interviewer scaffolding or cuing.
6. Such interviewing is not commonly offered in protocols for assessing older or nonhandicapped children.
7. Young children's methods of reporting may be judged less valid if the same interview format is used for all ages.
8. Young children's words alone are often not strong enough to sustain the weight of the full allegation's credibility.
9. Young children's statements need the buttressing of contextual information, including developmental history and current status, plus careful analysis of their sexual behaviors and behavior problems.
10. Young children are more susceptible to leading and suggestive questioning; thus, detailed information on the initial disclosure is needed, and subsequent interviewing must carefully control for this vulnerability.
11. Young children need assessment measures that allow accommodation to their rapidly changing developmental status.

Implications of the Research

1. **Assessment must shift from an emphasis on verbal statements alone to an emphasis on behavioral expressions as well as verbal utterances.** Verbal interview alone is not an appropriate assessment format for the young preschool child.
   We need to develop an assessment format that does four things:
   - evaluates children's statements in the context of their developmental status and history;

- recognizes the importance of behavioral repertoire in young children;
- does not place its sole weight on words alone;
- allows changes in assessment format that can shift over time, matching the changing competencies of the child.

2. **Assessment of abuse with very young children must shift from an emphasis on criminal prosecution to an emphasis on protection for the child.**

    Without eyewitnesses, confessions of perpetrators, or physical signs, small children's statements may be unable to meet the burden of proof for criminal prosecution. We need to develop a protective focus that does five things:

    - puts a priority on the protection of these children
    - demands careful evaluation of these cases
    - uses family or juvenile court to provide protective measures such as restricting contact, supervising visitation, and monitoring effects of contact
    - considers the burden of proof met by significant behaviors and statements
    - develops other arrangements outside the court system when less formal levels of protection are needed

---

NEW STRATEGIES FOR ASSESSMENT

The following conceptualization of assessment strategies for preschool children seeks to combine relevant theory, research, and applied clinical practice.

Very Young Children (18–36 months)

These Stage 1 children cannot successfully participate in a focused interview; they require a nonverbal assessment protocol. Such a protocol emphasizes documentation of behavioral repertoire (over time and across situations), collateral information, objective testing, and good developmental history. Assessment at this stage does not consider verbal disclosure as the only avenue of disclosure, although it does not ignore spontaneous statements. It carefully documents all behaviors and compares them to research-based norms for interpretation. It also

carefully inspects the situation around initial and subsequent disclosures for possible contamination. Assessment directed toward protection of the child versus criminal prosecution will require a major
departure from the present focus. Protection may range from no contact with an alleged abuser to supervised visitation, or to educa-
tion/prevention work that clarifies boundaries and develops safety
plans.

Young Children (3–5 years)

These Stage 2 children are in transition to interviewing capabilities,
and although they have some verbal communication skills, they do not
have all the skills necessary for detailed and specific interviewing.
They require careful assessment of behavioral repertoire, history, and
current developmental status in concert with a format that will prescreen for basic interview skills. Such prescreening is essential so the
interviewer can adapt the interview to fit to the child's capacities, and
not place the burden on the child to adapt to the interviewer's format.

Assessments at this level need flexibility in light of the changing
capabilities of the child. If a child has few interview skills, then the
behaviorally focused protocol used for the younger children may
predominate. If the child has demonstrated good interview skills, then
the information from the interview can be buttressed by additional
behavioral information. Some of these children can testify, but many
cannot, and data gathering should be for protective purposes, as well
as for prosecution.

Preschool Children (5 Years and Older)

These Stage 3 children can interview but they may need some minor
modification to adapt to their ability levels.

Chapters 4 and 5 present strategies for assessment in each of these
age categories. They begin with a case example of a child in a certain
stage, then list methods for assessment of that age child, and finally,
use case examples to apply the information presented in the chapter.
The methods proposed in the next two chapters attempt to bridge the
chasm between research and practice. These clinically developed
methods are not considered foolproof methods to give the truth about

abuse. They are offered as a more flexible, developmentally focused approach to assessment that will generate additional research and findings. Even though this framework can help in the assessment process, it should in no way be seen as a substitute for adequate training and supervision in this area of concern.

4

Assessing Very Young Children (18–36 Months): Children Who Cannot Be Interviewed

"My daughter, who is 27 months old, has been saying, 'Daddy butt. Daddy hurt butt.' The last time she said this, I repeated her statement and she said, 'Does this,' and grabbed at her nipple. My daughter has been resisting diaper change with my husband, but not with me. When I have to leave the house and leave her alone with him, she cries and cries. One time recently when she was naked, she put a strap from her car seat between the cheeks of her butt and moved her hips up and down and made noises, 'Uh, uh, uh.' I have talked to my husband about this and he denies he has done anything. I am concerned there might be abuse going on. I'm going to move in with my parents until this gets sorted out. Can you help me, please?"

What can you do with a case like this?

Before presenting an outline for evaluation of cases with very young children, I would like to clarify three bits of information. First, I work in a private practice setting and am a *second line* referral source; therefore, I rarely do initial assessments that are used for screening and documentation of cases of sexual abuse. I get my referrals after a case has been screened by police or child protection personnel, and I only do an initial screening if they request it.

My job is to assess the information about alleged abuse within the context of the child. Thus, my focus is both broader and more in depth than most initial interviews. I have the luxury of being able to conduct multiple sessions and can also use psychological tests. My assessment format has components that are different from those used by police or child protection personnel, so I will note throughout this protocol the things that are strictly part of a psychosocial assessment and may not apply to the typical initial interview.

Second, the emphasis in interviewing very young children is on history and behaviors, and a background in child development is needed to adequately gather this history. Whenever I have presented the following protocol to police officers, someone from the audience comes up and says something like, "I think every cop needs to hear this information, it should be mandatory, but I don't think I can do this stuff. I don't have enough background."

I refer such professionals to mental health workers or to professional interview centers that have staff with mental health expertise in very early child development. I believe it is critical to understand what needs to be done and how it can be done. I do not expect, however, that all professionals will themselves be comfortable with the assessment focus of this book. An important part of being a professional is to claim one's own strengths and limitations, and then share and balance these with other professionals. If you choose not to go forward with the following assessment format yourself, you will still have the information necessary to help direct another mental health professional in conducting an effective assessment.

Children who are under 3 years of age, as well as children with expressive handicaps or those who are electively mute, share many of the following characteristics:

- little language
- unintelligible speech
- an inability to report important concepts (who, what, where)

- play behavior that is sensory exploration, lacking detailed representation of actual events

Finally, before reading this chapter, please be sure to review the appropriate child development background I discussed in Chapters 2 and 3. References will be made to this material, with special attention to the research showing how developmental age affects the expression of sexual abuse and why we need to modify our interview format for young children. If you have read that, then you are ready to begin.

❏ Child Assessment Outline

The following assessment outline incorporates research and developmental theory into a prototype for abuse assessment with nonverbal children. Bill Friedrich (of the Mayo Clinic) and I developed this outline to use in research we completed on 2-year-old children. It has proven to be useful in clinical work, but it should be regarded as a work that is still in progress and subject to modification. (An outline form of this assessment is found in Appendix A.)

SETTING UP THE INTERVIEW

Your goal in this assessment is to gain as much knowledge as you can about the child and his or her family. The primary caretaker is usually your best place to start. Without adequate background, you will not know how to interpret statements the child makes or behavior the child may display. The words and behaviors of young children reflect the idiosyncratic experiences they have had. These children are embedded in the family context, and a careful and thorough knowledge of that context must be obtained.

As a clinician, I find that I need to schedule at least a 2-hour intake period with the primary caretaker, *without the child.* One of the first functions in this interview is to create a positive relationship with the caretaker and to reduce anxiety about the processes. Seeing the child without first having seen the caretaker raises anxiety in the parent and, subsequently, in the child. The better sense of relatedness you can develop in this session, the more comfortable the parent will be in letting you work with the child. I consider these first 2 hours critical, not just for the kind of information you will gather but also for the opportunity to develop future relationships with the child.

The assessment of abuse allegations involving very young children cannot rely on the child's statements alone. The assessment process is much like putting together a mosaic; as various pieces of information are assembled, a picture of the whole emerges. Eight different areas are critical to this process: developmental history, sexual abuse concerns, significant behaviors, rule-out hypotheses, objective measures, collateral information, contact with the child, and observations.

The semistructured interview outlined below surveys the past history and current status of the child. It focuses on important developmental milestones as well as shaping experiences from the child's history. The interview provides the foundation for your assessment as it helps you understand the ability of this child to function. It helps you evaluate the influence of the rest of the information you will be gathering.

SCREENING FOR DEVELOPMENTAL HISTORY

Was this child born via a wanted pregnancy?

Was there any drug or alcohol use during pregnancy? During what part of the pregnancy? Before the parent was aware she was pregnant? How much use, how frequent, and what kind of chemical?

Was there medical attention during pregnancy? What kind?

How long did the labor last?

Were there any delivery complications?

Was the child medically normal at birth?

Was there any placement in Intensive Care?

Have there been medical complications since birth? If so, please list these.

Children with medical problems (e.g., premature infants) place an increased stress on their caretakers and are at higher risk for abuse.

* * *

When did the child begin to walk and, if known, when did he or she begin to talk?

You are screening here for general developmental milestones. Most children walk at about 1 year and speak one or two words at about the same time. Many caretakers' memory for these events is not very reliable, but you can screen for major delays or problems in development.

Who has been the primary caretaker for the child?

What other caretakers has the child had, and for what period of time?

Has the child been separated from the primary caretaker for longer than overnight?

You are looking for information on the beginnings of attachment. A stable, consistent, nurturing, responsive caretaker is important for secure attachment.

* * *

Has there been a history of prior trauma in the child's life, including major medical procedures that might have been difficult for children, the witnessing of violence, or a situation of abuse or harm to the child or others?

Are there other factors that might have created the concerns that reported the case?

Through this basic history, you are also screening for other potential problems, besides abuse, that might affect a child's status and functioning.

SCREENING FOR CURRENT STATUS

Who is in the family?

Are the parents separated or divorced?

Who are the caretakers for the child?

How often is the child with each of them?

Have there been any problems with them?

Alexander (1992) emphasizes that the quality of family and relationship variables exacerbate or buffer the effect of sexual abuse. Other factors that appear related to the level of significance of abuse include lack of maternal warmth, support, and closeness; disruptions in the mother-child relationship; family cohesiveness; and the absence of family conflict (see also Friedrich, 1988; Paveza, 1988).

* * *

If the parents live separately, what is the visitation schedule?

Are exchanges between caregivers handled nonaggressively?

What kind of routines exist in the family?

What is the child's typical daily schedule?

We have found it interesting to ask who prepares meals for the child, what time the child goes to sleep, and if she has a specific bedtime, what she likes to eat, and so on. Once again, you are screening for major deviations. Many neglectful families do not have regular mealtimes or do not develop plans together.

What are the child's names for important people or things in his life?

Because articulation problems are common with this population, many children have shortened names as well as unusual names for people, places, or other body parts. Ask for the specific names that the child might call significant people in his life (e.g., grandfather, brother or sister, babysitter).

* * *

What does the child call his or her genitals? nipples? anus?

Does the child have specific names for genitals? It adds to assessment problems when the child has a "butt" both in the front and the back of their body or when both male and female genital anatomy are called "butts." If the child does not have a name for genitals, ask how the caretaker feels about assigning specific names to these parts. Children with vague names often have parents who are avoidant of reminders of sexuality. If a child does not have clear names, you may want to delay seeing a child until the caretaker has had a chance to help the child learn specific names (without, of course, bringing up the possibility of abuse as they teach these labels). You can encourage caretakers to do some of this education while the child is bathing or just out of the tub; this is a great time to teach eyes, nose, mouth, tummy, vagina, knees, and feet. Most parents will use "vagina" and "penis" for genital names, but some families resist this specific labeling. Letting them provide their own names is fine, the point of this labeling is to provide clear language for discussion of any abuse. Parents can also be encouraged to use these genital labels in a teaching manner in the same way they have taught eyes, ears, nose, mouth. Some parents have creatively exposed their young children to babies in the process of diapering. This has been especially helpful in teaching anatomical names for the other sex's private parts, and it is done in a nonintrusive manner. The parent may want to listen for any comments or remarks the child might spontaneously make at this time if there are concerns about possible abuse.

It is my belief that giving very young children specific names for their genitals is one of the first things we can do for the prevention of child abuse. It is a more helpful statement if a child is inappropriately touched and can tell you that it was in her vagina or on his penis (and not on the butt) where he or she was touched. People then can intervene in an appropriate manner.

* * *

What is the genital-care practice in the family?

"How do you wipe your child after toileting?" or "How do you bathe your child's genitals?" is helpful. Evidence of frequent enemas or rectal temperature taking is also important information.

Nancy Burson and Mark Everson of the Center for Child Abuse and Trauma at the University of North Carolina, Chapel Hill, have found this last question to be a good screen for some maternal sexual abuse, or for more subtle invasive practices that do not show up on a routine screen.

SCREENING FOR ABUSE HISTORY

Has there been any suspicion of prior abuse with this child? Has there been any prior report made?

Has the child witnessed abuse or has there been any abuse directly perpetrated on the child? This would include physical as well as sexual abuse, and any form of emotional abuse or neglect.

Most people are not really clear about labeling emotional abuse—they know what they think is abusive, but terms are difficult to apply. The APSAC Practice Guidelines for Psychosocial Evaluation of Suspected Psychological Maltreatment (1995) identify six forms of emotional abuse: spurning; exploiting/ corrupting; terrorizing; denying emotional responsiveness; isolating; and mental health, medical, and educational neglect. The Guidelines also provide guidance to professionals evaluating children and adolescents for psychological maltreatment.

* * *

Has the child been exposed to sexual activities?

Has the child witnessed intercourse?

Has the child seen X or XX pornographic movies?

Has the child seen sexually explicit literature?

ASSOCIATED RISK AND SAFETY FACTORS

Parent's Abuse History

Is there a history of chemical abuse with either parent? Is either parent currently using drugs or alcohol?

Has there been physical abuse in the family? Have either or both parents been physically aggressive with each other? Has the child witnessed this? How often?

Family Boundaries

Does the child have opportunities to sleep with the parent?

Does the child have opportunities to bathe with the parent? With what frequency?

With what regularity does the child see the parents without clothes? How many times a week?

Does the mother have a history of sexual abuse? Did this involve penetration? Did it involve force?

In two studies of abused 2-year-olds (Hewitt & Friedrich, 1991; Hewitt, Friedrich, & Allen, 1994), the maternal history of sexual abuse was a significant predictor of whether or not the child was "probably sexually abused." This does not mean that the maternal history of sexual abuse causes sexual abuse of the children. What it does mean is that maternal history may be an important risk factor. When a child is abused at a very young age, it is likely that she is growing up in circumstances characterized by more than the usual number of risk factors.

* * *

Does the mother have a history of physical abuse?

Does the father have a history of sexual abuse?

Does the father have a history of physical abuse?

History of Parents' Sexual Relationship

What has been the sex life of the couple?

Is there a history of compulsive or aggressive sexual contact?

Has the mother ever felt raped by the father?

Have there been unusual or atypical forms of sexual arousal present?

What is the use of pornography or videos in the process of sexual arousal?

"The marital relationship is a window into how intimacy is expressed in the family" (W. N. Friedrich). Unusual sexual needs, heightened frequency of sexual contact that is not comfortable for both partners, coercive sexual behavior, and exhibitionism suggest that sexual intimacy patterns in the family are distorted. When these patterns are present, sexual abuse of children is more likely, as well as excessive sexual behavior in the absence of overt sexual abuse. In cases of contested custody, a history of distorted sexual intimacy between marital partners is seen as a risk factor.

Maternal Connectedness

Does the mother feel supported by her own mother?

Does she visit her mother regularly?

Was there ever a period of time in which she did not feel supported by her? If so, when?

Studies by Mary Main and her colleagues (Main et al., 1985) indicate that attachment between a mother and child most often parallels the attachment that existed between the mother and her mother. Her Adult Attachment Interview must be administered by trained interviewers; it is not intended for screening interviews such as this. However, the WMCI (Working Model of the Child

Interview [Zeanah & Benoit]) offers the clinician a way of probing the quality of the parent/child relationship. By asking some specific questions, however, you may be able to get some idea of the earlier attachment pattern. Researchers have found that the quality of response detail to questions about maternal history of relationships is a good indicator of the quality of the relationship. Often the information is in how the mother says it; comments like, "My mother and I got along just fine," may be juxtaposed with other anecdotes that demonstrate an angry or neglectful relationship. The Working Model of the Child Interview (Zeanah & Benoit, 1995; Zeanah et al., 1997) is one measure specifically designed to assess the parent-child relationship through interview. It can be helpful for follow-up sessions when more information on attachment is needed. As you know from the theory and research in Chapters 2 and 3, attachment influences the kind of relationship children will present to you on interview, as well as the kind of expectations they will carry with them into life.

* * *

Does the mother have friends?

How many friends does she have?

With what regularity does she spend time with them?

Maternal connectedness is a measure of the quality of the mother's relationships. Dysfunctional families tend to live in isolation whereas healthier families have networks of friends and associates. The capacity to make and form friendships is one of the strongest buffering variables that one can carry into life. It is important to have the availability of alternate caretakers, especially when one has a young child. You want to know if this family has other resources available and, if so, at what level.

Family Arrest History

Has the mother ever been arrested? If so, for what? Did she spend time in jail? How long?

Has the father ever been arrested? If so, for what? Did he spend time in jail? How long?

SEXUAL ABUSE CONCERNS

Very young children may express themselves more eloquently in their behaviors than with their language. The purpose of this next, very detailed part of the intake interview is to get information about behaviors the child has exhibited over time and across situations. Most allegations are reported because of a specific incident or concern; however, earlier concerns are often also present. Begin to ask about early behavior because it can reveal the originating pattern to the abuse.

Initial Sexual Behavior

What was the *first* behavior or statement that your child made that left you concerned about sexual abuse?

Describe what that behavior or statement was. Where did it occur? When did it occur?

Describe exactly the child's behavior or the child's statements. What was the precipitating stimulus (or trigger factor)? What was the child's affect at the time?

How was this handled by the receiver? Did the receiver respond with anger? Did this person shame the child? Show fear to the child? Fall apart?

Because young children are so tied to their primary caretakers, they are also very sensitive to the primary caretaker's reactions. Very young children do not form their own sense of shame or embarrassment about their sexual abuse. Rather, they measure their own behavior by the quality of their caretaker's response. Therefore, it is critical to understand what cues the parent has given. Because caregivers may edit how they respond to the child, it is useful to ask general questions first. These are: How did you respond? What did you say? How did you feel? Did the child pick up on your feelings? Using their responses as a guide, you can then explore for the likelihood of more rejecting, angry, and shaming responses.

A parent who is more neutral may say, "What are you doing? Where did you learn that?" or "Who does that? Show me." These kinds of responses elicit additional information from the child and do not censor or frighten the child for any later follow-up. When an interviewer asks whether a child remembers the time she was in the bathtub, the child may feel comfortable to talk again about that experience if the past experience was accepting and calm. If, however, the child has been scolded, shamed, or blamed, she may feel she has done something wrong and may not want to talk about a painful past.

Because young children can be contaminated in their information, it is important to ask what kind of questions were asked of the child at the time of the initial disclosure. Were there leading and suggestive questions? Interviewing sexually abused children requires training and skill, and some parents do not understand that repeatedly asking a question may elicit a change in the child's response or alter the validity of the response. For example, suggesting issues may prime him for a particular type of response. On the other hand, simply asking a child yes or no questions may lead to misinformation as the child may respond to please the parent but not have specific content; the parent, however, may understand the child's agreement as evidence of a specific experience.

What words were asked in the questions? Was the parent using age-appropriate language? Was there anything about the words or the method of presentation that would seem biased or suggestive?

If the initial inquiry has been conducted in a leading or suggestive manner, this fact alone may not contaminate the whole case. If the child has a repertoire of spontaneous behaviors or statements, these may help clarify the extent and nature of the abuse even if the initial interviewing was not very well done. If a child has no behaviors and his abuse is documented solely on the quality of his statement, then the effect of the parent's early leading or suggestive questioning could disqualify the case.

Other Sexual Behavior

Repeat all the initial sexual abuse questions listed above for each incident described.

Carefully document each time the caretaker recalls where the child may have communicated information indicating possible abuse. Ask the questions in order. This simple, methodical history has always amazed me with its power to be so informative. Most cases are reported because of one target incident, but usually there have also been other examples across time, some clearer than others. When considering all such incidents, a more defined picture will begin to emerge.

SCREENING FOR SIGNIFICANT BEHAVIORS

As you know from reading the previous chapters, the little research that has been done on the behaviors of sexually abused children in this age group does indicate the potential for some behavioral problems. Clearly, more research is needed, however, to understand the extent of these variables.

Clinical experience has shown that acutely disturbed behaviors exhibited by very young children are often time limited. Acute symptomatology may dissipate rapidly over a period of about 6 weeks if there is no further abuse and the child is safe. Thus it could be lost to your history unless it is seen quickly. If the case absolutely cannot be seen within a week or so of the initial report, it is imperative that you ask the parent to keep good behavioral logs. (The Mannarino & Cohen [1996] behavioral report chart is very helpful in documenting daily behaviors.) Help the parent learn how to take clean, behavioral documentation and to avoid leading or suggestive questions. The parent should document what the child said and did, and in what context.

Sleep Problems

Has the child experienced any problems sleeping lately?

In many cases of sexual abuse, the child has been sleeping fairly well and then suddenly experiences an acute disturbance in sleep patterns. The child may awaken three or four times a night and scream, "No! No!" or "Don't!," "Owie!" "Hurts!" or "Stop! Stop!" This behavior may last for several days or weeks and then gradually subside. The disturbance may recur spontaneously if there is a trigger event for the child (see Chapter 3, the section on factors that affect recall) that raises concerns generated by the old material.

Sexualized Play

Have you noticed any unusual or repetitive play?

Repetitive sexualized play, independently initiated, has been associated with sexual abuse in the study by Hewitt et al. (1994; Schirvar, 1998). Even in a simple form, this play can be both graphic and helpful in understanding the child's history. Repetitive, almost compulsive-like play such as repeatedly poking a doll in the crotch, is of special importance.

In the Hewitt et al. study, a 2-year-old came home from his adolescent babysitter's home with a bloody anus. Penetration was confirmed by the physician, but the child's behavior also confirmed his own history. He began taking his Cabbage Patch Doll everywhere he went and to multiple people in his environment (including the check-out person at the grocery store). He would urgently point to the doll's bottom and say, "Owie bottom! Owie bottom!" His mother reported that it was difficult to get him to refrain from demonstrating his concern with the doll. It is this particular kind of reenactment that can also form the basis for future play therapy.

Toileting and Bathing Behaviors

Have there been any changes in toileting or diapering behaviors?

It is important to recall that certain situations might mirror the initial abuse context, and trigger a child's reactions. For example, children may abruptly cease to cooperate with diapering. They will hold their legs tight and cover their genitals, say "No, no!," and squirm away. Another child might suddenly begin to refuse a bath and scream and yell when her parents attempt to undress her. Ask carefully about behaviors in situations that might mirror the abuse situation, such as diapering, bathing, or undressing.

Fears or Phobias

Have you noticed any increase in fears or worries lately? How have bed-
times gone? Are there separation problems with the primary caretaker? Has the child become much more difficult to leave at childcare
with more clinging and crying? Are separations at bedtime suddenly
more difficult? Has crying been prolonged after the caretaker leaves?

*It is also common for children to suddenly become much more clingy and whiny
with their caretakers after abuse. They want greater proximity with their
primary caretaker and are especially disturbed when a stranger appears. They
may also have an increased resistance to separation at bedtime. Because such
behavior is common in young children, it does not necessarily signal abuse and
can be related to other environmental changes as well. Therefore, careful
screening to determine the origin of the behavior is important.*

*For example, one 2-year-old girl returned from a weekend visitation with her
father and was very subdued and quiet. She sat in a corner of her grandparent's
home and would not respond to her uncles or grandfather. She began crying
when she wet her pants and her genital area was found to be bright red and raw.
When taken to see her adored pediatrician, she was very fine with the nurse
examining her but went berserk when the male pediatrician entered the room.
This was a marked change from her usual cheerful greeting. Although that does
not in itself prove sexual abuse, it is one more piece of behavior and history to
add to the mosaic of the assessment findings.*

* * *

Does the child suddenly begin to approach strangers and act overly friendly
to them?

*This response is the opposite of the clingy behavior noted above, but this reaction
has been seen in samples of abused children. It is reflected in some of the
questions on the CSBI as well. Children with good attachment histories suddenly begin to go toward adult strangers in a very friendly manner. This may
be the child's attempt to make friends with a potentially threatening person and
check them out. This behavior is one that needs more attention and understanding not only for its dynamics but also because of the potential risk it may
present for very young children.*

* * *

Does the child exhibit compulsive behavior patterns? Does the child repeatedly engage in certain kinds of activities or behaviors such as insisting
on keeping a door to a specific room shut or open?

*Sometimes this compulsive behavior can be a form of undoing, in which the
child acts to be in control of a situation. By being in control, she tries to soothe
the anxiety or effects of the trauma associated with the abuse.*

A final word about behavioral problems in very young sexually abused children. Cases that medically indicate damage and "prove" sexual abuse has happened are rare in this age group, but they are often seen as the "gold standard" for future diagnosis. Children with documented medical conditions most often show Post-Traumatic Stress Disorder (PTSD) effects (sleep disturbance, phobias, repetitive behaviors) in response to aggressive sexualized contact. This cluster of trauma-reactive behaviors plus sexualized behaviors gives a signature profile for early traumatic abuse. But an important caution applies here. Not all sexual abuse is traumatic for young children.

Gentle but inappropriate sexual touching, rather than forceful penetration, is less associated with PTSD. When sexual abuse is coupled with attention and physical stimulation in an otherwise neglectful environment, a pattern that differs from the PTSD pattern is most common. In cases with nontraumatic touching, an increase in overt sexualized behaviors may be seen.

❑ Creating Rule-Out Hypotheses

During your intake history, it is often clear that there are other explanations, besides abuse, for some of the child's behavior. We find it very helpful to generate our own rule-out hypotheses. For example:

Is this child's reaction the result of exposure to a bitterly contested custody struggle?

Is this child's fear stemming from having witnessed physical violence rather than having experienced sexual abuse?

Is this child displaying certain behavior because he might have seen sexual intercourse?

Listing items as rule-out hypotheses can help you take a broader look at the case. It is as important to be able to identify when a case *is not* related to sexual abuse as it is to identify when it *is* related to sexual abuse.

❑ Using Objective Measures

We use three objective measures in assessing cases: the Child Sexual Behavior Inventory (Friedrich, 1997), the Child Behavior Checklist

(Achenbach, 1991a, 1991b), and the Child Development Inventory (Ireton, 1992). All these measures are to be completed by a parent figure. The validity of the information provided depends on this individual's objectivity and how accurately he or she has viewed the child. All information on the measures should be integrated with observation, history, and collateral resources.

CHILD SEXUAL BEHAVIOR INVENTORY (CSBI)

The CSBI is the only research-based measure that systematically examines a range of children's sexualized behaviors and compares these behaviors to a group of abused versus nonabused children. The CSBI solicits information from the mother regarding a range of sexual behaviors in her child. (Chapter 1 presented information on the kinds of behaviors that are normative and those that are clinical, according to the CSBI.) This measure requires about 10 to 15 minutes to complete, with the parent rating those behaviors seen over the previous 6 months.

This instrument lets you see the extent to which a child exhibits sexual behavior and whether the level of that behavior is more or less similar to nonabused or sexually abused children. Because the assessment of very young children must focus on behavioral repertoire, this measure is especially important.

Although these measures are usually given to parents after the intake interview, I often offer the CSBI to the caretaker toward the end of my intake interview to screen for any area of sexual behavior we may not have talked about. It has been interesting to watch some parents suddenly recall behaviors when their memory is jogged by the inventory. This adds a richness to the behavioral history that is being gathered.

CHILD BEHAVIOR CHECKLIST (CBCL)

The CBCL is a measure that compares the behaviors of a young child with those of other children of the same age and sex, and offers levels of significance for a target child's specific behavioral profile. It takes about 20 minutes to complete. The CBCL screens for behavior problems in multiple areas: social withdrawal, depression, sleep problems, somatic complaints, aggression, and destructive behaviors. The developmental sensitivity of the measure has been enhanced with the creation of a form specifically for 2- to 3-year-olds, in addition to the usual one for 4- to 18-year-olds. Clinicians use this measure to screen for significant behavior problems. It offers objective measurement to concerns like sleep disturbance that often present in abuse cases.

CHILD DEVELOPMENT INVENTORY (CDI)

The CDI surveys a young child's development in the following areas: social behaviors, self-help skills, gross motor skills, fine motor skills, expressive language, comprehension of language, skills in letters and numbers, and an overall general developmental score. It takes about 30 to 40 minutes to complete and is often the one parents find hardest to finish. Scoring compares a target child's ability level with the normative group of same-age children and provides a measure of the child's developmental process, including lags or problems in skill acquisition.

Clinicians use this information in multiple ways. The CDI screens for developmental problems the parents may not recognize or know about and gives an overall idea of the status of the child. If there are problems in development, the child's ability to present his or her information may be compromised or altered. This can then be taken into account when assessing the child's data. Knowledge about the child's expressive language and language comprehension scores will give an idea about how able the child is to be interviewed.

Data from the CDI is critical in cases in which abuse cannot be determined but risk factors are prominent (and this is a common category for many of these cases). CDI scores form a basis for referral to specialized services such as Head Start, Early Education Programs, or Special Education. Such settings can both remedy any delays and monitor and report any suspicious behaviors.

All these measures are subject to reporter bias. Some parents who have unresolved abuse histories are hypervigilant about sexual behaviors, and they can produce very elevated protocols. Other parents may be more repressed in their recognition of sexualized behaviors. When high levels of pathology are noted by the parent but are not echoed by a day care provider or sessions with the child, then we become concerned about the validity of the parental observations. Scores from objective measures are compared to our own clinical observations and experiences with the child, the history, and information from collateral sources.

❏ Noting Collateral Information

Which important people in this child's life, besides the primary caretakers, can provide information about the child's behaviors or symptomatology?

CHILD CARE PROVIDERS

Information from the day care provider or the sitter is very helpful. Abused children don't usually express their behavior to just one person. Asking a day care provider to fill out a CBCL, CBSI, or CDI can give an interesting, sometimes contrasting, perspective. When observations are consistent, they strengthen the validity of the case. When observations are disparate, this does not necessarily negate the primary caretaker's observations. Some children do not show critical behaviors outside their home. This may be because such behaviors occur during bathing or nighttime bed rituals and therefore not at day care or with the babysitter. If there are marked differences in perception, however, it is a cue to look at the primary caretaker's level of bias in interpretation.

RELATIVES

Are there relatives who have regular contact with the child and who might be considered alternate caregivers? Could they complete any of the objective measures? Is it important to interview them? Are they able to give impartial judgements?

MEDICAL INFORMATION

Has this child had a medical exam? What are the findings of that medical exam? Is it possible to get releases to receive that information? Were there significant behaviors that occurred during the course of the exam or were there statements made during this exam?

Medical exams for a child of this age rarely have physical findings. However, behavioral data observed during the examination may provide important information for your assessment. For example, children who have been frightened or hurt during their abuse often are very resistant to a medical exam. Some of them show clear differentiation in the sex of the professional they will allow to look at their genitals.

CHILD PROTECTION

Has there been an investigation by child protection? If the case has not been referred to you by child protection, can you have a release to talk to the child protection investigator? What did the investigator find? Who did she or he talk to? What kinds of behaviors or concerns were seen with this child?

POLICE INVESTIGATION

Have the police investigated? Have they talked with the alleged perpetrator? What's their feeling about the case? What did they find? What have they seen?

There are always at least two sides to a story involving child abuse. The scope and credibility of your assessment is limited if you don't examine all sides. If you don't have access to the alleged perpetrator, note this fact in your report and point out the limitations in your conclusions. When you can interview only one side, the rule-out hypotheses are important.

Putting together a case of sexual abuse with very young children is like putting together a puzzle. Each one of the above sources alone will probably not offer information powerful enough to draw a conclusion about the case. The whole picture is rarely reflected in one of the pieces; yet if all the parts are brought together, sometimes the overall picture is very clear. It is essential to gather information across time and across places in order to fully assess cases with very young children.

❏ Making Contact With the Child

Because these children cannot be interviewed, you may feel they do not need to be seen for they can offer little in one appointment. However, there are many things that can be learned from meeting the child.

OBSERVATION

What does this child look like? Is he or she age-appropriate in height and weight? What is his affect? What is his level of activity? How approachable is she? How does she interact with her primary caretaker? How does she explore her environment?

*Begin contact with the child with a powerful, yet underutilized tool: observa-
tion. Simply observing a child can alert you to problems the child may have that
the caretaker has not reported and that may be important to your attempts to
talk with him or her. If you do not have training in observation, The Classroom
Observer, 3rd Edition (1997) by Boehm and Weinberg can help enrich your
skills.*

THE CARETAKER-CHILD RELATIONSHIP

How do the caretaker and child interact? Does the child come to the
caretaker for help or assistance? Does he move closer to the caretaker
when he is stressed? Is there eye contact? Is affection expressed?

*Watch for evidence of the attachment quality in young children. On the first
visit, it's amazing to observe a child who begins to explore some of the toys in
your room, and when he experiences trouble and needs some help, he turns and
comes to you rather than the primary caretaker. When a child ignores his
primary caretaker to come to a stranger for help, you have just witnessed an
important marker for possible attachment disorders.*

CROSS-VALIDATION OF CARETAKER
INFORMATION

Do your observations of this child match the caretaker's reports?

*On intake, one mother described her child as "average" in all ways, yet when
the child appeared for the first appointment there were several signs of fetal
alcohol effects (widely spaced eyes, ears spaced low and turned forward, dental
problems). The child was lagging in many skills, though these were not reflected
accurately on the CDI because the parent overestimated her child's developmental capabilities. All the measures completed by the parents for this assessment
outline are subject to parental bias. As professionals, we can not only offer a
broader reference group but also provide avenues to specialized resources, if
needed.*

❏ Pre-Interviewing the Child

Even though these children usually do not have the skills to be
formally interviewed, some of the older 2-year-olds may tolerate a very
simple form of questioning. For best results, know their background
and history. Use language that is simple and concrete. Become skilled

at understanding immature articulation because children will not explain (and often won't repeat) their comments to you. Before actual interviewing, work to develop some relationship and assess developmental status and the presence (or absence) of skills needed to respond to a simple interview. As you do this ask several questions about the child and his or her status.

ESTABLISHING RELATIONSHIPS

How easy is it to make friends with the child? Is he comfortable and trusting? Is he anxious and does he cling to the caretaker? Does he disregard the caretaker?

You can begin contact with the child while the parent is in the room so the child has a secure anchor as he meets a stranger. Later you can quietly join the child on the floor to explore the various material you have available. You may silently watch or simply reflect what he is doing. You may ask a few questions or help him learn how a new toy works.

TALKING TO THE CHILD

Does the child have much language? How understandable is it? Do I need to have a parent in the room to interpret for me or am I able, with a little bit of time, to understand what she is saying? How frequently does she talk? Is she comfortable verbalizing or is this a very quiet and unresponsive child?

As you sit with the child, listen to her vocabulary, articulation, sentence structure, and language comprehension. To an untrained person this may look like just play, but it is a lot more—your initial assessment here shapes the direction of further interactions.

SCREENING FOR CONCEPTS

Can the child respond to questions about who, what, where? Does the child have the basic conceptual development that is needed to participate in an interview about abuse?

Some children who are almost 3 years old have very good language skills. If this is the case, then begin to screen for the kind of concepts a child needs to be able to interview: "who" questions, the idea of touch, and genital names. All these skills are involved when you have to ask the child, "Who touches your pee pee?" for example.

To see if the child has "who" concepts, you can ask the child, "Who lives at your house?" or, sometimes more interesting yet, "Who sleeps at your house? Who puts you to bed? Who helps you when you hurt yourself?"

Next, screen for the concept of "what." You can ask, "What color is that big bird on Sesame Street?" or, "What did you eat for breakfast?" If the child can answer your "what" questions, then go on to other prescreening issues. Some children readily answer questions, others are mute. **When a child cannot respond reliably to basic "who" or "what" questions, do not pursue interviewing.**

FREE PLAY OBSERVATION

How does the child play? Does she simply look at an object, feel it, put it into her mouth, try various ways of interacting with it (hitting, punching, coupling it with another toy), or does she use the human figure dolls to go to bed, sit on the potty, and so on.

Children who are simply exploring objects are at a very early stage of play and cannot be relied on to demonstrate experiences through play. You cannot expect to use props, anatomically correct (AC) dolls, dollhouses, and so on, as vehicles for communication when there are no representational play skills present. Representation of self—a capacity needed before AC dolls can be used to show self and other interactions—is not expected at very young ages.

PLAY SCREENING

Can the child use small dolls representationally?

You may ask a very young child to select (from a pool of small, say, 5-inch adult and child dolls) a doll for the mom, one for the kid, and one for the dad. Then watch how the child plays freely in a dollhouse with these dolls. Some children only play with the mother and child doll. At some point you can take the dad doll and say, "Here comes the dad. Show me where he should go," or "Show me what he does."

This simple request to "show me" what the dolls do is as close as I can come to integrating one of the formal, research styles for assessing children's memories. In Pat Bauer's (1996) work with very young children, she first demonstrates how several parts (i.e., a gong, a stand, and a mallet) can be assembled to form a working gong. Later, she assesses recall by showing the child disassembled pieces and asking them to "Show me what we can do with these." This request then elicits a sequence of behaviors that is used to demonstrate memory in the very young child.

Giving stimulus doll figures to the child and watching his play does not use neutral objects. It also requires some representational skills with dolls but does

not require self-representation. This free play exercise is one of the only ap-
proaches to data gathering for this age child that requires little verbal direction
and yet may elicit some meaningful behavior. Remember, no research has been
conducted with abused children to quantify this approach. Clinically, children
have been observed to do a wide range of things. Some children will put the dad
to bed, or have him sit at the table, whereas other children will refuse to play
with him.

While the child is playing in the dollhouse, you can initiate another activity
that gently gathers information. You can begin by saying that it is time for the
child doll to go to bed or take a bath. Ask the child, "Who should give the little
girl a bath?" or "Who should put her to bed?" You could also say that the child
doll needs her diapers changed and then ask, "Who should change the little girl's
diaper?" You can offer the alleged perpetrator doll as someone to help. Carefully
watch the child's reaction. A young child can sometimes participate in this very
concrete play with interesting responses. One child threw the dad in the basket
and refused to play with him. Can such interviewing prove abuse? No, but it
is one piece of information for your mosaic.

SEPARATION

Finally, watch to see if the child can tolerate separation from the caretaker. If at all possible, interview the child alone. You can ask the caretaker to announce that she has to go to the bathroom and will come back shortly. Some children are so caught up in play that they do not mind the caretaker's absence, whereas other children become anxious and do not allow their caretaker's exit. Other children may allow the departure but their play behavior is disrupted and regresses as they anxiously await the caretaker's return.

❏ Preparing Case Decisions

With information on language, behavior, concepts, articulation, responsiveness, play, and separation, the case is now shaped for two forms of action:

1. Behavioral documentation alone. Some children have little language (one-word or two-word sentences), their articulation is poor, they cannot stay on task with you or answer questions

reliably, they have little response to basic concepts (like who, what, where), and their play is exploratory rather than representational. In these cases, your evaluation focus is on the careful documentation of the child's behaviors and spontaneous statements over time and across caretakers and collaterals. The behavioral data reviewed above is the best expression of the child's history. Your knowledge of normal versus abnormal behavior, including sexual behavior, is critical here. Research on sexual behaviors, behavioral problems, and overall development helps to define the level of atypicality of your target child's presentation and the similarity of this behavior to that of other children who have known abuse backgrounds. This can be translated into risk factors and become an argument for some level of protection.

2. Documentation with words and behaviors. If the child has sentences with a few words, can respond reliably to concepts of who, what, where, and is beginning to use toys representationally (e.g., as you sit with the child, she takes the toy toilet in your dollhouse and puts the child doll on it saying, "Goes potty"), then you may attempt some limited interview to supplement your history and objective data. I have used the primitive inquiry described below to supplement the above outline. Interviewing very young children, however, is an extremely difficult task.

BEGINNING TO INTERVIEW

Body Parts

One simple interview format begins around body parts. Using a small doll, ask the child to show you the dolly's eyes. When he or she responds correctly, ask the child if *he* has eyes, and have him show you where his eyes are. Repeat this with the small doll's nose and mouth. Then point to the dolly's hands and ask the child the name of that part ("What do we call these?"), when he supplies the name, ask if he has hands and ask him to show you his hands. If he cannot supply the name, give him the name and see if he recognizes it. Repeat this for the tummy. Then point to the dolly's crotch and ask, "Do you have a part like this? What do you call it? Where is your part?" As the child points to his own crotch ask, "Does somebody tickle you where you go potty?" Follow up with, "Does somebody hurt you where you go potty?"

These are carefully worded target questions: the use of somebody versus anybody gives a more specific focus and does not require the child to excerpt from a larger pool of information. The use of anybody has also been shown to be associated with more "no" responses than the use of somebody, which is more specific and direct (Walker, 1994). The use of hurt or tickle is also more concrete and specific than the more conceptual, or global, term touch. Some young children may understand touch as something you do only with your finger. If you think the child may not understand these terms, prescreen this understanding first with tickle and then with hurt. We have found that most young children do not have specific genital names. Therefore, this body part reference is asked in a very concrete way. If your intake data indicate that the child has a special name for the genitals, then that name would be appropriately used here.

Follow-Up Questioning

If the child gives you the name of someone, then ask him to "Show me what _____ does." Some children cannot show you or give more information. It is tempting to ask, "How do they do that?" but remember the word *how* is also a broad-based conceptual term that will be hard for a very young child to answer. You can ask, "Where did the touching happen?" but the child may not be able to understand that you want geographic locations and you are not referring to his body parts. You could ask if this touching happened in his bedroom, or the bathroom, or somewhere else, but often children of this age will nod yes to all your questions, and you are left no clearer about location.

Follow-up questions become very difficult to ask with children of this age. Coupling their prior behaviors with their statements is the least directed route for gathering case information.

Supplemental Play Observation

When very young children have responded to the question "Does somebody hurt or tickle you where you go potty?" with a specific name but they cannot show what happened or list a setting or give other details, some details may emerge in structured follow-up play situations.

> Pat Bauer's (1996) work has a child replaying some experiences in sequentially related play. I have had limited success presenting some play scenarios. I will ask the child to select a caretaker doll and a doll for the target person (usually a mommy doll, a daddy doll, and a little girl or boy doll). Then I will take the child doll and say, "It's time for you to eat. Who should help this little girl/boy get his/her lunch? Show me." Or I will ask, "Who should help this boy take his bath, the mom or the daddy? Show me." I will continue with questions about going to the potty or going to bed. Some children become very frightened when I ask if the target doll should help them go to bed, go potty, and so on. Some children are very comfortable with any caretaking action by the target person.
>
> The responses do not prove abuse has happened, unless the child can demonstrate what the person does, and even then it is difficult to clearly substantiate an act. Atypical reactions of fear, avoidance, or aggression should be noted and, with the behavioral repertoire, a pattern may emerge that can argue for protection.

OBSERVING THE CHILD WITH THE ALLEGED ABUSER

In an earlier publication, Bill Friedrich and I wrote the following:

> This activity is optional, and is not desirable if it may be traumatic for the child; for example, if the child has been shown to decompensate in the past when in contact with the alleged perpetrator, and if such decompensation would compromise the child's present status. If the alleged abuse is not considered threatening or potentially harmful, then observations of the two [subjects] may be conducted. (Hewitt & Friedrich, 1995, p. 135)

There are conflicting opinions about the validity of observing a child with an alleged abuser, however. Haynes-Seman and Baumgarten (1994), in their book *Children Speak for Themselves*, claim that their method of interactional assessment, called the Kempe Interactional Assessment, is a "proven, highly-effective" process that "facilitates the emergence of reliable data without the pressure of directly questioning the child." Unfortunately, there is no research to document their claims and questions have been raised about the validity of some of their case examples. Behavioral reactions with young children are important, but the method of analysis advocated by Haynes-Seaman and Baumgarten ignores several important aspects of assessment that are noted above.

It is important to note that much more research needs to be done to determine what kinds of behaviors are associated with sexual abuse of varying intensity and duration, and how the passage of time affects their presence or absence on observation. Sometimes graphic behavioral interactions may be seen in an abused child, but the lack of such behaviors does not rule out abuse. Very young children are resilient and can regroup quickly with abuse-related behaviors. If the abuse is not reinforced through repetition, the child's behaviors may fade over time. (Hewitt & Friedrich, 1995, p. 135)

Parent-child interaction can, however, provide pieces to the puzzle. One parent can be contrasted with another regarding quality of play and interactions with the child. The alleged perpetrator may exhibit a broad range of very appropriate relational skills with a child who never looks distressed. The alleged perpetrator may be inept but nonthreatening and the child is similarly nondistressed. Both of these provide very different pieces of the puzzle from the questions raised by watching an alleged perpetrator whose range of interaction is limited to occasional hugs and kisses or other intrusive behaviors (e.g., retying shoes, tucking in shirts repeatedly) and whose child responds with a very limited or blunted range of play.

CONSTRUCTING A CASE FOR PROTECTION

This is the precise moment when you can come face to face with the fact that the child is too young to be able to tell specifically who touched them, where they were touched, and in what context. These are the elements needed to criminally prosecute a case; therefore, cases with children this young are rarely prosecuted criminally (unless there is a confession, a competent eye witness, sperm or semen with DNA analysis, or a uniquely competent child with clear behavioral information).

If a case can't be prosecuted criminally, is it still possible to protect very young children? Yes, but maybe not through criminal court.

The information you carefully gathered (behaviors, observations, collaterals, etc.) stands for the child's "statement." The child's few spoken words are then coupled with this "other language," their behaviors. Now, compare your data with data from samples of children with known abuse histories. If your data echo data associated with abuse, then you can argue a level of risk for this child. The aim here is to protect and "buy time" until the children have developed the skills that will allow them to better report. Getting protection for children who exhibit high-risk behaviors is difficult, and it will take changes in thinking and procedures in several systems to accomplish the task.

Our experience in court has found a wide range of response to assessment data, from restoration of full visitation with minimal supervision to suspension of contact. Much depends on the judge's knowledge of early childhood development and the importance of behaviors. If the court recognizes and supports the data indicating risk levels for the child, then several things can happen.

Suspension of Visits

When the court suspends visitation, then grounds for reinstatement are usually spelled out. This may be that the alleged offender receive an evaluation, therapy, education, or other forms of intervention to assess and reduce risk levels.

Contact Within the Limits of a Therapy Environment

For these cases, a therapist sets up and observes all visitation. The court's mandate for such therapeutic reunification directs the therapist to actively intervene in the child-adult relationship to correct problem behaviors. Contact is continued or delayed depending on the responses of the child to visitation and to the alleged offender's ability to alter damaging behaviors. The therapist can also recommend outside individual therapy or educational programs, with regular response back to the court. In some cases, if there is little or no progress in modifying problem behaviors, the court may suspend visitation until such time as the desired change is instituted. If positive change is noted, then visitation can be extended outside the therapy sessions with varying directives for supervision and length of contact.

Supervised Contact

Supervised cases provide monitoring but not intervention. Children and their alleged abusers meet at a safe location for their visits. One of the most popular sites for such contact in the St. Paul area is the Children's Safety Center. This center has several rooms, each equipped with toys and activities for different developmental ages. Trained volunteers observe and record the interactions in the visitation and enforce the rules of the Center. Visitation documentation is then forwarded to the court or a case manager, and it is used for referral to therapeutic intervention or to determine future visitation schedules. The neutral observer's charting provides an objective record to the court, and it is helpful in providing data about the child's needs as well as the alleged offender's responses (see the Children's Safety Center reference for organizational and procedural information).

Alternate forms of supervised visitation may be done by relatives, guardians, or by child protection workers at a county location. These options provide a protected environment for the young child, but they may not always have clear rules that must be signed by all parties involved, observational records, or strategies for monitoring the child's responses.

Sometimes these cases need ongoing professional monitoring of the child's responses and the custodial caretaker's concerns. Increased frequencies of nightmares, behavioral regression, or acting out sexual behaviors are important components in keeping the court informed of the child's well-being. A noncustodial parent's repeated attempts to frighten or alienate the child from a relationship with an alleged abuser may also need professional monitoring.

Monitored But Not Supervised Visitation

These cases are usually monitored by relatives or friends. They lack an opportunity for objective observation and recording, a clear set of rules for all parties, mechanisms for enforcement of the rules, pathways for therapy referral, and trained persons monitoring the child and alleged abuser's contact before, during, and after contact. This form of visitation is usually used when the court determines a low risk for the child.

Unsupervised Visitation

A child can be returned to the custody of the allegedly abusing caretaker with no supervision or monitoring. Such a schedule does not monitor the child's response or act to intervene in the risk factors associated with the case.

Responses to our cases with very young children who have high-risk profiles have varied. Some alleged perpetrators have readily agreed to supervision of visitation as a way of protecting themselves from further allegations while still maintaining contact with the child. Other alleged perpetrators have refused any form of intervention and demanded unrestricted contact. In some cases, the court's recommendations include cessation of visitation until the child is older, or clearly restricted and supervised visitation (visits on the child's birthday and at special holidays only within a supervised setting that can prepare the child and afterward monitor the child's responses).

If there is to be unrestricted contact with an alleged perpetrator and the case appears to be high-risk, it is *essential* to have good behavioral charting before and after the visitation. Often this requires the involvement of a trained professional to monitor the child. Sometimes the courts need to have "proof" of the damage to the child with contact, and the only way to do this is to clearly and concisely document the child's pre- and postvisit behaviors. Behavioral logs like those used by Mannarino and Cohen (1996) are especially helpful. Pre- and post-Child Behavior Checklists are another objective way of documenting such behaviors.

When a pattern emerges and the child's disturbances are clear, then resubmitting information to the courts can help modify contact until the child's healthy behaviors reemerge. When the visitation poses a significant disruption in the child's behaviors and adaptation, or when it begins to impede the child's ability to successfully grow and develop, it is time to advocate for visitation change. When children are older, use of the therapeutic management strategies in Chapter 9 may be employed. The object of advocating for the court's protection is to help ensure that young children have an opportunity to grow up safely and without the stress that can negatively affect their growth and development.

❏ Applying the Protocol: A Case Example

This case example demonstrates various issues that present in this age range and one way to organize a case. The details of all cases here have been modified to protect the confidentiality of the child and family.

THE REFERRAL

An attorney called to ask if I would review the file on a child age 2 years and 11 months and possibly testify in a family court matter. The child had been displaying some sexualized behaviors and making statements about possible sexual abuse by her father. When child protection investigated, the child could not give a clear account of any event, so no abuse was substantiated. Now the father wanted liberal, unsupervised visitation. The attorney was worried about safety and did not know what could be done to protect this very young child.

I agreed to look at the case and scheduled a 2-hour intake with the mother.

CASE SUMMARY

Mother and Dad are separated and in the process of divorce. Mother reports a rocky marital history with multiple separations and arguing. Both parents have extensive histories of chemical abuse. Mother completed treatment 2 years ago and has remained sober; Dad has continued to drink, moving from job to job. The child, A. A., lives with Mother and visits with her father. Prior to the allegations, weekends and midweek visits were unsupervised.

The allegations began about 5 months ago, when A. A. was 2 years 6 months old. She began exhibiting unusual sexualized behavior (poking things in her vagina, rubbing her vulva against furniture) and sleep problems after visits with her father. A specialized forensic interview at a children's center was ordered, but it was unsuccessful because A. A. would not talk. A medical check found no physical evidence of abuse. Child protection could not substantiate abuse and suggested A. A. see a therapist for follow-up and ongoing monitoring.

Dad's visits were suspended with the initial report, but once-a-month supervised visitation was later reinstated. After the first two supervised visits, A. A. showed signs of upset, with bedwetting and nightmares at home and aggressive behavior during day care. A. A. told her therapist, "Daddy squeeze me," and she pointed to her genital area but gave no specific information.

A 2-hour intake was requested with each parent. Father, on the advice of his attorney, did not participate. Mother did participate and all developmental information was obtained from her.

INTAKE INTERVIEW

Child's Developmental History

Pregnancy was not planned but A. A. was a wanted baby. Medical services were available during the pregnancy and there were no com plications. When Mother learned of the pregnancy at about 6 weeks gestation, she stopped all smoking and drinking. After a normal labor and delivery, A. A. went home with her parents. Developmental milestones were on target or accelerated and there is no history of any significant medical or physical problems.

After the birth of A. A., Mother resumed drinking. When A. A. was about a year old, Mother went to inpatient treatment for chemical dependency for about 2 months. A. A.'s maternal grandmother, a familiar caretaker, stayed with her and brought her for regular, if not daily, contact with her mother in the hospital. No significant problems were evident from this separation.

When A. A. was 24 months old, her parents separated. Before separating, the parents were physically aggressive with each other, but not in A. A.'s presence.

[Comment: This is essentially a normal developmental history, with the exception of maternal drinking and smoking during early pregnancy. There is no indication of any problems or deviations in development. A weakness of this history is the absence of the father's point of view.]

Current Status

A. A. lives with her mother in an apartment and she attends child care full time when her mother works. The maternal grandmother babysits on weekends when Mother works a second job. Daily life is structured around Mother's work schedule, whereas weekends are less structured. A. A. calls her parents "Mama" and "Daddy," and her grandmother "Gamma." She does not have specific names for her genitals; she calls them her butt, with one in front and one in back. Her nipples are "boobies" and her anus a "butt." Mother was directed to teach specific genital's names (vagina, butt, and penis) following the intake appointment. Mother worked on this at bath time, combining the new labels with other body part teaching (e.g., elbow, ankle). Mother also had A. A. at home when a friend with a baby boy came over and A. A. observed the diapering and was given the label penis. The genital care Mother describes is nonintrusive and appropriate.

Mother reports that as A. A. is getting older, her speech is rapidly expanding. She now talks about "Daddy hurts my butt," and "Daddy pokes me, Mommy." Her child care center reports more aggression after the visits with her father and she has been caught approaching boys in the bathroom to touch their genitals.

Screening for abuse history. There have been no prior abuse allegations. A. A. has not witnessed intercourse nor seen any form of pornographic material while in Mother's care. Mother did not know about A. A.'s experiences at Dad's house. Dad had a history of having pornographic magazines around and he did masturbate in front of A. A. when the couple lived together.

[Comment: Screening for prior sexual abuse is important here because any current behaviors may have to be evaluated in terms of past allegations.]

Risk and Safety Factors

Father has current evidence of continued alcohol and chemical usage, and Mother reports she is sober. A. A. has not witnessed family violence but she is aware of the tension between her parents. A. A. has had opportunities to bathe with both parents. As bathing was discussed with Mother, she recalled earlier concerns about A. A.'s bathing. Before the separation, A. A.'s father insisted on being the one to bathe her, and he would put her in the tub with him. After the bath he and she would walk around nude, and he enjoyed having A. A. touch his penis. Mother now bathes A. A. alone and also shields exposure to any nudity because of A. A.'s very active interest in this area. A. A. has been found sneaking a peek at Mother while she is undressing or showering.

There is no maternal history of sexual or physical abuse. Father has a history of extensive sexual abuse (starting in preschool years) by his babysitter, but specific details of the abuse are not known. He has had extensive sexual contact with females beginning in early adolescence. The father also has a history of physical abuse.

Mother states she has not been arrested, but the father was arrested and convicted for stealing at his last job. His sentence is pending.

Mother reports a good network of friends and work associates. She feels supported by her mother, visits with her regularly, and has never felt unsupported.

Marital sexual history shows frequent sexual contacts, which Mother did not enjoy. Some of the contacts were nonconsensual. Father also practiced masturbation compulsively and at one time voluntarily sought therapy to deal with this. He attended for a brief time and quit.

[Comment: This case has several important risk factors, including active chemical dependency that can loosen inhibitions and allow impulsive behavior. If Mother is accurate, Father would have a very sexualized approach to physical contact, and a coercive quality to sexual relationships. Marital relations that are forced reflect the way intimacy and caring are expressed in the family. Children in homes with forced and compulsive sexuality between partners can be at greater risk for improper sexual contact. The history of arrest and conviction is one of the psychopathy indices seen in the histories of known sexual offenders. A weakness of this history is again the absence of the father's report.]

History of the Concerns

When asked about previous concerns, Mother reported the behaviors listed on the intake. When she was directed to "go back to your very first concerns about the possibility of sexual abuse," a much more complex picture appeared. Mother often mentioned these behaviors out of sequence as the discussion seemed to trigger additional memories and concerns. The history Mother reported is as follows:

1. At her husband's insistence, Mother did no bathing of A. A. from 0 to 18 months. A. A. was always bathed with her father and after their bath he would be nude, enjoying it when she would touch his penis.

2. Between 6 months and 2 years, when the parents were still living together, Mother observed A. A. touch her father's penis (outside the bathing) when he was nude. Twice, when A. A. grabbed his penis, the father laughed in response. More recently, A. A. grabbed the crotch on one of Mother's male friends. When told not to do this, A. A. said, "Daddy let me do it."

3. After Father and Mother separated, when A. A. was about 24 months, there was a brief hiatus with no contact between A. A. and her father. When weekly visits were started (from 10:00 a.m. Friday to Tuesday evenings) behavioral changes were noted in A. A.

   (a) Night disturbances. A. A. began to awaken repeatedly at night screaming at the top of her lungs, asking to have her mother hold her, and often coming to Mother's bed in the night. There were frequent episodes of this behavior immediately after visits with the father but they would dissipate in the times between visits. Before visits began, A. A. slept comfortably in the dark; now she required the light to be on in her room and the door to be open.

   (b) Regression. Toilet training had been completed by age 2, but now A. A. began wetting again and she had to be put back into diapers.

   (c) Distractibility. A. A. no longer listened well, as noted by both the mother and an aunt.

   (d) Phobias or fears. A. A. suddenly became terrified of all tile floors. (This unusual fear decreased and then disappeared after visitation was stopped.)

   (e) Masturbation. A. A. began to masturbate by putting her finger into her vagina. She became preoccupied with her genitalia and talked frequently about her "front butt."

4. A more detailed description of the incident which precipitated the child protection call was elicited during this time. Mother said she and A. A. were in the living room talking together after A. A. had returned from visitation. A. A. was very quiet, resting on the couch. Suddenly A. A. pulled her legs up over her head, exposing her vulva. She put a small cylindrically shaped toy at her vulva and said spontaneously, "What Daddy do." A. A. then asked for her Mother's hand and put it down by her vagina. Mother asked about what A. A. was doing, and with questioning, A. A. told her it was what she did with her daddy at bedtime. (Mother added that this was so unnerving because the position A. A. demonstrated was her ex-husband's favorite position for sexual intercourse.) Mother reacted to A. A.'s words by crying and holding her, saying, "When you're home here you're safe, no one will ever touch you again." A. A. told her mother she did not want her daddy to touch her. Maternal grandmother witnessed this exchange from the kitchen. The next morning Mother called child protection and A. A. was referred for interview and later a medical exam. A. A. also began to display more sexualized behaviors toward other children at her child care.

5. Visitation was stopped after the call to child protection. Mother reported that A. A.'s sleep, masturbation, and toileting problems all gradually dissipated over the next several weeks.

6. Approximately 2 months after the precipitating incident, when no abuse was substantiated, supervised visitation was awarded to the father. This 2-hour visitation was held at a supervised facility that had an observer in the room at all times. The observer reported no problems or inappropriate behaviors on the visit. However, when A. A. returned home she wet her pants and other problem behaviors returned. She began to wet her bed at night, there was a recurrence of nightmares, and her child care reported increased anger and aggression. They also reported a new behavior: A. A. would make monster hands, bare her teeth, and talk about monsters.

7. At the time of the intake, 5 months after the alleged abuse, A. A.'s language capabilites expanded remarkably, and she spontaneously said unusual bits and pieces of information (e.g., "Daddy hurts me. I don't want to be with Daddy"). When Mother was asked how she handled these remarks, Mother indicated that she has been afraid to say anything. She has not talked with A. A. about her father except to tell her when the visits would be resumed.

8. Approximately 2 weeks prior to the intake, A. A. had attempted to insert the end of a fork into her vaginal introitus after her bath. She hurt herself and had difficulty urinating. When Mother told her not to do this, A. A. was hurt and defensive.

9. Roughly 4 days after the fork incident, a babysitter was coming to care for A. A. Previously, Mother had told A. A. that she was not to touch her genitals, that only her mother, aunt, grandma, or the doctor could touch her. When the babysitter arrived, A. A. went over to her and spontaneously said, "You can't touch me. Only my Mommy, my aunt, or my grandma can."

10. Three days before the intake, when A. A. was informed of an upcoming visit with her father, she plugged her ears and would not respond. Later that day, the visitation was cancelled and A. A. was told she would not be seeing her father. A. A. evidenced no unusual reaction at the time, but that evening she spent a lot of time in her room alone. When Mother checked on her, she found that A. A. had lined up her stuffed animals and was talking to them and saying, "Why does Mommy say 'no' if Daddy says 'OK'?" Later that evening, as she was preparing A. A. for bed, Mother checked A. A.'s bottom. It was bright red, the kind of redness that had been evident after the child had engaged in extensive masturbation.

11. Two nights before this intake interview, A. A. finished her bath, got dressed for bed, and was playing with her tea set. Mother saw her take a cup from the tea set and try to put it in her vaginal area, but because she had underwear on, the process was thwarted.

12. Most recently, A. A.'s father was awarded phone contact three times a week. Since her last visit, A. A. has been more willing to talk to her father, but she has also been heard to say, out of the blue, "Oh, my Daddy's nice. He won't hurt me."

[Comment: This historical review of all the Mother's observations greatly expands the context and importance of the single referral incident. Watching old memories be triggered by the questions in this format is very powerful. This observation weighs against the allegations of this being a fabricated story as the surprise, spontaneity and idiosyncracy of the various behaviors would be difficult to fabricate. Gathering information over time often provides a much richer context of unusual behavior, which if taken alone, would not have great weight. When viewed as a pattern over time, however, these behavioral incidents have greater importance.]

SCREENING FOR SIGNIFICANT BEHAVIORAL CONCERNS

Sleep Problems

A. A. had a history of sleep problems, being up at night and calling out in her sleep. These disturbances dropped off markedly during the hiatus in visitation with her father. When visitation resumed, the problems reappeared. At intake, A. A. was sleeping with her mother regularly because of bad dreams.

Sexualized Play Concerns (See section on Collateral Information, Child Care Providers)

Toileting and Bathing Problems (See above Sexual Abuse Concerns, #3 and #5)

Fears or Phobias (See above Sexual Abuse Concerns, #3 and #5, see also Collateral Information, Medical exam)

CREATING RULE-OUT HYPOTHESES

1. Father's attorney alleged that Mother had implanted or suggested material of the allegations.

[Comment: One of the biggest weaknesses in this case is that the initial information was gathered only from the mother and reflects only her point of view, although it was buttressed by the collateral material. The father was invited to come for an intake but he refused on the advice of his attorney. To address this rule-out hypothesis, care is needed in the history taking to screen for Mother's level of suggestion by leading or suggestive questioning of her daughter as well as how she or others handled A. A.'s behaviors and disclosures. Sometimes having parents take an MMPI-2 can clarify their personality structure and address their propensity for manipulation.]

2. This is a work of fantasy from the child.

[Comment: This can be refuted by careful discussion of child development information. Children this young are not capable of creating elaborate scenarios depicting abuse, nor are they able to integrate emotion into fabricated statements.]

3. The child was abused, but by someone else.

[Comment: Careful history-taking to determine who the caretakers and contact persons are in A. A.'s life is critical here. Asking if Mother has a boyfriend or if there are babysitters who have regular contact with A. A. is also important.]

OBJECTIVE MEASURES

Three tests were completed by the mother. Sexual behaviors rated on the Child Sexual Behavior Inventory (CSBI) were within the significant range and more similar to those behaviors found with children who do have a history of sexual abuse than those children who have not had such a history. The following behavior categories were observed at least one time per week: masturbating with the hand, touching or trying to touch Mother's or other women's breasts, touching sex parts when at home, trying to look at people when they were undressing, kissing adults they do not know well, being overly friendly with men they do not know well, hugging adults they do not know well, and seeming to be very interested in the opposite sex. Behaviors that were endorsed at the level of one to three times per month were inserting or trying to insert objects in the vagina or anus and showing sex parts to others.

Elevations on the Child Behavior Checklist (CBCL) were at the significant level in sleep problems and somatic complaints. The Child Development Inventory (CDI) indicated all developmental tasks within normal limits for her age. Maternal observations on the CDI and CBCL were consistent with the information provided by the day care and with other observations of the child.

Because this was a contested custody case, one of the concerns was Mother's propensity for creating false allegations with her child; therefore, Mother was asked to take an MMPI-2 to assess her own level of psychopathology. The valid MMPI-2 was within normal limits and no significant psychopathology was indicated. The only elevated scores were content scale score, specifically on the McAndrews scale, a scale measuring behaviors associated with chemical abuse. The mother's elevated scores would appear to reflect her past history of chemical usage because she denies any chemical usage in the past 2 years and her regular attendance at AA meetings was verified.

COLLATERAL CONTACTS

There were collateral contacts with A. A.'s child care center, the maternal grandmother, and the child's therapist. A. A.'s medical records were also reviewed.

Child Care

A. A.'s child care center offered a rich source of behavioral observations for A. A., as it regularly charted children's behaviors. Center notes show a marked disturbance of behavior, increased aggression, and defiance following visitation with the father. A. A. also told a child care staff member that she had seen a monster and she was mad. Later she said, "Daddy is a monster. Daddy hurts me." This was followed by wetting her pants. Child care staff also noted that A. A. seemed to know a great deal about sex and was precocious in her awareness. Shortly after the mother's report that A. A. had attempted to insert a fork in her vagina, child care staff noted that A. A. was playing with herself frequently. The play, however, was not just fingering herself; A. A. was also observed putting a toy figure in front of her underwear and then trying to hide it. She was also observed encouraging boys in the bathroom to engage in genital play with her.

Relatives

A. A.'s grandmother reported having witnessed A. A.'s disclosure to her mother, and the grandmother's report was essentially the same as her daughter's. Since that report, A. A. had also spontaneously shared bits and pieces of information, over time, with her grandmother stating, "Daddy hurts me. I don't want to be with Daddy." Grandmother also noted that when A. A. was bathing, she would push her labia aside and appear to poke her fingers into the vaginal vault. The grandmother told A. A. not to do this or she would hurt herself and A. A. responded, "It won't hurt."

Therapist

A. A.'s therapist documented increased levels of anger, aggression, and distance in A. A.'s play after visits with the father.

Medical Records

Medical charts record A. A.'s resistance to any form of vaginal examination by an adult male and the subsequent drugging to complete an examination.

Maternal Journals

Although Mother had noted several sexualized behaviors following the precipitating incident, she was instructed to keep a detailed daily behavioral log, adding information received from both A. A.'s grandmother and her child care. This extensive behavioral log was also reviewed.

Audiotapes

Mother made an audiotape of the conversations she had with A. A. the night she heard her daughter talking to her animals (the same night she had been masturbating vigorously). In this particular tape, Mother was angry with the child when she asked A. A. what she was doing. A. A. explained to her mother that she was touching herself, and then she spontaneously added, "I do it *after* Dad," indicating she does the rubbing after her father does.

[Comment: Checking collateral contacts in this case acts as a cross-check for Mother's veracity. Neutral observers such as A. A.'s child care center, the therapist, and medical records also support problems with A. A.]

CONTACT WITH THE CHILD

Observation

A. A. was seen twice for individual evaluation, roughly one hour each time. She appeared to be a child of average height and weight with lots of energy and a pleasant manner.

The Caretaker-Child Relationship

While in the waiting room, A. A. stood close to her mother and did not explore the toys in the room. She was reluctant to separate from her mother when it came time to meet alone, but engaged quickly when invited to play in the dollhouse.

Screening for Concepts

A. A. was observed to have good vocabulary and good language usage for a child who was just 3 years old. She demonstrated the presence of concepts important for any interviewing such as who, what, where, and genital-specific names that were appropriate.

Play Observation

Play was age-appropriate, as A. A. was able to symbolically use different dollhouse figures to demonstrate going to the bathroom, going to bed, and eating. She was unable to use a doll to represent herself or create specific, personalized interactions in the dollhouse play.

Interview

During the second session, A. A. was interviewed about various forms of touching in her life: hugging, kissing, tickling, spanking, and private part touching. She did not acknowledge any genital touching by her father or her mother, despite her mother's early repeated reference about checking her bottom and the doctor's exam that she hadn't liked. She avoided any questions about touch in this area. Her interview results were seen as having questionable validity. Just after this interview, however, A. A. needed to go to the bathroom, even though she had gone just prior to the interview. Because of the urinary frequency, I suggested that the mother double check with the doctor for any form of bladder problem. None was found.

[Comment: It is important to recognize that the interview about sexual touching was conducted after A. A. had resumed supervised visitation with her father and after she had seen him two or three times for the 2-hour duration. It is not unusual for children to no longer indicate sexual abuse if the relationship with the alleged perpetrator has been normalized during the interim between the initial reporting and my interview. As most young children are sexually abused by someone they know, they often have mixed feelings about the caretaker, and if the most negative aspects of the relationship (i.e., the sexual touching) have stopped, then the more positive aspects may regain salience. Young children cannot maintain two simultaneous, contradictory thoughts at the same time. Consequently, people are either good or bad, often depending on the quality of the most recent contacts.]

OBSERVATION WITH THE ALLEGED ABUSER

The father was invited to be a part of the intake process. He initially accepted but later declined and would not participate. Subsequently, he was court ordered to be observed with A. A. in a therapeutic playroom with a two-way mirror.

When A. A. entered the waiting room, her father was present, but she made no move to contact or join him. He gave her little eye contact as well. (It is possible that A. A. avoided contact with her father to maintain an overt loyalty with her primary caretaker, her mother, who waited in the waiting room.) Once the couple was alone in the playroom, A. A. did interact with her father. She explored the play therapy room, and her father joined. He would play with a toy just as she did. When A. A. went to play in the sandbox, she initiated activity in one half of the box while her father made his own productions in the other half of the sandbox. As A. A. continued her play, her father interrupted her and showed her how he was making things on his side of the sandbox. He made no comment on her play. Throughout the session, A. A.'s father was friendly and cheerful, but A. A. gave him little eye contact. Despite the request that he not have physical contact with A. A. unless she initiated it, he asked her for a hug rather than waiting for her to initiate one. When A. A. moved away from physical proximity with him, he responded by moving closer to her. At one point, A. A. wanted to draw on the easel. Her father set it up for her, but then he began to draw on it as A. A. stood by quietly and watched. Toward the end of the session, A. A.'s father took her hand and wrote her name on it, an act of his choice and not one initiated by A. A. Separation at the end of the session was quick, there was no physical contact, and A. A. did not bid her father goodbye as she left.

[Comment: There was no sexual abuse or sexualized interaction observed during these sessions. The father, however, did demonstrate an interactional style that indicated possible problems. He disregarded the rules set before the session for initiating physical contact. He showed an insensitivity or disregard for her physical proximity boundaries; when she moved away from him, he repeatedly moved again to be in her space. There were no examples of the usual parental role of expanding her chosen play or teaching her about the play material she sought to explore. He did not encourage or support the play she initiated, rather, he played in a parallel fashion with her or he redirected her play. A. A.'s father behaved more like a peer than a parent in his play with her; he took over the play both in the sandbox and at the easel. When taken together, these observations are seen as examples of high-risk behavior, given the allegations of abuse.]

CASE DECISIONS

Sexual abuse cannot be proven in this case, but many factors in the case speak toward the possibility of sexual abuse having occurred. Unsupervised visitation between A. A. and her father presents as very high risk. A report issued to the court regarding visitation between A. A. and her father included the following excerpt:

> This is a child who is too immature to specifically create a detailed report of any sexual abuse. Because of this immaturity, a careful history of her behavioral reactions over time and across situations was conducted. Results of this evaluation match very closely with the behavioral reactions seen in a research sample of sexually abused children and significantly raise the possibility of sexual abuse. Pros and cons related to the issue of sexual abuse are reviewed.
>
> Cons: The child does not acknowledge any abuse on direct interview, either at this specific interview facility or during this interview process. It is possible she could be displaying some behavioral reactions to the visits as there is tension between the parents and she could be reflecting that. There are also repeated medical examinations that could focus attention on her genitals. The mother is very vigilant about the child's behavior and forceful in her questioning, possibly pressuring the child to acknowledge abuse that may not have occurred. Finally, abuse could have occurred, but it may have been by someone else.
>
> Pros: Behaviors are one of the most important sequelae of child sexual abuse and the above questions or alternative explanations still do not explain the child's sexualized focus over time and across people. The child repeatedly and spontaneously emits behaviors that are consistent with a history of sexual abuse. She certainly may exhibit some anxiety about visitation and this could lead to some of the problems noted, but it does not explain the sexualized focus. Medical exams could focus attention on the genitals, but that would not explain the coupling of specific idiosyncratic acts (i.e., attempting to insert a toy in the vaginal area) while coupling her father's name with the act. Mother's questioning could force the child to answer in the affirmative about abuse, but

this would not account for the specificity or spontaneous detail ("I do it *after* Dad"). Someone else could have done sexual things, but the child is consistent in her link of the behaviors with her father and she displays significant behavioral reactions after visitations with him (i.e., behavioral regressions, anger, sleep disturbance). None of these responses is consistently related to anyone else.

The father appears to have several risk factors active. He has a history of sexual abuse and extensive sexual contact with multiple females. He has a history of drug and alcohol abuse, and he has continued to use chemicals. He has been charged and convicted for dishonesty at work. His play observations indicated a disregard for rules and a problem with boundaries. These factors raise concerns about his reliability and safety with a young child.

Sexual abuse of this child cannot be "proven" because she is too young to tell her history and we officially document sexual abuse by the way a child can tell us what has happened to them. Nevertheless, very young children are still sexually abused, in fact they are more vulnerable to abuse because of their immaturity and their needs for regular toileting and bathing help. Ironically, the more vulnerable of our children are those who are least able to protect via official documentation. It is my professional opinion that this child has a history that raises significant concern for sexual abuse and she is in need of protection. The court should help protect her safety now and "buy time" until the future when she is more capable of taking an active role in her own protection.

Recommendations include the following:

1. Supervised visitation only for limited time periods of up to 2 hours at a neutral and safe facility.

2. Monitoring her reactions to the visitation by a therapist, with the therapist allowed to space out or shorten visits if significant disruption increases for the child (i.e., nightmares, increased masturbation, increasing levels of aggression). The therapist should be able to call for a cessation of visitation until a later date should the disruption be deemed harmful to the child's emotional status and development.

3. The father should undergo an evaluation by a therapist trained and experienced in the evaluation of sex offenders and be addressed for the level of risk he poses to the child.

4. At some time in the future, when the child is better able to comprehend relationship boundaries, the father should do some prevention education work with her and explain that no one is to touch her genital area, that no one should tell her to keep any secrets, that those are her private areas and he will not touch them. Further, he should make it very clear that she should always tell if anyone does

that, whether in the past or in the present, and that he would not be mad at her. This kind of work should be a prerequisite for any consideration of extended visitation of any kind.

5. The case should be reviewed again after the evaluation is completed and any visitation has been monitored, with therapeutic documentation of the child's responses.

Postscript: Shortly after this evaluation, Mother accepted a job in a distant state and A. A. moved with her. There was little contact with the father. When A. A. was about 7 years old and in treatment for some behavior problems, she made very clear statements about her father's sexual abuse of her. The case was never prosecuted.

❑ Things Are Not Always as They Appear: Is It Abuse or Not?

An intake call from a foster mother asks to have a 28-month-old girl evaluated for possible sexual abuse because she has been masturbating excessively. Despite attempts by the foster parent to help B. B. stop masturbating, she masturbates pretty much constantly and to the extent that she has a reddened and raw genital area. Attempts to keep clothes on and to inhibit the masturbation have not been very successful. There is little information available as to developmental problems or milestones, but the Child Development Inventory scores show at least average levels of functioning for a child her age. The Child Behavior Checklist indicates some problems with aggression and a sleep disturbance is noted. Other areas are not significant. The Child Sexual Behavior Inventory (CSBI) indicates the increased frequency of masturbation but no acting out of sexual behavior with any other children or in any situations other than the masturbation with herself. There is no evidence of sexualized activity toward other adults or other caretakers, and the play is not repetitive or sexualized in nature.

On intake, the foster mother indicates that this child has come out of a home where there was excessive drug use, and B. B. has been exposed to repeated episodes of fighting between the mother and father. At times the police had been called. The child has had multiple caretakers and some separation from both of her parents. She has stayed at the homes of relatives when the parents have been fighting or have had difficulty managing their drug usage. The parents deny any form of sexualized contact with the child, but the possibility of abuse occurring when the parents were on drugs, or at the homes of various relatives, cannot be ruled out. During the times B. B. was living at home, her mother was her primary caretaker. The foster mother gives a detailed history of the child's repeated masturbation in multiple situations but most frequently when the child is under stress. The child does not seek adults for comfort or safety; instead, she sits alone, often looking sad. The foster mother also notes sleep disturbances, with the child awakening and crying; however, during the past 6 weeks these have been lessening in frequency and duration. The child has little language and her articulation is extremely difficult to understand, so she is not appropriate for interview.

This case presents an interesting problem. Although this child has compulsive masturbatory behavior and she has shown some level of sleep disturbance, she does not show a generalization of any form of sexualized activity in other contexts. It is important to recognize that in these cases, absolute determination of sexual abuse by a specific perpetrator is extremely difficult to prove, and most often you are left with a supposition of abuse rather than proof of abuse.

In this case, because there is no other evidence of sexualized behavior, the case was eventually determined to be a child's use of masturbation for self-soothing rather than an indicator of sexual abuse. Strength for this viewpoint came from the child's history of having viewed parental violence and having had multiple caretakers. Her avoidance of adult caretakers points toward an avoidant attachment disorder in which the child would not use adults for comfort or security. Young children can find genital touching an anxiety reducer, and if their repertoire of self-soothing behaviors is limited, they may, in fact, use this as a way to calm themselves. Sexual abuse could not be ruled out in this case, but the foster mother was directed to help provide other forms of intervention for the masturbation that included distraction, other forms of tactile soothing, minimizing the stress factors in the child's life, working to create a healthier attachment style, and careful assessment of the visitation structure as much of the child's masturbatory activity occurred after the visitation sessions. Attempts to redirect and refocus the child's attention were initiated. With time, the behavior decreased, and there was no further evidence of sexual abuse.

Not all sexualized activity that young children show may have its origins in sexual abuse.

❏ What's Happened to My Child?

One evening when Mother was supervising a bath with her 36-month-old daughter, the child stood up, spread her labia and said, "You want to touch my 'gina?" Mother said that she did not want to do that, that was not her place to touch, and only the child should be touching herself there. Then the mother asked if somebody touches her there. C. C. said, "Yes, John Mark." (referring to an older boy at her child care). Mother was alarmed, but her demeanor remained calm while she told her daughter that it was not OK for John Mark to touch her there. C. C. replied, "I want him to and he wants me to touch his pee pee." Her attitude during this disclosure was very confident, and very bossy. C. C.'s statement to her mother was less a comment and more a directive. The mother, not knowing what to say, got her child out of the tub while C. C. continued to talk about John Mark, saying, "I eat him up," and later, "He eats himself up"; during this time, C. C. became increasingly silly. The mother did no more questioning and put the child to bed.

The mother requested an evaluation for her child for possible sexual abuse. On intake, Mother reported that C. C. had no history of sleep disturbance and no sexualized play in other contexts. There were no levels of regression in toileting behavior, but C. C. had shown some problems with separation lately, as she did not like to be alone in her room and needed to be in close proximity with either of her parents, both when they were at home and other places. Child care staff indicated a history of multiple problems with John Mark, ranging from aggression to different types of sexualized contact with other children. They had not observed any genital touching between C. C. and John Mark, and they had not heard other children report such observations.

John Mark's mother was unwilling to cooperate in an assessment of her child, but support staff for the child care had observed him and they recommended placement in a specialized classroom.

Following an intake meeting with the parents, the child came for her first session. C. C. presented as a very verbal, articulate, 36-month-old child with an excellent grasp of concepts and ideas. She easily answered all the screening questions about concepts and her play was detailed and imaginative. When she was seen the second time, she began the session by looking at the dolls in the dollhouse and saying, "Oh, look, this girl needs panties," and then she handed me a doll. She asked me to put the panties on. Usually I do not begin a session with a targeted question about possible sexual touch, but in this case the situation presented itself and I pointed to the doll's genital area and said, "Does somebody touch you here?" The child responded, "John Mark *wants* to." I asked if John Mark ever touched her and the child responded, "He didn't touch it, he always wants to." I asked what other girls were at her child care and C. C. named them. I then asked if John Mark touches any other girls' 'ginas and used some of the girls' names C. C. had given me earlier. C. C. said he had not. I asked if she had touched John Mark where he goes potty and she said, "No, he just wants me to." I asked C. C. who was in charge of her 'gina and she said, "Ummm, probably I am!" Collateral contact with the child care indicated the children had not been observed to be sexual with each other at any time; bathroom visits were carefully monitored.

I was very lucky with this case in that this young child could deal with intent. She clearly stated that John Mark had *wanted* to touch her but that he had not and she could also deal with my question about whether he had touched other children's bottoms. The whole concept of intended versus actual touch is a tricky one to be using with very young children, but this child's good ability and language skills made it possible to conduct a more advanced style of interview with her.

This case demonstrates the presence of clearly sexualized behavior (i.e., exhibition and talk about sexual touch), but there is no spillover into initiated contact with other children, or other contexts. The sexualized contact is with another child, but only in the context of the other child asking to touch the genital area. There appears to have been no actual contact. Case follow-up over time indicated no evidence of specific genital touch.

The general taboo about young children speaking of specific sexual acts (e.g., "suck my dick") have held that only older children, usually with sexual exposures of some sort, do this. Some new observations have called this thinking into question. An informal poll of my friends in child protection intake indicates a rise in this form of allegation. They attribute it to more discussion of previously forbidden topics, even among young children. Children at the bus stop or on the playground may frequently hear other children yell, "Suck my dick!" and thus a heretofore unimagined act is suggested. Usually, simply talking about genital touching does not create sexualized behavior, but in this case the request for genital touching was made but did not result in actual touching, even though there was a subsequent behavioral display. Again, not all sexualized behavior can have its origins in actual sexual touch.

❏ Can You Believe the Reporter?

Twenty-seven-month-old D. D. was found to have evidence of traumatic vaginal penetration when examined by her pediatrician following visitation with her father. Her case was referred by her mother's attorney for evaluation of possible sexual abuse by the father. The father maintained that he was innocent and that abuse had been perpetrated by the mother's boyfriend.

D. D.'s mother, a developmentally delayed 30-year-old woman, was interviewed in a 2-hour intake session for D. D.'s history and developmental status. She indicated an absence of sexualized behaviors or problems for the child. Because of her disability and low reading level, she was unable to complete a Child Development Inventory, Child Behavior Checklist, or Child Sexual Behavior Inventory, but oral administration of the Child Sexual Behavior Inventory to her (with attention to specialized needs relevant to the mother's handicap) indicated no problems. In similar fashion, questions about development and behavior revealed few problems. Because the mother was home full-time, she was the primary caretaker; consequently, there was no available cross-check through collateral contacts such as child care or other babysitters.

The child was brought to the office and observed but she had little speech, mainly one- or two-word sentences, and her articulation was difficult to understand. Her play involved picking up the various dolls in the dollhouse, looking at them or mouthing them, and then setting them down while she picked up another doll. It was determined that

D. D.'s speech, language, and play skills were such that this young 2-year-old was unable to be interviewed. Preparation was made to notify the court that there was no behavioral evidence of possible abuse with the father and, in fact, the child showed few of the signs that would be expected given the evidence of physical penetration. While the father's attorney aggressively pushed for his client's rights and held forth on a refusal of any observation between D. D. and himself, it appeared that there was little data to support limiting visitation between this father and his child.

One last appointment prior to writing the report on this case held a surprise that would change the course of the case. When the mother came for the final appointment to discuss the findings and recommendations regarding her daughter, she brought her long-time case aide with her. This case aide had frequently visited both mother and D. D. in their home, and she came to offer support to the mother. When a final check was made about the observations of any unusual behaviors the mother had seen in her daughter, the home aide interrupted. The home aide reminded the mother of specific behaviors and reactions that D. D. had produced during the aide's visits. The aide's observations included the presence of multiple sexualized behaviors, sleep disturbances, fears, and regression in toileting. The aide could also place these behaviors in relation to the father's visit. The aide's observations of the boyfriend's interactions with D. D. and D. D.'s reactions after his visits indicated no problem behaviors or reactions to the boyfriend.

D. D.'s mother's mental handicap—and possibly her own history of violent and prolonged abuse—had resulted in a virtual "blackout" of the numerous cues her child had presented that did, in fact, support sexual abuse.

This case is important for three reasons. First, it reminds us that objective measurement data as well as history can be skewed by a primary caretaker, either by overendorsement and hypervigilance about abuse matters or by underendorsement and a muting or denial of abuse cues. Second, it stresses the pivotal nature of collateral contacts if you have an impaired primary caretaker whose observations may have questionable validity. Finally, it underscores the critical level of reliance on the validity of the caretaker's report when a child cannot be interviewed.

This case example *does not* mean to indicate that parents with handicaps are inadequate caretakers. Many handicapped parents are able to adequately take care of their children. This case does, however, stress the importance of caretakers' past history as they respond to allegations of abuse. It has been my clinical experience that caretakers with a history of their own abuse may either over- or underreact to abuse concerns with their children. For some caretakers, the "red flags" that their children emit may be muted into denial or minimization by the caretaker's own unresolved abuse history. Young children are so embedded in the context of their environment that successful evaluation of very young children must always consider their environment as well as their behaviors and statements. In cases such as this, involvement of collateral sources is important. In an age of dwindling dollars for child abuse work, work like this takes time that is often not billable but still significant for the final disposition of the case.

5

Assessing Young Children (3–5 Years Old): Prescreening Children With Transitioning Skills

Children ages 3 to 5 are in transition. These young children are Stage 2 children; they are more competent than Stage 1, or very young, children who can participate only minimally in an interview, but they are not as competent as the older, Stage 3, preschool children. Three- to five-year-old children are in the process of acquiring interview skills.

It is important to understand what is typical at this age. These children usually have a good working vocabulary to describe basic elements and acts in their environment (although they cannot abstract well and do not articulate the relationships between various elements), their articulation is understandable, they have some concepts (who, what, where), but they offer little spontaneous or well-organized narrative. They may lack genital names but appear capable of learning such specific labels. They do understand basic forms of touch and at 3 years they have some beginning representational play (they will put a dolly on the potty, or pretend to put it to bed). It is not until about 4 years, however, that they are able to demonstrate actions or reactions identified specifically as their own.

The demand by professionals for specific information from children with sexual abuse allegations (who, what, where, when, etc.), remains constant across all ages, yet the young child's skills for responding to these questions changes greatly across these early years. It is important to understand what abilities are central to good interviewing, how these skills are developing during this time, and how they affect the nature and outcome of the interview process.

For example, what would you need to know if you were presented with the following case?

E. E., a 4-year-old girl, had been found in a closet, panties off, with a male peer. Mom was worried about a possible history of sexual abuse, so E. E. was seen for a one-session, standardized-format interview, using the Touch Survey (an interview format described in Chapter 7). E. E. was very verbal and cooperative in the session, but she did not always respond to specific interview questions. During an initial screening of faces expressing different feelings, E. E. gave a jumbled account of her current life events, often adding conflicting or confusing responses. For example, she said that she had been spanked, but she added a happy face to the drawing about spanking. "Do you like being spanked?" I asked. "Yes, I'm happy. It doesn't hurt. I don't cry." (Mother's intake had indicated very little spanking with this child). At times E. E. would disregard my questions; often she could not track a logical sequence of questions.

When asked about genital touch, if anyone ever tickled or hurt her "privates," she said her old baby sitter "put a curling iron in my butt." With very structured questioning, E. E. said the incident occurred in the sitter's bedroom, and, "No one watched. Nanny and the kids were the only ones home." When asked about the other children who were also being cared for with her, E. E. consistently denied their presence (several other children were always in the day care with her). E. E. was able to give information about what she was wearing: "My pants were off, but my shirt was on." She pointed to her vulva and said, "Nanny touched me right here." Then she spontaneously added that her cousin (a 14-year-old male babysitter) had touched her there as well (new information). She said the touching happened to her when she was about 3. She felt sad about it. When asked for details or further information, E. E. had difficulty remaining on task and sustaining attention.

At age 4, E. E. could give some limited but seemingly accurate information about her earlier experience. Unfortunately, she also gave other confusing, questionable, or unreliable information, and she offered new information but without detail. E. E. could not give good free narrative accounts of either incident she described.

Inaccuracies in her statements, inconsistencies in her responses, her short attention span, and her inability to provide good narrative about her experiences meant nothing could be done legally about her case. E. E.'s 4-year-old behaviors demonstrate why it is sometimes difficult to effectively respond to young children's allegations.

This chapter will first survey the various skills developing during this stage and discuss how they affect a child's ability to interview, then it will offer practical, clinically based suggestions for screening a child's status in each of these areas. This prescreening can help the interviewer determine each child's unique pattern of growth and allow the interview to be shaped to the child's skill level.

We will return to E. E.'s case later in the chapter, but first a look at the various skills that are developing during this stage and how they affect a child's ability to give more detailed or precise information to an interviewer. If you do not have a strong background in child development for this age group, and if you have not read Chapter 2, then read that chapter now. The ideas about conceptual development provide an important foundation for the material that follows.

❏ Understanding Skills Necessary to Interview

Because young children are so embedded in their context, that is, their history, background, and current status, it is often impossible to understand their statements without clearly understanding their past. I recommend that before seeing a child, you review the outline in Chapter 4. Without a clear history of the child's development, previous experience, and exposure to trauma-causing experiences, children's interview information can be misinterpreted.

The following skills are emerging in children of this age and need to be prescreened:

- language (amount, articulation, vocabulary)
- concepts (who, what, where)
- attention span
- memory for past events
- representational play
- real and imaginary thinking
- remembering or forgetting concepts
- truth or lie understanding
- monitoring of self and others
- use of symbols

LANGUAGE

Children from 3 to 5 years old are understood by most adults, have good working vocabularies with many labels and names, and are beginning to explore the relationships between things. They have moved from the two-word combinations evident at 18 to 24 months to full sentences with longer utterances and more complex grammar. Their articulation is better, but they often have trouble with l, s, and r—consonants that mature later. These children often "wub you," or want to "weally gib you thumthing thpethal." Recognizing this pattern can help you better translate unusual sounding words. Young children often speak in several word sentences, and create long chains of thoughts. The best way to "speak their kind of language" is to match your length of utterance to theirs. If a child is speaking in three or four word sentences, pose your queries in that same form.

CONCEPTS

Children may exhibit good articulation and vocabulary skills, but their use of certain underlying concepts is important to interviewing. By age 3, children usually understand basic ideas about who, what (as in "what is this?" but not the more complex "what happened?"), and where (Peterson, 1990). These conceptual words are essential to basic questioning about abuse. "When" and "how many" are concepts that mature much later. Good understanding of enumeration and ordinal scaling (i.e., the first act is number one, the second is number two, etc.), doesn't begin until about 5 to 6 years, so asking a Stage 2 child for information delivery skills that are not yet developed can make the child look incompetent. Asking if something happened one time or more than one time is a better way to approach the subject of incidence level. Expecting a date or specific time reference also requires a more mature level of concept development. Asking for dates makes a young child appear incompetent; instead, you can ask for time or date information by inquiring what the child had on, who was in the house, where mom was, and so on. The younger the child, the more concrete the form of the question needs to be.

There may be wide variability in the acquisition of communication skills (Fenson et al., 1994). In a study of 1,800 children between 8 and 30 months of age, they found wide variability across children in the time of onset and course of acquisition of these [communication] skills. This research challenges the meaningfulness of the concept of the model child. Age should not be the sole indicator of skill level. Some children from impoverished backgrounds are old enough to have basic concepts in place, but they may lack the teaching or experience to develop them. Delaying an assessment, if the child is in a safe place, may be helpful for these children; the foster parent can work to develop concepts and vocabulary needed for successful interviewing. The individual skill level of each child must be considered when interviewing.

ATTENTION SPAN

One of my friends said that trying to get a preschooler to stay on task for an extended period of time is "like nailing jello to the wall." Young children typically do not have long attention spans. If they are forced to stay on a task when they can no longer concentrate, or if they want to get away, they may give answers they think the interviewer wants, or they may give false information just to stop the process. Care must be taken to allow the child to move off the topic of abuse concerns, regroup, and then be guided back. Some children have very long attention spans, whereas others, often children who have been badly abused, have short attention spans. Some forms of attention deficit

with hyperactivity can be emotionally induced from prolonged exposure to abusive or stressful situations. For children with abuse histories, hyperactivity is a common condition. For such children, it is better
to have a couple of short, comfortable interviews than to attempt to
keep a child on task and risk invalidating the interview material.

MEMORY FOR PAST EVENTS

Young children's memories do not have the internal cognitive structure that allows rich, detailed, and spontaneous narratives of their
experiences. Adults need to provide the framework or structure for
their memories. This is referred to as "scaffolding," and the younger
the child the more dependent she is on the interviewer's structure for
her memory retrieval (see Fivush & Hamond, 1990; Nelson, 1993; this
volume, Chapter 3). Understanding this need allows for better tailor-
ing of interview questions to the child's capacities so that more accurate information can be obtained. Care to avoid awkward, leading, or
hard-to-process questions must be made but, when used with care,
directed and focused questions can help facilitate a child's ability to
relate experiences without distorting memory.

A second factor in children's ability to give narrative accounts of
their experiences is the quality of their caregiver's interactions with
them. The way a parent talks to her child about past experiences
organizes the experience of the event and its representation in memory
(Fivush & Hayden, 1997). Meaningful narration can help children
understand and remember events because the adult provides a structure and comprehension of the event. The adult also organizes relationships among the actions and offers an understanding of why they occur
(Fivush, Pipe, Murachver, & Reese, 1997). Fivush et al. point out that
the parental style of narration can also influence the quality of a child's
recall. *Low elaborative* mothers tend to repeat the same question over
and over in their attempt to get the 'correct' memory response. Because
these parents provide less information, there is less contextual support
for their children overall. This book is just out and unavailable to me,
so I've had to paraphrase instead. In contrast, a *high elaborative* mother
confirms the child's response and then poses questions to help her
child fill in information. Such a mother might ask her child to discuss
an event they had experienced earlier that day. This helps organize and

construct not only the experience and its rehearsal but also the format for discourse. Children of high elaborative mothers have richer narratives, and those narratives are retained longer.

This finding is important to those of us who assess young children. Children who have low elaborative parents may have more difficulty organizing and sharing their recall. Hesitancy or lack of fluency should not be interpreted as a sign of invalid information. Clinical experience often finds fewer high elaborative mothers and more low elaborative mothers in the backgrounds of young sexually abused children.

Memory ability matures over time and with experience. Chapter 3 discussed early memory capacities in detail; important issues to remember for interviewing are the emphasis on routine sequences (Fivush & Hamond, 1990; Nelson, 1993), the beginning of autobiographical memory (Nelson, 1993), and a focus on more unique or different events versus event sequences (Fivush & Hammond, 1990).

REPRESENTATIONAL PLAY

Children with limited vocabularies, who have difficulty telling about what has happened to them, are often better at showing what has happened instead. Play is seen as a symbolic expression of knowledge (McCune-Nicolich, 1981). The ability to use dolls or other objects in a symbolic way is called *representation*. This ability matures with age (Corrigan, 1987; McCune-Nicholich, 1981; Watson & Fischer, 1977).

Play behavior starts at about 12 months, along with the emergence of language and the ability to use symbols. This early play moves from the infant exploration of an object (putting it in the mouth, poking fingers into holes, etc.) to a display of the child's own experiences (e.g., pretending to drink from a cup). Play behavior such as feeding a doll was noted by McCune-Nicholich (1981) in children 12 to 18 months old. Children of about 18 months of age were able to engage in pretend play, directing their pretense toward a person or an inanimate object such as a doll or stuffed animal (Belsky & Most, 1981; Fenson & Ramsay, 1980).

By about 24 months, McCune-Nicholich noted the active use of a doll, as well as the substitution of objects, to give the needed play (being able to use a stick as a horse). Younger children would pretend at their own everyday activity ("self-pretend"); but as they matured, they could begin to act out someone else's activity, (pretend to wash dishes like Mommy). At age 3 children would pretend with another passive recipient of their acts ("passive other"); a 3-year-old pretends her dollies are having a tea party and she talks to them—and for them— as she plays.

By age 4, children can pretend with an "active other" (a child puts a comb in the doll's hand and pretends to have the doll comb its own hair). When children use one dolly to act out someone else's part while another dolly acts the child's own part, the child is able to "represent himself externally," that is, the child can use a doll to stand for himself. This aspect of play development, a *representation of self*, is probably the most important aspect of play for child abuse investigators. When a child is handed two dolls and asked to show what the perpetrator did to them, the capacity to self-represent, as well as show active participation of another doll in interaction, is needed.

The ability to represent the self externally does not emerge until about 3 years 6 months, and it is usually in place by age 4. The work of Steven Ceci and Maggi Bruck has pointed out major problems in the use of anatomical dolls for interviewing very small children (Bruck, Ceci, Francoeur, & Renick, 1995). The experimenters asked children who were just 3 years to demonstrate, by using an anatomically explicit doll as a representation of themselves, what a physician had done on their last exam. They found that adding dolls "increased inaccurate reporting because some children falsely showed that the doctor had inserted a finger into the anal or genital cavity."

This study points to the critical issue of timing children's use of anatomical dolls to their proper stage of development. The Bruck et al. (1995) experiment was specifically timed to the early months of age 3, when the capacity to represent self is emerging. It would be *expected* that children that age would have difficulty using dolls to represent themselves. Using dolls as representative of self in young 3-year-olds is inappropriate and may lead to inappropriate conclusions.

This does not mean, however, that dolls can never be used with children. They can (American Professional Society on the Abuse of Children [APSAC] Guidelines, 1995), but their use must be in specified appropriate ways and in concert with emerging developmental skills (see section on dolls here and in Chapter 6).

What about the spontaneous play behaviors of children? Sexualized behaviors are one of the more common sequelae seen in young sexually abused children (Kendall-Tackett et al., 1993). Although young children may not be able to tell you something (explicit knowledge), they may demonstrate their experiences in play behavior (implicit knowledge). Research by Hewitt et al. (1994) found that spontaneous sexualized play was the factor that best predicted whether a child was in a group of probably abused versus probably not abused 2-year-old children. DeLoache and Marzolf (1995) also note that young children's knowledge can be represented in their play.

The fact that children demonstrate the experiences they have had in their actions is consistent with both theory and research. Young children are not sophisticated creators of new and novel sequences of actions. They are not well enough integrated to planfully hide all their responses.

REAL OR IMAGINARY THINKING

It is not uncommon for a young 3-year-old child to give information that appears to be coherent and based on reality, and then suddenly add fantastical sounding elements: "And then him dad came-ed in and kicked him." When this occurs, interviewers commonly shake their head and moan at the thought of what a defense attorney might do with this information.

Understanding children's development of the capacity to understand real and pretend is critical to this situation, and the work of Wooley & Wellman (1993) and Welch-Ross (1995) is relevant here. When children are age 2 their words are tied to concrete objects, but when they reach age 3, they are suddenly capable of internally generating thoughts and ideas. It is about this time that children's fantasy play begins to emerge. However, young children are not good monitors of the origins of their thoughts. They do not distinguish between thoughts that are internally generated and thoughts that come from reality. Some of this lapse is due to the normal structure of preschool thinking, which is very self-focused and assumes one's own reality is the same as everyone else's reality. Children under age 4 are not skilled at monitoring the origin of their thoughts, so the constructions of 3-year-old children can be subject to fantasy interjection.

The 3-year-old's lack of understanding that these events may be constructed by the mind creates a significant problem for interviewers. Research on the emergence and development of an understanding of real and pretend indicates 3-year-old children are prone to errors with real and pretend ideas. The skill of telling fact from fiction develops gradually. Children below 3 years 6 months are not aware of the origin of their thoughts, but children of this age are transitioning into this skill. By 4 years of age, most children can see imagination as a fictional state.

By 5 years of age, children can think about their own thoughts, but they still do not necessarily recognize, or have the ability to identify, the source of their knowledge. By 6 years of age, true thinking about real and pretend, as a form of internal thought, begins. The ability of children to think about their own thinking is one benchmark of the shift to a more advanced level of cognition.

Three-year-old children also interject fantasy material from their own internal processes into accounts of sexual abuse for a variety of reasons (for a more thorough review of fantasy in children's statements, see my discussion the work of Dahlenberg (1996) and Everson (1997) in Chapter 3). Some children need to protect their sense of self or to buffer the effect of the abuse they have experienced, whereas others may be relating unclear or misunderstood events in a primitive language structure whose reality base is not immediately apparent. Fantasy interjections, however, create havoc in a criminal justice system, and imaginary interjections bring into question a child's separation of real versus fictional events. When a child's interjection of fantasy events into real experiences is recognized as a normal process of development, however, the focus can be shifted from the issues of fabrication and false allegations. Support for the child's reality-based experiences may be found in their behavior, play, or spontaneous utterances. This information can be obtained by extending the behaviorally based assessment outlined in Chapter 4, because it documents the children's sexualized behaviors, post-traumatic stress behaviors, spontaneous language utterances, and play behaviors. Supplementing statements with these important behavioral markers removes the need to rely solely on the verbal accounts of children who may intermingle real and fantasy material. The focus then can be on helping create a situation that promotes protection for the child, even though the material may not be appropriate for immediate criminal prosecution.

REMEMBERING OR FORGETTING CONCEPTS

For adults, the act of remembering involves "metacognition," or thinking about your own thinking. This is an advanced cognitive skill. Often, however, we ask young children to remember a past event. Is this a question understandable to children? Is this a concept that is appropriate to ask children?

Children first begin using words referring to memory at about 18 months. Research by Bauer and Hertsgaard (1993) has shown that when 14-month-old children are told to remember or "not to forget" a certain event, they show greater recall at a later time. These young children are obviously understanding the word "remember," but not necessarily in the same framework as adults. Children at 2½ years begin to use words regarding remember and forget, and by age 3, most understand that remember means to "successfully search after a delay" (Wellman & Johnson, 1979). By 4 years of age, children generally understand that remembering means having success in finding something, but it is only at age 4 that children also recognize that they need prior knowledge to be able to forget something (Lyon & Flavell, 1994). The capacity to remember means recognizing "what was." Older preschoolers understand also that remembering involves learning and retention over time.

The emergence of complete understanding of this skill can result in interesting interpretations of the concepts of remembering and forgetting. Walker (1994) cites a case in which a young boy was asked if he remembered an earlier event and he said no. When additional questioning was done, he appeared to show evidence of recollection for that earlier event. On further inquiry, he explained that he did not remember it because "he hadn't forgotten it yet."

The idea of memory as an internal process is fairly well understood by 5 years of age, but it is not until 6 years of age that there is a clear recognition that remembering depends on a prior exposure, not just general knowledge. Six-year-old children are capable of understanding that you can't remember what you didn't experience.

Understanding the developmental course of remembering and forgeting is important to interviewing. Although we can ask children questions about memory, we have to understand how children will respond to our questions. We cannot assume that their memory is the same as an adult's. We cannot ask a child about remembering in the same way we query an adult. Walker (1994) notes that "do you remember?" is often followed by a series of ideas that have to be remembered and processed by a child. For example, the sentence "Do you remember *when you were at James's house* and *your mother came over*, and *people were playing together*?" chains multiple events and makes responding to a "do you remember?" question exceedingly difficult for a young child to answer. Sometimes "do you remember?" can be deleted by an interviewer and children can be asked, "Did your mother go to James's house?" This is a more straightforward question and can be answered yes or no by the child. When questions are complicated, children may say they do not remember when, in fact, further exploration shows that they do.

TRUTH OR LIE UNDERSTANDING

The judicial system is dependent on an understanding of truth and falsehood on the part of its witnesses and their ability to tell only the truth. It is not uncommon in a voir dire to question a child in the following manner: "What color jacket am I wearing? Yes, it's blue. If I told you it was red, would that be a lie or the truth?" This type of questioning may tap the child's knowledge of colors, but it does not effectively tap their knowledge of deceit and intent—critical elements in forensic cases (Walker, 1994). Children as young as 2 years (Garvey, 1984) have a sense of deceit, yet they cannot articulate it. Preschool children can recognize truth or deceit when given an example, yet they have difficulty explaining the abstract ideas of truth and justice (Lyon, 1996). Interviewing must be adapted to the child's more concrete skills (for a better way to present the truth or lie issue, see Prescreening Children for Interview Capabilities below).

MONITORING OF SELF AND OTHERS

Young children are very egocentric, or self-focused. They are not capable of thinking about their own thinking. They do not recognize when they do not know something, and they do not recognize when you do know something. They assume that you have the same experience and perspective as they do, so they see no need to explain the context of their thoughts or to correct your misconceptions. It is easy to misunderstand young children's responses if you do not double-check. You can do things to ensure that you have accurately understood a young child's intent, and you can encourage them to "catch you" if you make a mistake (see Prescreening interview format).

Preschoolers also do not monitor the truthfulness of adult's statements to them. Because children are so dependent on adults for all their needs, they assume that adults are truthful. Children may endorse items an interviewer is pushing because they want to please or because part of the question is true, but not necessarily because the whole question is true. It is helpful to explore a child's level of suggestibility to see if he is clear about what he believes, and not totally dependent on your comments. Encouraging children to maintain the integrity of their own observations is an important permission to give.

USE OF SYMBOLS

Children can comprehend more than they can report. They can have an implicit knowledge but not the ability to express it explicitly. When we want children to demonstrate something, we often turn to the use of symbols. Children's ability to use symbols is involved, for instance, when we ask them to "show me what happened," and we offer a dollhouse as a demonstration tool. We also ask for symbol use when we tell children, "Use this dolly and show me where you were touched," or, "Use this drawing of a man and put a mark on the place where you were touched," or, "Let's draw a map of your house and you show me where you were." There are several important milestones involved in children's use of symbols. The work of Judy DeLoache and colleagues, discussed below, has helped clarify children's use of symbols.

Dollhouses

Very often, interviewers will use a small dollhouse to have a child show where and how an event occurred. Children age 2½ typically fail to understand the relationship between a scale model and the larger space it represents (the dollhouse as a model of their house). DeLoache

(1989) suggests that young children do not have the ability to respond to a model both as a real thing and as a representation of something else. DeLoache (1991) has shown that children who are age 2½ tend to respond to a scale model not as a copy of a larger space but rather as a stimulus in and of itself, that is, a dollhouse. They do not relate to it on an abstract level and they are not able to use it as a format for depicting events in their own home.

DeLoache (1989) has demonstrated this by presenting 2½-year-old children (30–31 months) with a scale model of a separate, larger room. Using the model, she shows them how she hides a toy dog behind a piece of furniture. Then she opens the door to the real, larger room, ushers the child in, and asks the child to find a larger, stuffed dog like the one they hid in the larger room. Children who are 2½ years of age have difficulty accomplishing this task, but children 3 years of age (36 to 39 months) are able to "map" from the scale model to the actual room and successfully find the toy. When the scale model and the actual room are no longer exact replicas and the model differs from the actual room, however, then 3-year-olds have more difficulty.

Abuse investigation often asks children to demonstrate an experience using a dollhouse; remember, older preschool children are more capable of setting up a dollhouse as a model of a specific place, but explicit demonstration is more difficult for a child under the age of 4. Children under the age of 4 can still use a dollhouse, but with less specificity than older children. Young children may show spontaneous play in a dollhouse that reflects their experiences in the original abuse situation because parts of an interviewer's dollhouse may evoke specific elements of their abuse (a bed, a bathtub, a potty). The use of a dollhouse as an interview aide must be adapted to the level of the child's capacities and representational skills.

Dolls

DeLoache's (1989, 1991) tasks involve having a child "map" her knowledge from a scale model to a larger model. Sexual abuse interviewing, however, focuses on a reverse mapping skill: a child is asked to demonstrate, with a smaller model, something that happened in a larger, reality context.

Can young children show what happened to them on a doll? In one experiment, stickers were placed on the bodies of children ages 2½, 3, and 4 years. The children were then told to place the stickers on a doll that was specifically accessorized to be similar to the child (DeLoache & Marzolf, 1995). Ninety-two percent of the 4-year-olds placed the stickers correctly, and 71% of the 3-year-olds placed the stickers correctly, but only 41% of the 2½-year-olds could place the stickers correctly. The majority of the older children were capable of using the dolls to show what happened to them, whereas few of the younger children were able to use the dolls successfully. When asked to show on the dolls where they were touched during a Simon Says activity, 53% of the 2½-year-olds accurately showed the correct responses on the doll, whereas 67% of the 3-year-olds and 81% of the 4-year-olds also did so. Children in all three groups were quite good at answering leading questions accurately, and even the 2½-year-olds answered 89% of the questions correctly.

Results obtained by Bruck, Ceci, Francoeur, and Renick (1995) in their use of anatomically detailed dolls with young 3-year-olds also show that this group has difficulty using AC dolls. Understanding the emergence of representational skills can help direct the best timing for use of the AC dolls as interview aids so as to avoid misinterpretation of a child's behavior (for a more detailed discussion of the uses of AC dolls, see Chapter 6).

Pictures of People

Sometimes figures of nude adults are used to represent a perpetrator (Forensic Mental Health Associates, 1984). Children's abilities to use a drawing as representative of themselves or others would appear to mature in concert with other representation-of-self skills, as noted above. Children under 4 years of age may not comprehend that the specific forensic drawing is to be a representation of the actual perpetrator or that the child drawing is to represent his- or herself. Older preschoolers, about age 4 or 5, can usually mark specific body parts involved in their abuse and use the drawings appropriately.

Drawing a picture and saying, "Let's have this be you," may be inappropriate for a child under 4 years of age, or for some delayed 4-year-olds. Using a drawing as a representation of themselves is difficult for most 3-year-olds. Before specifying a figure drawing as that of the child, it is important to carefully assess that child's capacity for self-representation.

Asking children to draw a picture of their perpetrator, or of an object involved in their abuse, is also an age-related request because children's abilities change dramatically (Berk, 1994). Prior to age 5 or 6, children are unable to draw with much specificity or exactness. When we ask young children to use pictures or dolls to represent themselves, we must remember that these are skills that emerge at a different rate for different children.

Although very young children have trouble using dollhouses, dolls, or pictures as symbols of themselves, DeLoache (personal communication, 1996) has also found that some can respond to snapshots of a person. The younger children do not have as much difficulty with dual representation with a snapshot as they might with a more abstract picture or model; thus snapshots could be a better prompt than line drawings or pictures across changing developmental capabilities.

Maps

By age 4, children are able to use models and some very concrete maps. The full ability to create and use maps does not usually emerge until a child is about 7 years old. Then he can begin to draw spatial maps (a map of the route from his home to school). Younger children can use some symbols depending on their level of concreteness and specific representation of the original situation.

Symbol usage needs to be understood against the background of a child's history. If children have had exposure to symbol practice in one environment, that exposure may help younger children transfer the skill from an easier symbolic task to a more difficult one (Marzolf & DeLoache, 1994). Good history about the child's background and experiences can help the interviewer better anticipate the child's capabilities. If the child is from a white, middle-class environment, the research findings best match their group. However, if the child comes from a low-income population, then skills associated with the use of symbols may be delayed (DeLoache, personal communication, 1996). Further work on the acquisition of symbol skill is needed with children who have been abused or neglected.

In the same vein, asking a child to draw a map of their home or of the route taken during an abuse episode may be impossible for 4-year-old children. This interview technique is best left to children who are school age.

❏ Prescreening Children for Interview Capabilities

Using the same format for interviewing across all ages does not take into account children's changing skills. Prescreening children for their competence in interviewing skills before presenting them with an interview format can allow us to tailor our interview to their capacities. *A developmentally adapted interview ensures the most accurate assessment of the child's experience.*

CAUTION

1. Prescreening does not mean that some children are "screened out." As used in this context, prescreening means the profiling of a child's abilities to allow an interviewer to best adapt his or her interview format to the child.
2. Some children are not capable of following a formal prescreening format (see Case Example 2 at the end of this chapter). That does not mean they cannot reveal their information, but they may need a manner other than a structured interview format.

One benefit of this proposed prescreening is that it can be a way of preparing for targeted information queries that will occur later. For example, having a child tell you about some neutral event she remembers can not only help you understand her capacity for free narrative but can also rehearse a skill that she will need later in a more crucial context.

CAUTION

The material that follows is developed from clinical practice, with some integration of various research procedures, where such application is possible. These ideas are not meant as final, research-substantiated methods. It is my hope that the ideas will prompt research to test their efficacy or to offer more effective techniques.

How can we prescreen? There is no best way to do this, but the following format surveys the status of basic skills needed in interviewing. It is for use during the "warm-up" time with a child, the first 20 to 30 minutes. While you are getting to know the child, developing rapport and comfort, you will be assessing important developmental capacities and rehearsing the various structures you may use in your interview.

PREPARING FOR THE PRESCREENING

Before you see the child, have available the materials that you will need. I like to have a couple of small doll figures (I use the 5-inch plastic doll families by Rumple, listed in the references under Kidsrights, the company that carries them. I like to use these dolls because some of them have molded genitals and they are available in multiethnic groups—Caucasian, Black, Hispanic, and Asian). To assess general play skills, I also have some small play dishes, toy beds, a couch, and a bath and toilet. The child and I sit on the floor and attention is focused on the toys and not directly on the child. This indirect focus is more comfortable for a shy child and the play allows time to get acquainted.

SCREENING FOR DEVELOPMENTAL SKILLS

The techniques that follow were created to assess the level of development for each skill area listed above. Again, I want to emphasize that these techniques are clinically based strategies and they are not meant as final, research-substantiated methods.

Language

While children explore your toys, just listen and watch what they are doing. Sometimes I make a neutral comment like, "You're putting that dolly to bed," or some other remark that reflects the general activity but does not require a response.

If the child talks while he is playing, listen to his language. I am listening for several things:

Can I understand him, or will I need an "interpreter" at this session?

How long are his sentences? (I will match my inquiries to his sentence length.)

What kind of vocabulary does he have? (I will try to match his vocabulary level.)

What kind of narrative does he offer?

Does he respond to open-ended questions or does he need more structure?

How spontaneous are his comments?

Does he need prompting?

After some initial play observations and questions to get more language sampling, you can begin to screen concepts. I like to proceed from open-ended to more focused questions, so I may ask the following (some of these are repeats of the questions outlined in Chapter 4):

Who: Who lives at your house? Who sleeps at your house? (This helps you understand whether the child can respond to a "who" question, and it also provides information about the child's home and their ability to document who is there.)

What: As the two of you continue to talk, you can ask if the child watches TV. "What do you watch on TV?" (This is an open-ended question that does not restrict a response.)

Some children do not answer, so you can move from an open-ended question to a more focused one:

"Do you watch *Sesame Street* (or *Barney*)?" If yes, then go on to ask "What's the name of that bird, the tall one?" or

"What is the name of Barney's friend?" "What does Barney do with Baby Bopp?"

Where: You can ask anything that might tap the child's general knowledge, such as

"Where do you live?"

"Where do you sleep?"

"Where did you put your car when you came to see me?" or "Where did you get on the bus?"

You can ask some other "who, what, or where" questions as well, if you want to build more rapport, hear more language, or encourage more expression.

CAUTION

Some children cannot complete even a brief question and answer interchange. When a child is not able to respond to a basic screening or discussion, *stop* the interview-focused assessment and move to a psychosocial evaluation to get more information (see APSAC, 1997, *Guidelines for Psychosocial Evaluation of Suspected Sexual Abuse in Children*). In that context you can explore more of the child's skills, use objective measures to look at skill development, and check on emotional status. Children raised in very chaotic living situations may be emotionally disturbed and they should be evaluated in a more extended situation so their credibility is not judged only by their response to one interview session.

As you ask these questions, monitor the ability of the child to respond to questioning and listen carefully to articulation, length of utterance, and language capabilities. As children "warm up," they usually become freer in their speech and language.

Style of the Child

Your next step in prescreening is to focus on the style of the child:

How open and relaxed is he?

Does he seem anxious or afraid?

Does he look to you for help rather than to their caretaker? (This might provide some information about level of attachment.)

In a short period of time, you can assess language, explore several of the concepts you will use later, and get a feel for how competent, open, and available the child is.

Attention Span

How long a child can stay on task will determine how long your interview session will be. I like to note how well the child sustains attention as I begin my interaction.

Can she stay on task easily and for enough time to allow me to finish my question and give me an answer?

Is she easily distracted? Is she monitoring noises in the hallway or other rooms?

Is she listening to parts of my questions and not the whole?

Does she need frequent breaks or can she attend for a period of time?

Does she actually play and explore her relationship to the toys, or does she move rapidly from one thing to another, maybe even around the room?

Remember, many abused children are hypervigilant and may have developed some hyperactivity in response to prolonged exposure to threatening environments. You may have to gently ask the child to look at your eyes or to repeat a question if he has trouble attending and you want to be sure he is "tracking" your questions. Some children left to play freely will quickly move from one toy to another, not really exploring it. To test the limits of their level of attention, you can try playing with them around a toy or game and see if you can prolong their attention span.

All of this watching and playing is important knowledge as you prepare for your target interview. If the child cannot stay on task for this part of the assessment, you may need to do more individual status assessment or create more rapport before you try to interview. I do not force children to stay with my questions. If you persist when the child is disinterested or unwilling, you run the risk of getting invalid information. I allow the child free play and come back with my structure later. Pacing yourself to the child's rhythm and respecting his reaction to this new situation is important for rapport building.

Memory

Spontaneous narrative is difficult for young children, as I mentioned above, for they do not carry enough internal structure or organization to deliver a detailed description of things that have happened to them. To determine a child's capacity for spontaneous narrative, I like one of the Step-Wise Interview techniques (for further discussion of this interview format, see Chapter 6). Before I meet the child, I will ask the caretaker to tell me about an event the child has experienced roughly 2 to 3 months ago. I will then ask the child about that event during my prescreening time. A discussion of past events provides a good chance to listen to the child's ability to relate events in a narrative. Some children will need more structure from you to allow them to give you their information.

The following example illustrates some of the difficulties an interviewer faces in trying to get an event narrative from a young child. This example is taken from case notes with a boy who was almost 4 years of age at the time of his interview:

> F. F. was involved in sucking penises with other boys at the playground. The children were interviewed separately and F. F. was determined to be the initiator of the action. When his mother asked him where he learned about this, he said his father did that to him on visits. F. F. was interviewed by child protection, but the case needed further corroboration so I did an evaluation of the boy. Just prior to the session, when I planned to prescreen, I asked the mother to tell me about some experience within the last 6 months that she thought her son might remember and be able to talk about. She reported that he had gone to the stock car races with his grandmother and aunt about three months earlier and she thought he would remember that. So I asked F. F. some questions.

1. "Do you have a grandmother?"
   "Yes."
2. "Where do you go with her?"
   No response.
3. "Do you sometimes go places with her?"
   "No."
4. "Did you ever go to the races with your grandmother?"
   "Yes."
5. "Do you have an aunt?"
   "No."
6. "Do you have an aunt Sarah?"
   "Yes."
7. "Do you go places with your Aunt Sarah?"
   "No."
8. "Did your Aunt Sarah go to the races with you?"
   "Yes."
9. "What did you do at the races?"
   No response.
10. "Did you see cars at the races?"
    "Yes."
11. "What did the cars do?"
    At this point the child took a small car, began to make large circles on the floor with the appropriate sounds and noises. He spontaneously added, "It was so noisy that when you put your fingers like this (and he stuck his fingers in his ears), you could still hear the cars."

This is an interesting example of a young child's problems with articulating or narrating his memories. The problem that this young child had in providing narrative details is related not to his memory for an event but to the kind of questions he was asked. Some of the questions asked have a lack of specificity (questions 1, 2, 3, 5, 7, 9)— they require this young boy to search memory for an appropriate response and they leave too many options for a reply. When provided with more scaffolding or structure (questions 4, 6, 8, 10, 11), he was able to not only acknowledge experience but also provide idiosyncratic and specific evidence of experiencing a specific situation.

Knowledge from prescreening in this manner helps set the format for the subsequent target interview. The prescreening of this child would indicate that asking questions that have a lack of specificity (e.g.,"Did somebody do something to you?") might easily elicit a "no." Asking questions about specific people may, in fact, be a better method of inquiry. Concerns about leading questions or about suggestibility can also be countered by the fact that this child has demonstrated a need for scaffolding and external cuing.

Play

Representation of self is the most important concept to prescreen in this category, because its presence or absence determines how you use AC dolls in your interview. This ability can be prescreened in several ways. Sometimes just watching a child play in a dollhouse can give information about his or her representational skills. When a child uses one of the dolls to speak for her, she displays representation of self. To explore this ability, have a child pick three dolls, one for the father, one for the mother, and one for the child (adapting this for children from single-family situations or other family constellations). Then ask the child to show you what these people do in the dollhouse. Watching how a child uses the dolls reveals self-representational abilities.

I have also screened for this ability in a more focused way. I ask the child to pick out a mother doll and a doll that looks like himself from my selection of dolls. I then take the child doll and say, "Let's have this doll be you. Show me how your Mom (or Dad) puts you to bed." Children without representational skills will not have the child doll talk or act the way they would in that situation.

When I tried this technique with the 4-year-old boy referred to earlier, he took the mother doll, straightened her arms out so they were in front of her, then laid the child doll in her arms and had the mother say, "Now it's time for you to go to bed." Then he said, "I don't want to go." The mother doll said, "You need to go." The child doll said, "I don't want to go!" and the mother took him up to bed, laid him down, and said, "You go to sleep!" The child said, "I don't wanna, I don't wanna!!" and jumped all over the bed. "Oh all right," said the mother, "five more minutes." By having the dolls behave in such a realistic way, this boy demonstrated clearly that he had reached the representational stage of play development.

Some children will not talk with dolls, so that kind of play won't work. But if a child is age 4 or older and comes from a reasonably stimulating environment, most probably the ability is there.

Another way I use to screen for representation is to draw a child, label it with the child's name, and ask the child to help me put the right feeling face on the drawing, such as, how does the child feel? Young 3-year-olds are unable to respond to this invitation, whereas older 3-year-olds often talk easily about themselves. If I am going to use anatomical dolls as an interview adjunct, I find it helpful to try to screen this ability with some kind of small doll, although it is not essential.

Real and Pretend

Understanding that 3- to 4-year-olds internally generate thoughts different from those generated by their actual experiences is a critical aspect of interviewing preschoolers. An intermingling of truth and fantasy in a 3-year-old should not be seen as negating the child's capacity for relating their experience. A careful screening may be able to clarify what is real and what is fantasy.

When a child begins to intersperse what seems to be fantasy into an otherwise factual account, I use the following clinical technique. I stop the child's disclosure, shift topics, and encourage some free play. After a few minutes I say, "I wonder if you know the difference between real and pretend?" (Most young preschoolers have a difficult time putting this understanding into words.) Then I explain that I want to see what they know. To check on this, I ask questions about experiences that I know the child has had versus those I know he hasn't had. I usually frame them around his past interaction with me. "When you came to see me last time, you got cookies at the end of the work that we did. Is that real or pretend?" (Sometimes I use "real" or "not real," depending on the child's understanding.) Sharing cookies at the end of the session is something I do, and if the child answers "real," we proceed.

If the child has not been in before, and she is disclosing on a first session, I ask her about something that happened just prior to our meeting; for example, "When you came today, you played with Duplos while I talked with your mom. Is that real or pretend?" She usually says that is something that really happened. If she has trouble focusing on the task, I may ask her a couple of "real" questions, and then switch to a pretend question. To do this, I ask about something that is clearly not reality based, such as, "When you were playing in my waiting room a big clown came in and did tricks. Is that real or pretend?" Often the child will appear puzzled, and then laugh and say, "That's pretend!" I persist with questions like, "Did we play with my dollhouse when you were here?" (real), "Was there a big crocodile under the chairs in my waiting room?" (pretend). Some very young children are unable to accurately respond to real and pretend, and they are very suggestible, endorsing all questions. In these cases, I return to the type of assessment used for smaller children (behaviors, spontaneous statements, behaviors over time and across situations).

If the issue of real or pretend information surfaces in the target interview, I use the above format to review the child's mastery of real versus pretend. After we have practiced distinguishing this concept, I ask the target question. "You told your teacher you touched your mom's boobies. Is that real or pretend?" When children come at the target information from a new direction, it forces them to think about it in a new way. Often the veracity of this statement can be documented, although sometimes their earlier utterances cannot be validated.

Again, I must emphasize that not all children respond to this specific technique. I have presented one framework from which to consider an exploration of this issue, but it does not rule out other approaches. Assessing fantasy-like statements with 3-year-olds is difficult but important work. It warrants additional exploration and understanding.

Truth or Lie Understanding

The following idea of developmentally appropriate screening for children's concepts of truth or lies comes from Walker (1994), and I have taken the liberty of putting her idea in a preschool context. The heart of the voir dire questioning is the child's ability to grasp the concept of falsification, and the following series of questioning does just that.

Using hypotheticals I already know about the child and the family (a preschooler with an older brother and a family cat), I construct the following vignette.

> "What if your brother pulled your cat's tail? And what if your cat meowed? And what if your brother said *you* did it? Is he telling the truth, or a lie?"

Most children interrupt when you get to the part where the older sibling says the child did it, and the child yells, "He's lying!" Reminding children that they are only supposed to talk about true things, not lies, helps meet the demands made of a witness.

Suggestibility and "Correct Me"

Some children are easily suggestible, and prescreening the robustness of a child's ability to maintain his own point of view can also provide the opportunity to set some of the ground rules for the interview situation. You can probe suggestibility by asking a child if you are supposed to do something not usually involved in the interview procedure. For example, I ask the child if we are supposed to brush her teeth today (or cut her hair). The child will usually say no. You can press your point and see how robust her suggestibility is by telling her you really thought you were supposed to do that. Is she sure you're not supposed to_____? Isn't that what she was told?

The above questioning can show whether children are able to maintain their own understanding in the face of suggestive adult questioning. Clinically, I have found that some children will acquiesce to any form of question that I raise, whereas other children will be very clear and resolutely maintain their expectations about our meeting. After this discussion, I either praise the child for staying with what they believe and reiterate that it is important for them to stay with what they know as part of the rules for our time together, or I become watchful for fantasy statements and ground my assessment in the Stage 1 assessment.

After this screening, I follow up by explaining the rules for the interview. (Young children do not monitor the accuracy of other persons' perceptions. Pointing out to them that you make mistakes and need their help, and then practicing mistakes and corrections, can help increase the child's ability to monitor.) I tell the child I may ask several questions. If he doesn't know the answer, I'll tell him that "I don't know" is a good answer in our sessions if he does not know. I also tell him that if I make a mistake he should correct me. Then, to practice this, I deliberately make a mistake and refer to one of his friends by a different name. When the child corrects me, I will offer him praise and support for having caught my error, and I will marvel at his sharp ears and ability to listen and catch the mistakes that I make. Sometimes I may deliberately misstate a fact that the child has told me to see if he is able to contradict me and, again, I will support his ability to discern mistakes that I have made.

Correcting adult errors, or recognizing his own lack of knowledge, is not a preschool skill. Practicing this specifically with young children can sometimes help shape their abilities to monitor, while other young 3-year-olds may not be able to do this.

* * *

In proceeding with this prescreening, not only is the level of the child's different developmental skills screened but also a precedent is set for the target format that will follow. Questions and answers will be conducted, and children will be asked about their memories. Prescreening allows an understanding of the child's capabilities in the area; also, the child, because she has already experienced that type of format, may more easily be able to respond to the type of questions posed. Prescreening of this nature can take anywhere from 20 to 40 minutes, and is easily interwoven into the initial discussion and rapport building with a child.

Again, let me caution, there is no research on this particular form of prescreening and although, clinical evidence shows that it has promise, it awaits further, more rigorous examination.

If you are currently using a single-format interview to question 3- to 4-year-olds, it is my recommendation that you first have good developmental background and history. Then you can add this prescreening format to the initial rapport building you have provided. Based on what you know about emerging interview skills in this age group, you can consider adapting your current interview format to the needs of less well-developed children. Examples of different forms of interviews and methods for their adaptation are the topics of the next chapter.

Applying the Protocol: Three Case Examples

❏ Interviewing Again

E. E.'s initial consultation is described in the introductory paragraphs of this chapter. Her case is included here because it was done "backwards"—a single standardized interview was done before any background gathering (the Touch Survey outlined in Chapter 7) or prescreening was done. Following the initial, one-shot interview, the mother pressed for more information and a different process was followed. Mother was interviewed for background and developmental status and E. E. was seen again, this time for prescreening and a second, modified target interview. What emerges from the information gathered on background and prescreening gives additional, important information Completing a prescreening and conducting a second target interview, modified to E. E.'s developmental status, gives a richer view of E. E.'s allegations. (Fictitious names were added to this case history for ease of reading.)

MOTHER'S INTERVIEW

Mother was seen alone for information on E. E.'s early background and development. She presented as a concerned, caring parent, but she had difficulty completing responses to questions—she often gave rambling, far-ranging responses to focused questions and she was frequently caught in her own emotional reactions to E. E.'s behavior. The following history was pieced together after her interview.

Developmental History, Current Status,
Risk Factors, and Test Findings

Mother reported a normal pregnancy, birth, and delivery, with developmental milestones on target and no major medical problems. There was no history of prolonged separation, trauma, or exposure to sexual information. Mother was now married and had just had her second child. She described good relations with her family and a sensitive and caring mate. She observed no sexualized play with dolls, no sexually focused bathtub behavior, and no other unusual sexualized behaviors with her daughter. The CSBI was elevated with item endorsement regarding sexual play with other children, a history of attempted insertion of the curling iron into her vulva, and talk about sexual touching. The CBCL showed no significant elevations on any behavioral scales.

History of the Concerns

When E. E. was 2 years old, Mother was a single parent who cared for her daughter during the day but worked a 4 o'clock to midnight shift in the evening, so E. E. went to her day care provider's home to sleep. One night after picking E. E. up, the mother put her sleepy daughter on the potty before tucking her into bed. As E. E. began to urinate she started to scream. She said it hurt when she went potty. Mother checked her bottom, saw small spots of blood on her diaper, and a new redness in the vaginal area. Mother remembered that recently E. E. had been saying her butt hurt, but Mother thought E. E. meant her anus and thought the problem might be constipation, which lasted only a few days and then dissipated. Now, seeing the vaginal redness and the small drops of blood, Mother worried that it might be sexual abuse her daughter was telling her about.

Early the next morning, Mother took E. E. to her doctor for a physical exam. The doctor confirmed a reddened and irritated area with a small laceration along the edges of the vaginal introitus, which was the source of the bleeding. He indicated the laceration was quite small and would heal very quickly, but he saw the medical findings as indicative of probable penetration and reported the case to child protection. The child was too young to give meaningful responses to the doctor's questions. Child protection investigated. When the day care provider was interviewed regarding possible abuse, her statements were, "You can't blame me for what another child did," referring to a 5-year-old child who was also receiving day care in her home.

Given the physical findings, the case was substantiated but nothing was done because the child could not give sufficient information about her injury or its origin. Mother did not return the child to the day care home.

Shortly after leaving the day care, E. E. gave the following spontaneous behavioral demonstration. She took her mother's curling iron from the bathroom sink, and began talking and gesturing. "Like this," she said and pointed the curling iron barrel toward her vulva. Mother told her not to do this. A few days later, E. E. repeated the same actions and statements to an aunt. Then all demonstrations ceased and Mother thought everything was over, until just recently.

About 2 weeks ago, Mother surprised E. E., now 4 years old, and a neighborhood boy in the closet, with their jeans pulled down and E. E.'s panties off. Mother set boundaries and limits for the children, but did not follow up around possible abuse because she did not consider the behavior related to any sexual abuse. But then Mother and E. E. unexpectedly drove by the former day care provider's home, a location they had not visited in almost 2 years. From the back seat E. E. spontaneously said, "That lady was naughty; she put a curling iron in my butt."

Mother was stunned by E. E.'s "out of the blue" comment and asked E. E. why her baby-sitter did this. E. E. replied, "Because I was naughty." Mother assured her no one was to do such things even if she were naughty, and that it was not OK for someone to touch her privates. E. E. then replied, "Well, _____ (her adolescent cousin and former baby-sitter) touched my privates," but she would not give additional information. A week later, Mother again drove past the baby-sitter's house, and again E. E. spontaneously talked about the naughty lady who "put a curling iron in my butt."

Mother now began to worry about long-term effects from early abuse and about any future sexual acting out.

E. E.'s statements and behaviors at age 2 are consistent with the physical findings of penetration. Her behavioral reenactment and her limited verbal responses are characteristic of 2-year-olds. Although she had previously complained about a sore butt, mother had not understood her concern because E. E. could not elaborate. Although E. E. was too young to give much specific information about what had happened to her, her actions provided insight into her experiences. Her current 4-year-old status is a time when children are naturally more focused on genital concerns, and genital play between children is not unusual. E. E.'s surprise exposure to her former day care home probably acted as a trigger to old memories and E. E., now able to talk much better, could give voice to her recall. It is not unusual for clinicians who treat children for sexual abuse matters to see a child who, at age 4, is acting out abuse experiences they had at age 2 but could not talk about. Mother's concern that old experiences might now be expressed in new sexual behavior is a valid worry. Additional work to determine E. E.'s status and treatment needs was needed.

E. E.'S SECOND INTERVIEW

In contrast to the first interview detailed above—a standard format structured interview—the second interview centered on the prescreening areas.

Language

E. E. again talked easily and rapidly. She had some mild articulation problems, but she was readily understandable with a good vocabulary and age-appropriate sentence length. She had good usage of the essential concepts involved in abuse assessment: who, what, where. Despite being very verbal, E. E. was not well organized.

Narrative Capacity

E. E. had difficulty with narrative accounts. She did not organize information around the question presented, she would add unrelated bits of information, and she had to be regularly brought back to the question presented to her. E. E.'s narrative style was similar to her mother's style during the intake. Most likely, E. E.'s mother is a low elaborative mother who does not ask E. E. to organize her past experience into a story (what happened first, what happened next, and what the point of the story is), and she also does not model such behavior.

E. E. needed extensive structuring to keep her on task and to help her respond to questions. She needed short, directed questions; she became very disjointed and she rambled when given open-ended queries.

Memory

E. E. could remember, but her memory was not organized as adult memories would be organized. E. E.'s memory capacity was assessed by asking her about her birthday party, an event 3 months before the prescreening interview. When asked about her birthday, E. E. chatted easily about the people who came to her party, but she mixed elements from two parties—her third and fourth birthdays. She adamantly insisted all information was from her most recent birthday party, and she could not separate information temporally. (Time, or "temporal," distinctions are very difficult for preschool children; good mastery of temporally managed accounts do not emerge until most children are in elementary school, and it is not unusual to find children of E. E.'s age having trouble with this organization.) At the end of the session, when E. E. and her mother were seen together, E. E. surprised her mother by adding other accurate details of both birthday parties that her mother had forgotten!

Even more interesting than the first memory event was a second memory event that E. E. spontaneously talked about. She described bits and pieces of a fishing trip she, her mother, and her new stepfather had been on. Her account was vastly different from her mother's account of the same trip, and this time mother identified several errors in E. E.'s account.

Does this invalidate E. E.'s capacity for memory? No. Parent and child memories of an event do not always match. Children's memories are focused on things *they* see as important, and these things may be quite different from a parent's focus or interpretation. Children may also intersperse information from other experiences. Careful work is needed to sort out their organization—an organization that is not like that of an adult. Young children can remember, as E. E. demonstrates by providing additional details her mother had forgotten in the description of the birthday parties. They can also forget and add different details.

Fantasy or Reality

E. E. had real difficulty with this area; she endorsed all real or pretend questions as real. When she was asked about her presession play in a park adjoining my office building ("Did you see Barney when you walked to the park outside my office?"), E. E. adamantly maintained that she had seen Barney. When asked if she *really* saw this with her eyes, E. E. said, "He was in the car sleeping." Given her overendorsement and difficulty separating the concepts, it could be expected E. E. might have some difficulty mixing fact and fantasy into some of her accounts in a later target interview. Asking her to show versus tell, and to demonstrate a sequence of actions, could help separate fact and fancy, and looking for supportive behavioral repertoire for some of her statements or other corroborators would also be important.

Correct Me

E. E. also had some difficulty in correcting my mistakes. She was encouraged to have her "ears open and be pretty sharp," to be able to catch my mistakes as I mentioned both accurate and inaccurate elements of our last visit. She did not appear to have good monitoring skills, but she was pleased when on one or two occasions she was able to correct me. I took some time and we practiced this skill and soon E. E. was happily catching and correcting my errors. I supported and encouraged her corrections.

Play

E. E. demonstrated an excellent ability to use dolls as demonstrators of actions as well as a representation of herself (to use her words and create interactions in the first person). At age 4, emergence of this ability is right on target and E. E. did a nice job with it.

CONCLUSIONS

Several things emerge from this prescreening. E. E. cannot give good narrative accounts, her questioning will have to be very concrete and focused, she will need much structure from the interviewer. If she is left to organize and direct her responses to open-ended questions, she will appear incompetent, although she demonstrates a good and accurate memory when the questioning is carefully structured. She also has difficulty sorting information in a time frame and separating actual events from made-up accounts. She has demonstrated some tendency to elaborate on information that is false (the Barney response) when she is pressed for a response. She will need cautious interviewing and her verbal responses will need to be coupled with good behavioral and historical data.

E. E.'S THIRD INTERVIEW

After the prescreening interview, this interview was scheduled to focus on the target material, issues of sexual abuse. E. E. is very verbal, but not well organized and does not give good narrative. She is better with concrete, show-and-tell demonstrations and she has good representation of self. In light of the above information, I decided that a paper-and-pencil format that required verbal follow-up might be too difficult for E. E. Instead, she may better reflect her experiences by using something that was more concrete and emphasized showing versus telling. I decided to use small dolls to replicate a downward extension of the Touch Survey used in the first session (see Chapter 5). Dolls are more concrete and E. E. had demonstrated good, accurate use of the dolls and self-representational skills.

The second session began by talking with E. E. about her early life. Before this interview, her mother had given me physical descriptions of the people who were important in this interview (Nancy, the day care provider; a 5-year-old girl, Annie; and her cousin, Craig). When we were alone I asked E. E. to select dolls from a large assortment of 5-inch dolls to represent Nancy, herself, her cousin, her mom, and Annie. E. E. refused to find a doll for Annie.

We began the target portion of this more concrete interview by reviewing body parts on the small doll she had chosen to be herself. She was responsive during this period of the interview, and as we went through the various body parts she labeled them correctly and called her bottom her butt and identified her front as her private area. I pointed to the vulva of the small doll and asked E. E. if somebody had ever tickled her there. "Yes," she said, "but they didn't hurt me." Then she added, "Nancy was mean to me. She would pinch me and get mad at me." When asked if anyone ever hurt her in her private area, she said, "Yes. Nancy." I asked E. E. to show me, using the Nancy doll, how Nancy did that. E. E. sat the child doll down, spread its legs, and pointed to the crotch. As she did this, she again stated that Nancy had touched her with her curling iron.

Next, I expanded the interview to ask about E. E.'s cousin. I asked about his hugs, kisses, tickles, spanks, or private part touching. To concretize this last area of questioning, I picked up the E. E. doll and again pointed to the vulva, followed by the butt. I asked if her cousin had ever touched her in these places. E. E. said yes he had and she spontaneously spread her own legs and pointed to her crotch. "He did it," she said, "at night when I'm trying to go to sleep and he did it." I asked which house or bedroom she was in and she said she was "in my bed." She then began spontaneously undressing some of the dolls. She picked up a doll we had designated as Craig and she opened the pants to look at the genital area. She pointed to the molded penis and scrotum on this small plastic doll and asked me what that was. "Is it a private part?" I said, "Yes." I asked if Craig had one, and she said, "Yep, a big one." Then she turned away from me and would not discuss any more information.

I let her free play to gain equilibrium again, and I proceeded to ask target questions about her mother. E. E. denied any form of abusive genital touch by her mother.

After a brief interlude of play, I asked if it was OK for me to talk with her about her cousin again. E. E. now appeared quite comfortable and said it was. I asked if anyone would be mad if she talked about touching. She said no one would be mad. She turned back to play and I let her free play briefly. Then I redirected her focus back to the target questioning. I asked E. E. to please correct me if I got any of the information wrong, and I repeated the information she had just given me, using small segments and asking for her monitoring. She affirmed her earlier statements. As I was unable to interview about Annie, I could not rule out possible genital touching by her.

CONCLUSION

Using a more concrete interview format and encouraging demonstration rather than narrative, E. E. was able to give a clearer, more detailed, and more credible account of her experiences. She still does not have good skills to give a detailed, contextually embedded account of her experiences. Her account will need buttressing by behavioral and historical data. Even with such data, she will still not make a good witness for a court case, and no charges were brought forward on this case. Child protection was notified about the day care provider but no action was taken. Concern for E. E.'s safety with her cousin remains, however, and the need for intervention focused on protection versus prosecution issues.

Recommendations to E. E.'s mother centered around possible sexual acting out and protection from her cousin. Mother was encouraged to continue to monitor E. E.'s behavior, and to not allow her to play dress-up with other children without adult monitoring, to make clear rules about always keeping underwear on if she did play dress-up. We also discussed having Mom use a prevention education program with E. E., which involved using genital names and making clear rules about E. E. being in charge of her own private parts and not touching other children. I suggested there be no contact with Craig and that the issue of sexual abuse of E. E. be discussed with her sister and with Craig. Mother also expressed concern about any other children Craig might have been baby-sitting and said she would check with her sister about this. She was also going to talk with E. E. specifically about Craig not touching her private parts, and to let her know if Craig or anyone else wanted to do such touching with her. E. E.'s own heightened interest in sexual areas was to be monitored and structured but not shamed or censured. Clear boundaries and appropriate behaviors were to be emphasized, and E. E. was to be encouraged to "take good care of herself." Mother was invited to call back if she had questions or if E. E. should engage in more acting-out behavior.

❏ **Is It Mistaken Identity?**

When questioned about some sexual talk and play with neighborhood children, 4-year-old G. G. spontaneously told her father that J. J.,
her mother's new fiancé, had kissed her "china" (J. J.'s adaptation of
vagina). Father and his new wife then both talked to G. G., trying to
get additional details. As G. G. maintained her story, father became
quite concerned and brought the child in for a physical exam. During
the exam, G. G. again stated that J. J. had kissed her china, but she could
give little detail and some of her information was inconsistent; she
added that her future stepsister had also done this to her. She stated
J. J. had kissed her with her clothing "on—no, it was off." Additional
evaluation was needed to determine whether G. G. had been abused
and to determine the level of risk in returning G. G. to her mother's
home.

Initial meeting time with G. G. found her to be a bright, verbal, and
outgoing young girl. She easily drew a representative picture of her
father's family but did not have much detail (she did not draw the
house, or her bedroom, etc.). Her language was understandable; she
had good narrative for her last 2 weeks summer experiences with her
father; she could describe the time when J. J. moved into her mother's
home and the change in her room (she moved to another bedroom,
farther from her mother); and she showed easy mastery of who, what,
and where questions. She could distinguish truth and lies, and she
would comfortably correct me when I misstated her cat's name and
later her baby stepsister's name. She could not, however, tell the
difference between real and pretend, and she showed great vulnerability to leading and suggestive questioning. For example, when asked if
she played with Duplos in the waiting room (this was observed), she
said that was real, but when asked if there was a clown that walked
into the room where she was playing with Duplos (a fictitious event),
she also said that was real. This questioning format was repeated in
later questioning, and again she displayed the same difficulty. Because
the skill of real and pretend is usually in place at about 4 years of age
in middle-class Caucasian children (and J. J. fit this category), an
attempt was made to teach this skill during a second interview. Real
was described as what you see with your eyes and touch with your
hands and what you feel on your body. We exchanged "real" feeling of

touching on each other's forearms. G. G. was better with this concrete task. She was then interviewed in a standardized format and she again stated that J. J. had kissed her genitals. Her statements were spontaneous. The kissing happened in her bedroom and no one was around. She also gave a more detailed description of kissing by her stepsister, saying they lay on the bed (she demonstrated with small plastic dolls two figures lying face to face, and then the larger doll kissing the "china" with clothes on; her stepsister told her this was how they loved). When asked if the kissing J. J. did was real or pretend, she said real; her stepsister's kissing was also real.

J. J. willingly submitted to a psychological evaluation and he was seen as open and straightforward, with no prior history of molestation, no drug or alcohol use, and a history of regular but not overly frequent marital sexual contact in his previous marriage. He acknowledged adult, heterosexual fantasies, he was committed to his Christian faith, and his history showed evidence of thoughtful, deliberate planning. His ex-wife was also interviewed independently and she corroborated his description of their marriage and his sexuality. She saw no problems with any form of deviant sexuality during the 8 years they were married. Psychological testing confirmed the presentation and history. J. J. did not look like someone who might offend.

These are very difficult cases to evaluate. Are G. G.'s statements true reflections of reality she has experienced? Could she be transferring information from an experience with her new stepsister to her new stepfather? Because she has repeatedly demonstrated problems with real/pretend, does this make her statements more prone to fantasy? It is tempting here to re-interview G. G. about the allegations with her father, but multiple interviews can lead to problems. G. G. could feel that repeatedly asking the same question means adults do not believe her or that they do not like her response.

In cases like this, alternative ways of approaching the issue can be explored. The use of multiple modalities and multiple approaches can come at the information in different ways. In this case, several alternative methods were used: free and structured dollhouse play, exploring individual characteristics of various family members, "helping" the examiner see if there were people in her life that needed help to know about the "rules" for touching "chinas" (G. G. had previously demonstrated a clear idea that "chinas" were not to be touched by others).

In addition, psychological testing was also used to clarify relationships and overall emotional status. Working at the underlying relationships and understanding them while the focus is off the specific abuse questions helps create a better relationship as well as offer better understanding of the child and his or her history. Having multiple interview formats is helpful. They can also be substituted for the initial style; thus, less repetition is required. For example, a young child's memory might be triggered by different approaches to his or her memory store; one interview may emphasize touches on the body, another may ask about relationships, and yet another may use drawings of a home. Different approaches can offer differing avenues for memory retrieval.

In this case, G. G. was seen again and asked to help me see if there were people who needed to know about the rules for touching. Together, we drew pictures of her sister, her mother, J. J., and her future stepsister. Again G. G. talked about J. J. and her stepsister not knowing the rules about touching "chinas" and that they needed help. (This manner of exploration also reframes a child as a helper for someone else, rather than focusing on whether he or she has engaged in touching. Four-year-olds are aware of blame and of having done something wrong and they, just like adults, do not like to be in positions of "fault." This shift in focus to a helper, rather than a wrongdoer, is useful in facilitating cooperation.)

Again, in this context, G. G. gave content and description to the things her future stepsister should be told about the "rules," whereas she gave less elaboration about J. J.'s need for rules. Because of this discrepancy, G. G. was first asked to demonstrate with small dolls what her future stepsister did and then later to contrast that with what J. J. did. This contrasted showing was very revealing. G. G. first demonstrated, using a bed, how her stepsister would lie down with her, and how they would hug, how the stepsister would tell her this was how they loved.

Then she carefully showed how her stepsister would move down the bed and put her face in G. G.'s crotch and kiss her. When asked to show what J. J. did, she laid the dolls on the bed and moved to put J. J.'s face in her crotch. Then she stopped, looked uncomfortable, and took the J. J. doll away. G. G. said, "J. J. doesn't do that, _____(stepsister) does." Back-to-back contrasting depictions helped to clarify the individual actions of the different people and, in this case, appeared to help G. G. separate spillover between her new stepfather and her new stepsister's actions.

More than one interview is often needed to clarify the statements of preschool children. Multiple interviews that repeatedly ask the same questions can lead to false endorsement over time. Offering multiple modalities (verbal, written, dollhouse, drawings, etc.) can tap different parts of the memory store and give additional details, as well as broader information about an abuse situation. The need for multiple interviews is a reality in many preschool cases; the way in which these interviews are conducted is the critical issue.

❏ In Her Own Way

Three-year-old H. H. and her five siblings had just been removed from their home for neglect. With her 2-year-old sister and her 6-year-old brother, H. H. was placed in foster care. The second day in foster care, she was found by her foster mother with her brother in the garage. She had her panties off and her brother was putting his hands in her vulva. When asked about this activity, the brother said the grandfather did such things. H. H.'s language was so poorly developed at the time of this discussion that her comments made no sense. The brother was placed in a separate foster care home. Over the next 8 months, H. H. took off her younger sister's diapers and rubbed the child's vulva until it was reddened, she smeared feces on the clothes she wore after visits with her parents, and she began deliberately urinating on her bed or floor after visitation with her parents. Visitation was halted. When H. H. was almost 4 years of age and her sister almost 3, H. H.'s language had improved so that most of her speech was understandable, and she began talking about her father hurting her by poking a stick up her vagina. The foster mother's behavioral logs indicated repeated spontaneous comments about H. H.'s grandfather and father touching her vagina and butt in hurtful ways. There were other incidents of sexual touching with other children as well as with the younger sister. Because H. H. now had sufficient intelligible speech to be interviewed about her history, she was referred for a single-session forensic interview about possible sexual abuse.

FIRST SESSION

H. H. appeared as a cheerful, talkative, active almost-4-year-old. She was of average height and weight. She readily separated from her foster mom and chatted almost nonstop once in the playroom. On careful listening, however, her chatter was noted to be very tangential and poorly organized. She did not respond to direct questions, nor did she track adult conversation. Initial prescreening efforts with H. H. were abysmal failures. H. H. had good language, using complex sentences of at least eight words with age-appropriate articulation errors on s's and w's. She did not respond to any of the conceptually oriented questions that asked, "Who lives at your house?" Who do you play with?" "What did you eat for breakfast today?" "Where do you sleep?" H. H. simply ignored all questions and continued with her talk. She would also try to take control of the session by telling me what to do and what she wanted. She did not know body parts—she pointed to her toes when asked where her fingers were. H. H.'s responses could have been interpreted as control and avoidance, and they may have been, but she did not seem angry or afraid. She loved the individual attention and initiated several interchanges. H. H. seemed not to know how to exchange conversation, especially conversation about herself.

The foster mother supported this observation, stating that when H. H. came to foster care she talked only to her younger sister and did not use adults for any help. H. H. had shown little recognition of her name, and her younger sister responded only to H. H.'s name, not recognizing her own. Both girls displayed a remarkable lack of basic skills; they ate with their hands, ate out of the garbage, did not know how to wear underwear, showed little evidence of having been bathed, and had not had toilet training. H. H.'s unorganized environment had failed her in many ways; she had little clear sense of self, or self in relationship to adults. She did, however, take some dolls, all males, and said, "This one is naughty! He gets in trouble." She handed the doll to me and said, "You keep him. He's bad." When asked what he did, H. H. responded, "He do it. Hitting people." She accompanied her statement by grabbing her crotch, looking directly at me and saying, "My dad touches me right there." She could not find a doll to represent her father, and she did not repeat her statement. She could not give responsive narrative about her life experiences. H. H. could not complete prescreening.

When a child cannot attend to, or comply with, directions around prescreening, they need a format different from a structured interview for assessment. Although H. H. spontaneously set up interesting play and obviously had information to relate, she lacked the skills to respond to a structured interview and these techniques were abandoned.

SECOND SESSION

A second session, one with a free play situation that allowed H. H. to continue her play about the bad dolls, was set up. In this session, H. H. would be allowed to direct the session's content and to play with the items she chose.

H. H. began the session by selecting several action figures, exploring them and their weapons. She informed me that these were bad guys and very carefully took the daggers that came with the action figures and jabbed them in their crotches. She lined them up and said, "He's bad, he hurts me!" After some repetitions of this, I suggested maybe he needed a time-out. H. H. was delighted with this idea and she told me where these figures should be put. She went through five or six various action figures, again repeating the same statement with each one—they were bad! To one of them she said, "He's bad—he touches me." I asked H. H. to show me where he touches her. She pointed to her crotch, grabbed her vulva, and gave me a straight-on gaze. I said, "It's not OK for other people to touch your body or to hurt you. I think this one needs a timeout. Where should we put him?" She instructed me to put him in the corner with the others. H. H. repeated this play about five times, going through a series of maybe six to eight dolls, moving them from one part of my office to another, turning them with their faces to the wall, or sometimes just lining them up. She always instructed them to stay in that place because they were bad and they had hurt her. I repeated her statements and assured her that it was not OK for anybody to hurt her. Toward the end of the play, as H. H. again regrouped the dolls and picked out those that she said had touched her, I asked her if anyone had ever touched her. She nodded solemnly.

I asked who had touched her, and she replied, "My daddy." I asked where he had touched her and she grabbed her vulva.

H. H. could not complete a prescreening, but her actions and words in this free play session were a very powerful reflection of her experiences. Behavioral data about her sexual acting out and her spontaneous statements in her foster home were used to buttress an assessment report that was anchored in behaviorally oriented assessment strategies and supplemented with her spontaneous statements and play demonstrations.

Not all children are able to be interviewed directly. Some very disturbed or disorganized children will need other, nonverbal, possibly play-oriented formats, to allow access to information about their experiences.

6

Current Interview Formats
With Adaptations
for Preschool Children

I. I., almost 5 years old, was in an early childhood program to help prepare her for kindergarten. She had been adopted 18 months ago out of a background of chronic neglect but, despite her earlier history, she was doing quite well in her new home. During the past few weeks, however, she had begun to grab other children's crotches. She also asked a boy if she could touch his penis, she took her underpants off, and she began displaying her vulva to other children. The school psychologist initiated a referral for abuse assessment. After intake history with I. I.'s adopted mother and father, she was scheduled for an appointment.

When I. I. appeared in my office waiting room, I saw a tall, sturdy preschooler who spoke rapidly and excitedly. She had lots of language but she misarticulated several initial consonants, making her speech only partially understandable. As the pattern of her errors became clearer, she was easily understandable, and the enthusiasm she exhibited while exploring the contents of the playroom was contagious. While she worked on setting up a picnic for the dollhouse family she had just created, I. I. comfortably answered basic screening questions. Despite her early background, she appeared well informed, bright, task oriented, and engaging. She easily chatted about who lives at her house now, and spontaneously interjected information about her old family, too. Her sentences were long and complex, full of ideas and her opinions. "You know, today at thool we had to do thowart thories, and I wobed it thoooo mush!"

As I. I. was observed playing, she spontaneously initiated talk between the various doll figures as they had their picnic and she successfully used one of the dolls to represent herself. She talked to the family as she served them cake. Her attention span was excellent and she was interested in talking about the things she knew and enjoyed. Her information about her old family showed a good grasp of narrative format and solid factual information (as verified later by her adoptive mother). I. I. is a good example of a Stage 3 child, a child who has the skills that allow her to be interviewed using a standardized interview format.

Interviewers of children like I. I. can come from many different professions—law enforcement, child protection, medical, and mental health. Some child abuse interviewers have a great deal of training and experience in working with children, and interviewing is a major part of their job, whereas others have no such background and interviewing is only a small part of a much larger job.

Some interviews given to children are standard, forensic-type adult interviews whereas other interviews are developed out of research on children's memory and retrieval skills. Most interviews are of the single-session type, directed at gathering sufficient information to determine if a case should be pursued or not. Preschool children are at a disadvantage here because they often do not give complete, detailed information during such sessions. On the other hand, multiple interviews increase the likelihood of gathering false information or they expose a child to leading and suggestive questions or cross-contamination.

There is no one way to interview a child about abuse. Each child and each interviewer presents a unique match of personalities and

styles. **What is important is the match between the child's capacities
and the interviewer's needs.**

One of the most common and effective ways of assessing for child
sexual abuse is through the use of a standardized interview format. In
larger, more urban areas, the use of professionally staffed interview
centers (Stern & Walsh, 1995) has become increasingly popular. Most
of them use single-session interviews with children ages 2 to 12, and
these formats have been carefully honed to meet the investigatory
demands of a specific state or locality. The use of a familiar format
across these ages creates a more unified method of assessment. It is
important, however, to recognize that the ability of young children to
respond to the demands of interviewing changes significantly during
the preschool years. Single-session interview protocols need to be
reviewed for their developmental appropriateness and, if necessary,
adapted to match the specific status of the child. That is the focus of
this chapter, in which four issues will be covered.

1. The definition of Stage 3 children
2. An outline of the components of an interview for this stage
3. A review of some interview formats that are currently in use, followed
   by a discussion of their strengths and weaknesses for young children
4. A discussion of other relevant assessment issues, such as psychosocial
   assessment, research in interview questions, statement validity analysis,
   and the use of anatomically correct dolls

❏ Who Are Stage 3 Children?

Stage 3 children are those who can be successfully interviewed using
standardized formats, understanding that some modification may be
required. These are children whose age range varies from very bright,
almost-4-year-olds to children who are older—most often 5 and above.

Characteristics of Stage 3 children are intelligible speech, sufficient
language and concepts, representational play with representation of
self, narrative capacities, responsiveness to an interview situation
(appropriate attention span and directedness), and competence in the
prescreening areas.

Although Stage 3 children can be interviewed, remember that they
are still young children. There are some competencies that have not yet
developed: they do not handle complex sentences well, they do not

have large vocabularies, they do not have the ability to abstract, measurements are very subjective and concrete, and reasoning is "on the basis of what they see, not invisible concepts of suppositions" (Saywitz, 1994). Children ages 5 and 6 cannot draw abstract maps very well, and they do not have the thought flexibility to see things from a variety of perspectives. They rely on adults for basic needs as well as for structure and organization, and their responsibilities need to be monitored and taught. Concrete, simple dialogue interviewing can give good accounts, but demands for abstraction, integration of information, synthesis of various opposing bits of information or discrepancies in stories, and evaluation of their own or others perspective are all skills best left to older children.

❏ Effective Interview Components for Stage 3 Children

Standard interview formats often need modifications to accommodate the immature skills of Stage 3 children. First, before interviewing, get a good background that includes early development and experiential history (use the outline for Stage 1), assess current behavioral adjustment (does this sound familiar?), generate rule-out factors, determine competence in the prescreening area by a brief screening (as in the case above, some children spontaneously demonstrate their competencies in a very short period of time), and, finally, practice any required formats if they haven't been done in a formal prescreening.

All the elements for good assessment components mentioned above are detailed in previous chapters, except how to warm up with practice formats in the absence of formal prescreening. That is the focus of the next section.

❏ Warming Up With Practice Formats

In the above example, I. I. spontaneously gives memory information and demonstrates representation of self. A full prescreening is not needed because her competencies are easily demonstrated. Even if competencies appear to be present, it is still wise to check some of these basic areas:

MEMORY

Yuille, Hunter, Joffe, and Zaparniuk (1993) and Yuille (1996) suggest asking children about past experiences that are unrelated to the suspected abuse (e.g., their birthday, a trip, a holiday) as a way to assess their capacity for language and memory skills. Asking preschoolers about such events, and encouraging them to share information about "what happened next," and "what did you do?" or "what did your mother do then?" also helps set a framework for later questioning. Structuring children's recall to "just what really happened" can be helpful if the child tends to wander or integrate tangential information. If children add fantasy extension, then reviewing the real/not real parameters is important. Rehearsing memory for past events and clarifying the format by asking questions that parallel the target interview queries ensure much smoother interviews.

SHOW ME

Children may not have words to fully describe what has happened to them, so showing actions can bridge this gap. Having a child show something from the memory rehearsal again practices a skill that can be used later. One of the major concerns regarding this category is the use of anatomically correct (AC) dolls with preschoolers (see discussion later in this chapter).

CORRECT ME

As mentioned in Chapter 5, young children do not monitor their own thinking, nor do they monitor the accuracy of another person's thinking. They will not correct your mistakes, but with prior explanation of this request and some practice, you can strengthen their ability to monitor.

You can structure and encourage the child's active participation in checking for accuracy of his or her own words. Repeat the child's statements after the target interview and ask the child to "make sure I got this right." One interviewer of a 4-year-old deliberately misattributed another person as the abuser when repeating the child's statement that his father had sucked on his penis. The child loudly and clearly corrected the interviewer, "No! I said *my dad* did it!" This restatement was important in anchoring the child's allegations.

In I. I.'s case, for example, I might explain that I need to be sure I am getting things "just right" when I listen to her story about living with her mom and brothers. I tell her that I'm going to check with her to see if I get things "just right" and if I do not, I want to know if she can help me. I might practice with her by telling her I think her name is Y. Y. and I wonder if I got that right. Most children will immediately yell, "That's not my name, that's not right!!" Some very passive children may never have been given permission to correct an adult, and it may take more encouragement and practice for them to correct you.

LANGUAGE

Long, compound sentences are confusing to the child; speak with shorter, direct sentences instead. Do not use negations (He didn't do that, did he?) and use nouns instead of pronouns whenever possible. These are simple, common admonitions for communicating with young children. Ann Graffam Walker's essential book, *Handbook on Questioning Children* (1994), thoroughly explores the use of language with children.

❏ Interview Formats With Research

One example of an interview format for preschool assessment is offered in chapter 7, along with adaptations for use with younger children. The following section reviews several other commonly practiced interview formats in light of their strengths and adaptability for use with young children.

NARRATIVE ELABORATION

Narrative Elaboration (NE) (Saywitz & Snyder, 1996; Saywitz, Snyder, & Lamphear, 1996) is a procedure designed to expand children's spontaneous reports of past events by using structured retrieval strategies to improve recall. It was initially created for use with children ages 7 to 11. "It is a procedure both designed to prepare children to be questioned, and a format for interviewing them" (Saywitz & Snyder, 1996, p. 1348). The authors recognize that children's free recall statements offer the most reliable information but that these statements are often incomplete. Because children do not have elaborate retrieval strategies, they are more dependent on adult structure; thus, they are more vulnerable to leading or suggestive questioning. In this format, children are taught "a strategy for retrieving details by organizing the elements of an event into categories . . . that guide event recall . . . (participants, setting, actions, conversation/affective states, consequences)" (p. 1348). Children are instructed to use visual cue cards, with line drawings to represent the various categories, and to report as much detail as possible from each category. The children practice on mock recall tasks and later, when the target event is presented, they are asked for an uninterrupted description, followed by presentation of the cue cards. The children are asked, "Does this card remind you to tell anything else?"

Narrative Elaboration combines a number of experimental procedures that have enhanced children's memory performance:

1. *Memory strategy instruction.* Children can be taught strategies for memory retrieval that they would not necessarily use but that could be used to enhance their recall.
2. *Visual cues.* Verbal reports underestimate children's knowledge, but pictorial aids can help children systematically focus on specific categories for recall.
3. *Strategy training.* Children are taught the importance of the NE strategy, they practice it, get feedback, and are reminded to use the strategies in follow-up situations. When narrative elaboration was used with school-age children, their accurate spontaneous recall increased 53% over the control group, without increasing unintended error.

Dorado (1996) has explored the use of NE with two new populations: preschool children, ages 4 and 5, and children from both middle and low socioeconomic status (SES). As most of the work done on children's memory—as well as work on the Narrative Elaboration technique—has been done with a sample of middle-class children, it was important to see if the benefits of NE would extend to children in lower SES levels as well. Of particular importance is the fact that more of the children who are reported for child abuse come from lower SES levels. Having the earlier noted benefits of NE extend to this population of children is important because Saywitz and Lyon (1997) found that children from lower SES environments had significantly lower scores on a test of receptive vocabulary than children from higher SES environments. Expecting children from distressed or low-income populations to function in the same manner as children with more resources is to discriminate against their ability to disclose their history.

For the study, all children were exposed to a staged classroom event designed to simulate characteristics of events that children are often asked to recall during forensic interviewing. A week after the event, the children were divided into two groups: experimental and control. Both groups were exposed to a storybook and video, but whereas the experimental group received training, feedback, and reinforcement in the NE procedure, the control group did not. They were instructed to "try hard and do your best."

The visual cue cards used for this younger group were slightly altered from the initial NE studies with older children. They were now called "remembering cards" and depicted four topic areas: participants, setting, action, and conversation drawings.

One day after training, the children were interviewed about what they had seen a week earlier. This interview was preceded by a brief booster session in which the children were reminded about what they had learned the day before. In the process, the children were interviewed using free recall (an uninterrupted narrative account of what happened), cued recall (presentation of the "remembering cards" while the child was asked, "Does this remind you of something else?"), and probed recall (open-ended follow-up questions). Narrative Elaboration training almost doubled the amount of information on cued recall, and the same findings extended across socioeconomic levels. No increased error was found with the procedure's use. The study did find, however, that lower-SES children made more errors than middle-class children, especially on probed recall.

Strengths of the Procedure

Narrative Elaboration is one of the only interview formats that has specifically extended the research on a promising technique with school-age children so that it can be used with preschoolers. It has also shown that the technique is equally valuable with children of middle and lower SES. This process is also one of the few with a good developmental foundation because it applies theory and research about the nature of young children's memory. By structuring recall across four categories, it provides the scaffolding necessary for more effective memory retrieval with young children. Adoption of this technique could help child protection, law enforcement, and mental health workers to elicit a more complete and accurate record of children's experiences because it minimizes the number of possible leading or suggestive questions that might be asked. Getting more complete information in the beginning can limit the need for multiple interviews, and it can add consistency across interviews. In addition, gathering complete information at the beginning of a case can shorten a child's wait to enter therapy while evaluation is being completed.

The presentation of the categories in visual cuing uses symbols and a mapping of that category to strengthen young children's event recall. Narrative Elaboration thus serves as an important model for the task of interviewing.

Weaknesses of the Procedure

This is a promising interview format, but it has not yet been tested directly in clinical and forensic settings.

Adaptations of the Procedure

This procedure has already been adapted for preschool use, although Dorado (1996) indicates that additional research is needed.

BOISE, IDAHO CARES PROGRAM INTERVIEW

The CARES Program of St. Lukes Hospital in Boise, Idaho, is a regional specialty interview center for child abuse victims. It is affiliated with the National Network of Children's Advocacy Centers, interviewing children of all ages. This interview situation is unique in that the Idaho Supreme Court recommends interviews be conducted "without bias, recorded on videotape, and use only nonleading questions." To address interviewer bias, CARES personnel began conducting "allegation blind" interviews in 1990. The interviewer must begin the interview having only the knowledge of the child's name for his or her own body parts and the names of significant others in the child's family. Once the interviewer has gathered as much information as possible using this approach, the interviewer breaks away to review the allegations and meet with the referring agent, if possible. The interview is resumed to follow up on any remaining concerns or problems. The interview protocol may be adapted to individual needs but the basic format is as follows:

1. *Introduction and warm-up:* The child is asked his or her name, where he or she lives, age, and so on. Responses are used as a general indicator of the child's capabilities.

2. *Truth or lie:* The child is asked if he or she understand what a truth is, what a lie is, and what happens if there is a lie.

3. *Reason for interview:* Why are you here today?

4. *Introduce the subject of touching:* The child is asked if he or she knows about touching, if he or she can demonstrate it, and if anyone ever touched him/her.

5. *Body parts:* If the child is unable to respond to questions, the interviewer may draw a body. The child is asked if there is any place on the body that people are not supposed to touch, and if that has ever happened to him/her.

6. *Evasive child:* If a child is evasive, questions are posed to decrease the onus on the child by changing from present to past tense, such as, "Did touching *used to* happen? How *would* it feel if it had happened?")

7. *Disclosure of the incident:* If the child talks about an incident, he or she is allowed to tell the story in its entirety. Follow-up questioning goes from more general to more specific.

8. *Specifics:* After disclosure, follow-up asks about where, who, what, when, and—if indicated—about the offender's genitalia, foreign objects, and lubrication.

9. *History of the abuse:* The child is asked about frequency and duration of the abuse (e.g., how often it happened, when it started).

10. *Secrets, punishments or threats:* The child is asked, "Would this be a secret?" "Would you be in trouble?" and so on.

11. *Pornography:* The child is asked if he or she has seen pornography.

12. *Alcohol or drugs:* "Do you know what alcohol and drugs are?" "Do you know anyone who uses or sells alcohol or drugs?"

13. *Pain:* "How did it feel?" "How did it feel to go pee or poop after ____ happened?" "Did it ever hurt or feel different?"

14. *Feelings:* Ask about the touching, self, parents, and perpetrators.

15. *Break:* The interviewer excuses herself from the child, leaves the room briefly, and checks with law enforcement or child protection for details about the allegation and any additional inquiry that may be needed.

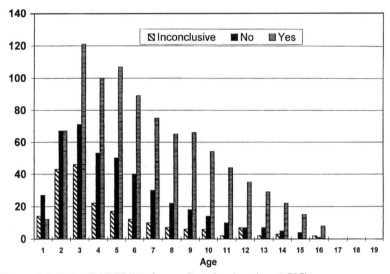

Figure 6.1. Boise CARES Disclosure Rate by Age (n = 1,535)

SOURCE: From "Outcome Based Practice: Disclosure Rates of Child Sexual Abuse Comparing Allegation Blind and Allegation Informed Structured Interviews," by J. Cantlon, G. Payne, and C. Erbaugh, 1996, *Child Abuse and Neglect, 20*(11), 1113-1120. Used with permission.

16. *Closure:* The interviewer returns and interviews for any missed details or other information the child might have to offer. The interview is closed by thanking the child and appreciating his or her work.

Because of the unique interview structure recommended by the Idaho Supreme Court, Cantlon, Payne, and Erbaugh (1996) were interested in analyzing the interview center's interview data. When they compared the disclosure rates of the "allegation informed" interview with those from the "allegation blind" interview, they found that the allegation blind interview technique yielded a higher disclosure rate. They also found something else.

The protocol did not work well for children ages 2 and 3. Interview disclosure rates with 2-year-olds were more likely to be rated as "no" or inconclusive, than "yes." Disclosure rates for 3-year-olds were equal for "no" and inconclusive responses, but both rates were higher than "yes." Once a child turned 4, disclosure rates for that age and all subsequent ages had significantly higher levels of "yes" disclosures. Did this mean that children younger than age 4 were not abused? No, it did not. It meant that the protocol used did not effectively assess abuse with these very young children. Graphed data from the Boise study demonstrates these important findings (see Figure 6.1).

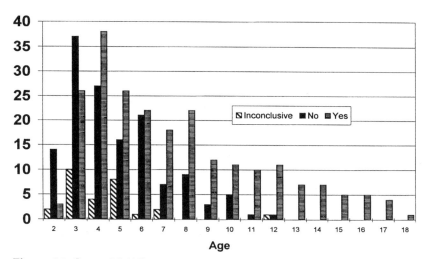

Figure 6.2. Center M (Allegation Informed) Disclosure Rate by Age (n = 397)
SOURCE: From "Outcome Based Practice: Disclosure Rates of Child Sexual Abuse Comparing Allegation Blind and Allegation Informed Structured Interviews," by J. Cantlon, G. Payne, and C. Erbaugh, 1996, *Child Abuse and Neglect*, 20(11), 1113-1120. Used with permission.

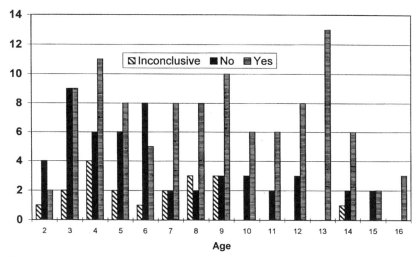

Figure 6.3. Center I (Allegation Informed) Disclosure Rate by Age (n = 176)
SOURCE: From "Outcome Based Practice: Disclosure Rates of Child Sexual Abuse Comparing Allegation Blind and Allegation Informed Structured Interviews," by J. Cantlon, G. Payne, and C. Erbaugh, 1996, *Child Abuse and Neglect*, 20(11), 1113-1120. Used with permission.

The same results have also been found in data analysis from two interview centers located in other parts of the United States (see Figures 6.2 and 6.3).

Strengths of the Procedure

This is a structured format that is not leading or suggestive. It provides an opportunity for open-ended discussion of possible abuse and allows for specific, abuse-related questioning. It is an effective format for children ages 4 and above.

Weaknesses of the Protocol

There are numerous areas in the protocol that require skills that are not present in children ages 2 and 3:

1. Very young children do not give good spontaneous narratives of their experiences. They do not know where they need help in disclosure. They do not present information in a temporally or logically ordered framework—they commonly give bits and pieces and require adult scaffolding to facilitate disclosure of memories.
2. Very young children do not give good histories of abuse and they do not have the concepts of before, after, dates, numbers of times, and so on.
3. Very young children often do not have specific genital names, and they may not know about rules for touching. Because of diapering, toilet training, and bathing needs in this age group, genital touch is common. Differentiating abusive touching from appropriate caretaking functions is difficult when there is little language.
4. Very young children may not fully understand the more conceptually oriented term *touch*. They may see it as only something you do with your fingers and not with other parts of your body.
5. Very young children, as discussed in Chapter 5, do not effectively understand truth and lies.
6. Very young children do not have enough experience to differentiate between pornography or drug or alcohol use. (This question is omitted for children 2 to 3 years old by the CARES staff.)
7. Very young children do not often provide information about their own feelings or the feelings of others. Reporting on actions, objects, or persons is the most common form of their disclosure. Emotional states come later in a child's development.

Adaptations of the Procedure

This protocol is difficult to adapt to the very young child. The above comments do not negate this interview format as a valid protocol; it is a workable structured format for interviewing many children with abuse issues. But the Boise CARES research showing that this protocol is not effective with children 3 and younger is a significant finding and its validity is supported by similar findings from two other centers. Young children do not have the capacity to put their experiences into words to be measured by a verbally oriented interview. A more effective way to assess possible abuse with very young children is to require that an assessment be broader than a single verbal interview. Protocols, like the ones offered in Chapters 4 and 5 are more appropriate.

❏ Interview Protocols Without Research

THE STEP-WISE INTERVIEW

The Step-Wise Interview (Yuille, 1996; Yuille et al., 1993) has received attention as a format for interviewing children because it is designed to "maximize recall while minimizing contamination." In fact, it has been recommended for adoption as the national standard for interviewing in Great Britain (1993). The protocol itself has not been subjected to research but its use in the field has been examined.

Field research conducted on the Step-Wise Interview involves teaching the interview (in combination with Statement Validity Analysis) to child protection workers, police, and prosecutors in British Columbia and contrasting the interview quality with the tapes of untrained workers. Preliminary results indicate that untrained examiners produced interviews that were inadequate because of scant or contaminated information 30% of the time, whereas trained workers produced inadequate interviews only 5% of the time.

The goals of the interview are to minimize trauma for the child while maximizing information from the child, to minimize the contamination effects of the interview, and to maintain the integrity of the investigative process. The format of the interview moves from the most open, least-leading form of questioning to more specific forms of questioning; hence, the name Step-Wise. The goal is to give the child opportunity for free narrative recall before other forms of questioning are used (research has indicated that free recall, though less lengthy than structured recall, produces the most accurate information). Follow-up questioning is conducted to "elaborate on details already described or introduced in the child's earlier free narrative report" (Yuille et al., 1993, p. 99). This interview format attempts to incorporate knowledge of child development with memory techniques, and it is this regard for background information that makes the format increasingly appealing to child abuse investigators.

Following are the principal steps of the interview:

1. *Introduction.* After recording devices are started, the interviewer states the date, time, and location of the interview and the names of all present. The protocol suggests two persons be present in the interview with the child, one to record the interview and the other to direct questions to the child. The two participants should describe their professional roles.

2. *Rapport building.* Asking about a favorite pastime or school helps put the child at ease while gathering baseline information about children's language and ability. The child is asked to describe in detail two events, unrelated to the allegation, to give the interviewer a picture of the quality and quantity of detail the child offers about a past event.

3. *Interview rules (optional).* This step is not appropriate for preschool children and not necessary for adolescents, but it can be considered for school-age children. It involves telling the child the rules that the interviewer is following. These rules include:

   a. Ask the child to tell the interviewer if the interviewer has misunderstood something.

   b. If the child does not understand, he or she should tell the interviewer.

   c. If the child is uncomfortable, tell the interviewer.

   d. Even if the child thinks the interviewer knows something, he or she should tell the interviewer anyway.

   e. If the child is not sure about an answer, do not guess. He or she should admit to being unsure before giving the information.

f. The child is to remember that the interviewer was not present during the incident he or she is describing, and the more the child can tell about the incident, the more the interviewer will understand.

g. Assure the child that the interviewer will not get angry or upset with him or her.

h. The child should only talk about things that are true and that really happened.

4. *Establish the need to tell the truth.* The child is asked to describe the meaning of truth and the consequences of telling lies. If the child cannot give a definition, then the interviewer can provide a definition and inquire about the child's capacities by asking about the color of their clothing and misstating the colors. The child is then asked to determine the veracity of the color identification.

5. *Introduce the topic of concern.* This is done in a gradual, step-wise fashion.

a. Do you know why you are here?

b. The interviewer explains his or her professional role and asks, "Do you want to talk to me about anything that's happened to you?"

c. The interviewer asks the child if he or she can tell about something that has happened to him or her, something good followed by something bad.

If the above questions do not elicit information about the allegations, then the interviewer can introduce alternative techniques.

d. Review the names and roles of various adults in the child's life (older children).

e. Draw the outline of a human figure, the same sex as the child, point out different body parts, and have the child tell the name and function.

f. Repeat for the opposite sex.

g. If more inquiry is needed, the interviewer can ask the child who has seen and/or touched various parts of the child's body.

As a last resort, the following questions may be required but should be pursued with care, recognizing the child's vulnerability to suggestive questioning.

h. "Did (a neutral adult) touch you there, or did your Daddy touch you there, or did nobody touch you there?"

These questions should be asked again, later in the interview, altering the order of the alternatives.

6. *Free narrative.* This is the most important part of the interview and the child must be given the opportunity to express his or her own version of the event. If the event is a single episode, the child is instructed, "I want you to tell me everything you remember about what happened, starting from the beginning." The child should not be interrupted. The interviewer may take notes regarding inconsistencies or follow-up questions.

If the allegations are of multiple events, the child is asked to tell "what would usually happen." This can be followed by asking about other particular incidents, with the same process as noted above. Follow-up questioning may be about the differences in place or manner or about the actions. First and last incidents should be queried. After the description of an event, the child and interviewer should mutually agree on a label for that specific event. Care should be given to allow the child to freely offer his or her narrative of the experience. Any distress noted in the child is acknowledged and a break is encouraged. A "stop sign"—raised hand with palm out—can be demonstrated for the child and the child is encouraged to use the sign if there are areas of inquiry that he or she feels uncomfortable about.

7. *Open questioning.* After the child has delivered a narrative, the interviewer asks open-ended questions about the event(s) described—"Do you remember any more about (a specific incident)?"—or who, where, when, and what questions.

8. *Specific questioning (optional).* These questions are asked only to clarify and extend previous answers. Multiple-choice questions

are avoided or offered only when the question is repeated and the order is varied. Care is taken to avoid cross-contamination.

9. *Conclusion.* The child is thanked, asked if he or she has any questions for the interviewer, and the interviewer can explain to the child what the next steps will be.

Strengths of the Procedure

This interview carefully spells out specific steps in interviewing children that are designed to maximize recall and minimize contamination. Care is taken to encourage free recall as the basis of the child's disclosure, and leading and suggestive questioning is minimized. Initial field trial research indicates better interview quality with trained professionals.

Weaknesses of the Procedure

The authors do not specify age ranges for this interview. Comments are offered indicating that some of the specific procedures in the interview may be inappropriate for preschool children (see step 3 above); however, other comments (Yuille et al., 1993) indicate that preschool children have somewhat different skills than older children and that the interviewer must be "sensitive to and tolerant of these differences" (p. 102). The reader is left understanding that this interview is appropriate for use with preschool children.

There is only one point in the interview protocol at which the need for specific preschool focus is mentioned, and that is in the delivery of the interview rules (Yuille, 1994). (These rules involve encouraging the child to correct misunderstandings, indicate lack of understanding of a question, etc.) This caution is appropriate, as the rules demand metacognition (a skill not developed in preschoolers). The authors caution that "this step would not be appropriate with preschool age children (it would confuse them)" (Yuille, 1994, p. 8). However, the inclusion of this statement in the interview directions implies that the rest of the interview procedures *are* appropriate for preschool children. It is this implication of usefulness for young children that makes the presentation of this interview format especially problematic.

Research repeatedly finds that free recall is an inadequate measure of young children's knowledge. They require scaffolding and memory retrieval cues from the interviewer (see Chapter 3). The emphasis on free recall as the only source of the child's allegations leaves young children very vulnerable to underreporting.

Although attempting to avoid the dangers of contamination, open-ended questioning presents a danger for failing to elicit sufficient information about a young child's experience. The structure of the inquiry ("I'd like you to tell me everything you remember about what happened, starting from the beginning"), the generalization of events ("Tell me what would usually happen"), and follow-up questioning that demands conceptual organization ("Do you remember any more about the time it happened in the kitchen?") are all in opposition to the way young children organize and deliver their recall. Preschool children lack the conceptual framework to organize broadly defined categories; they also do not have skills to self-cue in order to generate additional information. Temporal relationships are very difficult for young children and they lack the skills to give information for when, or "the next time," or "the first or last time." For young children, organizational framework is required from the interviewer.

Elaboration questioning is done only on information provided by the child in free recall narration. Again, this creates a bias against the manner in which young children present their information.

Lyon (1996) found young children were unable to give a definition of truth and lie but could demonstrate competency when presented with statements that were examples of truth or lie telling. Requiring definition of such abstract concepts by preschool children represents another subtle form of discrimination for age-appropriate development. A frequent practice for discriminating between truth and lie in children is to ask them the color of various things and then deliberately misstate the color. This approach measures correct color recognition, but it does not actually measure truth and lie capacity (see Chapter 5 for a more appropriate screening strategy).

For children who have been raised with neglect, poverty, or prolonged exposure to traumatic events, the rigid expectations for them to respond to multiple categories of information may be discriminative, considering their organizational and narrative abilities.

Having two adult interviewers in the room with a small child may be overwhelming. Young children do not understand various professional roles; they develop relationships dependant on the qualities of the interviewer, not because of his or her title. Having one adult do the interview and the second sit quietly and write things down may seem intimidating.

This protocol does not recognize the use of standardized measures to document the quality of the child's behavioral presentation or developmental status, nor does it emphasize detailed developmental history as a critical context for understanding preschool children's allegations. A preschool child's response to sexual abuse may not be delivered in verbal descriptions, so for some preschoolers, developmental delays and behavioral problems may be the only available form of presenting symptomology. Because this interview format does not survey the whole status of the child, it does not place the child's statements within a developmental context. Lack of appropriate documentation of developmental status and any behavioral or skill problems do not allow the option of referring a child to available services for monitoring if abuse is suspect yet not discoverable. Furthermore, this protocol does not address critical aspects of effective interviewing for preschool children and does not suggest specific age limits for use.

Adaptations of the Protocol

Multiple aspects of the Step-Wise protocol are inappropriate for use with preschool children, but there are some suggested techniques that are effectively used in preschool interviewing. Procedures such as getting baseline information on a child's language and memory skills; surveying a child's memory capacities as demonstrated in event recall about two unrelated experiences; and monitoring affect, body language, and eye contact are all good interview skills. In fact, some of them are recommended in this volume.

Nevertheless, these good techniques do not negate the potential danger of using this protocol for preschool children. Based on what we know, this is *not* an appropriate interview format for the developmental needs of preschool children—and it should be labeled as such and

not publicized as appropriate for this age. Its use could greatly minimize a young child's reporting capacity, leaving them in danger.

COGNITIVE GRAPHIC FORMAT

Cornerhouse is a specialty interview program in Minneapolis, Minnesota, that is part of the National Network of Children's Advocacy
Centers. Cornerhouse uses an interview format that combines verbal
interview structure with an enduring written record of a child's history.
This produces a "cognitive-graphic" interview format that engages the
child in creating a written work, takes the direct focus off the child and
helps the child to relax so information gathering is enhanced. The
interview format is as follows:

1. A child who has made allegations of abuse is brought into a room
   with an interviewer. The room has been set up for interviewing,
   it is sparsely furnished and there are no toys. An easel with a pad
   of newsprint and a marker is available for the interviewer. The
   interviewer begins by drawing a circle and filling in eyes, nose,
   mouth, and physical details specific to the child (short hair, long
   hair, barrettes, crew cut, etc.). The child is invited to consider who
   the interviewer is drawing. When he guesses that it is himself, the
   examiner and child together discuss the details of the drawing.
   The paper is then flipped so a clean sheet emerges.

2. The child is told that only things that are true will be written
   down on the paper on this easel. The child is then screened for
   knowledge of truth and lies.

3. Once that competency is demonstrated, then the interviewer asks
   the child to name who lives at his house. Faces for the various
   members are drawn by the interviewer, and names of the different people are written below each face. Other people important
   in the child's life can also be explored (e.g., if the child visits with
   a parent in a split custody situation, then a separate drawing of
   the other family can be made). Then, the child may be asked
   where he lives, and a picture of the house (or the houses) is drawn
   by the interviewer.

4. After the family and location drawings are completed, the interviewer takes two line drawings that have male or female child faces with front and rear views. The rear view is differentiated because it has no facial features and has a line drawn to indicate the buttocks. Then the interviewer asks the child to identify the names of body parts, including genitals on both sexes, and the names are written in. The interviewer next asks the child if the drawing of the same-sex child can be used to represent him (i.e., "Let's have this be you"). The interviewer then points to the areas of concern, usually the genitals, and asks if the child has ever been touched in this area, and if so by whom and in what way.

5. To further aid a disclosure of abuse, the child is given two anatomically explicit dolls and asked to demonstrate what has happened to them.

6. Specific follow-up questions regarding details of the abuse are asked.

7. A telephone in the room is connected to an adjacent room where, behind a two-way mirror, police, child protection, medical or legal personnel may observe the interview. Any of these professionals can call into the room with questions for follow-up or further elaboration.

8. The interview ends with the child being appreciated for his or her involvement in the work of the interview. The interviewer then takes the initial drawing of the child, rolls it up and offers it to the child to take home. The interviewer also offers the child one of his or her business cards to close the interview.

Strengths of the Protocol

This is a structured, nonleading, and nonsuggestive interview format. It is an effective format for use with children 4 to 5 years and older. It creates a concrete record of a child's statements that may effectively be used in court, in a manner that comfortably engages a child's attention. The focus on a written product removes the direct attention from the child and helps lessen the pressure of an interview.

Weaknesses of the Protocol

When applied to children under age 4—and to some less well developed 4-year-olds—difficulties may arise. For example,

1. Asking children to have a drawing represent themselves is a capacity that emerges at about age 3½ to 4 in a population of white, middle-class children. The request of a 3- or young 4-year-old to use drawings as representative of self may not be understood.

2. Very young children (e.g., 2- and 3-year-olds) may not understand the use of a face as a symbol of someone. This concrete representation of various family members may not be helpful or understandable to them.

3. Young children do not have an abstract understanding of truth and lie—they will need a more concrete discussion of this. They do not understand the intentional nature of lying and the motivation to falsify, which is at the heart of this voir dire-type questioning.

4. Young children may not be able to sit and attend to the task for the 30 to 40 minutes that this interview requires.

5. The format does not involve gathering background or developmental data; it does not use objective measures as screening for problems; and it does not emphasize behavioral presentations of abuse. Without effectively evaluating the full context of the allegations of abuse, the young child's full presentation of information is not adequately assessed.

In summary, this interview format is fine for children 5 years and older. It may work for some 4-year-olds, but it is not appropriate for 2-year-olds, and several aspects of it present problems for 3-year-olds, especially if they are developmentally delayed or have been reared in environments devoid of stimulation.

Adaptations of the Protocol

A protocol such as the one in Chapter 4 is recommended for 2-year-olds. This protocol can be adapted for some delayed 4-year-olds or some 3½-year-olds who do not have good representational skills. Adaptation is done by making certain tasks more concrete and adding some of the prescreening procedures to the process.

1. The discussion about the family members can be preceded by the feelings screen used in Chapter 7, so the child's ability to relate to the feeling faces as a representation of self can be screened. For children who do not use the faces as representative of themselves, the focus can be on recognition of the feeling state.

2. Next, a drawing of various family members, done in full length, can be made with the child's assistance (e.g., "Are they short or tall?" "A lady, or a man, or a kid?" "Do they have long hair or short hair?"). The child should direct the completion of drawing the mouth and tell the examiner what type of feelings each person has. This concretizes the drawings for the child and makes them clearer representations of specific people. Understanding the emotional expression attributed to each family member may be clinically useful. (If the child is not able to use drawings, then move to the procedures suggested in Chapter 4). After drawing members of the family, other people may be added as well (e.g., if a specific person is an alleged perpetrator, this person may be added). This makes a concrete representation of various people who may be involved in possible abuse.

3. Questioning about individual body parts can be done by again making the task more concrete. The interviewer can create the generic body drawing, put in some body parts, and ask the child the names of the parts, but make the questioning more representational by asking the child to point to his or her own body part that is the same as the one in the drawing. Questions can be asked of the child by referring to his or her own body parts. If the child cannot follow this interview adaptation, return to a Stage 1 format.

4. Because demonstration with anatomically specific dolls to represent the self is difficult for 3-year-olds, the format needs to shift the use of the dolls for young 3-year-olds or older but delayed children. This can be done by asking the child to choose an anatomical doll to act as the perpetrator and letting the child use

his or her own body to demonstrate what happened to him or her. Caution: Very young children readily remove their pants and expose their genitals, so examiners must be prepared to deal with this. If specific body part identification is needed, a medical exam that also involves interviewing about touch can help young children show just where they were touched.

This interview format is good for children who are 4 years old and above. Younger or delayed children should be prescreened for their capabilities to tolerate the interview. Professionals have found this format capable of good downward extension in presentations adapted to younger children. There is no research available on this protocol.

❏ Other Interviewing Issues

PSYCHOSOCIAL EVALUATIONS

Not all children respond to initial interviews. Some, because of their emotional status, poor mastery of speech and language, or their censure, require additional assessment of their allegations. Such cases are usually referred to professionals trained in child development and the assessment of young children, such as psychologists, developmental specialists, or other mental health personnel. *Guidelines for Psychosocial Evaluation of Suspected Sexual Abuse in Children*, published by the American Professional Society on the Abuse of Children (1997) addresses multiple aspects of a psychosocial interview including characteristics of the evaluator, components of the evaluation, the interview procedures, the child interview, and general principles of the evaluation. A psychosocial interview should seek to establish good data on the status of the child; the child's cognitive, social, emotional and physical development; and information on his or her speech and language, attention span, and level of cooperation. Coupled with a thorough history, this information is then used as a background against which to craft an individually focused interview and to understand what the child is saying. Often it is difficult to fully assess allegations in one or two interviews, and it is quite possible that several attempts to address abuse material will be needed. Such attempts should not involve repeated administration of the same questions and techniques. Multiple modalities and varied media can all be employed to sample children's knowledge in differing formats (e.g., play in a dollhouse, drawings, anatomical doll interviews, discussion of pictures, etc.). Behavioral reactions after evaluation sessions should also be monitored. The protocols outlined in Chapters 4 and 5 are all appropriate for use in an extended psychosocial evaluation.

NATIONAL CHILDREN'S
ADVOCACY CENTER (NCAC)—
FORENSIC EVALUATION PROTOCOL
AND RESEARCH PROGRAM

Recognizing that some children do not disclose abuse in one interview, NCAC has developed an 8-week forensic evaluation (Carnes, Wilson, & Nelson-Gardell, 1997). This evaluation protocol is carefully crafted to address Faller's (1996) controversies in child sexual abuse interviews: interviewer competence, child competence, interview structure, and decision making in child sexual abuse cases. Integrated into these categories, NCAC has woven relevant research in interview components, child reluctance to report, memory, suggestibility, fantasy, and interviewer influence. The eight sessions allow the gathering of information over time, thus allowing the child to become more comfortable and trusting with the interviewer. The first two sessions cover essential information about the child: background and history from the primary caretaker, objective behavioral measurement, and individual developmental assessment. The third and fourth sessions build rapport using play and art therapy techniques and introduce education about good, bad and secret touching—as well as body part interview and touch screening. The remaining sessions employ "abuse focused, but non-leading questioning" to learn more about the child's experiences. The last session shifts to body safety and prevention education and other closure work. At the conclusion of the Forensic Evaluation, the therapist summarizes all information in a final report.

Besides creating a process that incorporates theory, research, and practice experience, NCAC has also conducted research on this protocol and is continuing the process of data gathering on a larger sample, including data from at least 30 other sites in the Children's Advocacy Network. Initial findings indicated that 8 rather than the 12 original sessions were needed for the evaluation and that various components used in the evaluation combined to clarify outcome categorization. Use of this protocol offers an underlying conceptual and research structure for the process of assessment and data categorization. Work of this quality is powerful refutation for critics who would characterize the assessment process in child abuse cases as flawed. This protocol is an important addition to the national need for a structure that is more respectful and sensitive to the needs of young children.

ASKING APPROPRIATE INTERVIEW QUESTIONS

Certain questions can result in different responses from preschoolers versus older children. Chapters 3 and 4 discussed the format of various questions and their association with children's development level. Walker's forensic linguistic work (1994) has focused on appropriate questioning of children.

Few research projects have focused on the assessment of real interviewer questions and child responses, varying across ages. Hunt, Komori, Kellen, Galas, and Gleason (1995) analyzed the responses to 42 North Carolina and Tennessee Child Protective Services interviews with a sample age range of 2 to13 years. They found some interesting developmental trends in children's responses to various questioning techniques.

Faulty Questioning Techniques

When an interviewer modified a child's statement (reworded a child's statement in a way that changed its meaning or claimed that the child made a statement that he or she had not made), children ages 2 to 4 were three times more likely to agree than disagree, whereas children ages 11 to 13 were equally likely to do either; in other words, younger children less often corrected or challenged a questioner's modification of their statement.

When an interviewer asked a forced choice question (a question that presents a limited number of response options), children ages 2 to 4 and 5 to 7 were significantly less likely to provide their own answers than to choose the interviewer's options. Children ages 2 to 4 were significantly more likely to choose the first option presented to them, whereas children ages 5 to 7 did not differ in their choice of the first or second option. Older children may be able to look beyond the limits of an interviewer's questions, whreas young children cannot.

When interviewers presented a multipart question (i.e., two or more inquiries with potentially different responses contained within the same question), children ages 2 to 7, who were able to provide an answer, tended to answer only the second question, whereas children over 8 years were likely to answer either question.

Nonproductive Questioning Techniques

Nonproductive techniques are those that do not generate interpretable answers. Specific questions that demand a certain type of answer (e.g., "What do you do after school?") were more likely than other questions to elicit nonverbal responses. These questions were especially problematic for younger children. Specific questions accounted for 64% of the 2- to 4-year-olds' nonverbal responses, whereas they accounted for 48% of the 11- to 13-year-olds' responses. The researchers interpreted their results as supportive of the use of open-ended versus specific questions.

"Can You . . . ?" Questions

These questions (e.g., "Can you show me X?" or "Can you tell me what you call that?") created problems because they ask for a broader, more conceptual response (can you perform a certain function?) even though the interviewer is probably seeking a specific piece of information (what do you call that?). This last question seems to ask for metacognition, for a child to think about their thinking (the child would have to sort through their experiences, find an item, and then evaluate whether he or she is capable of telling about it). This type of questioning is difficult even for older children, but it is more problematic for younger children. Children over age 4 were able to overcome the complex structure of the question and give specific information, but "members of the 2- to 4-year-old group were significantly more likely than members of any other age group to answer 'yes' or 'no,' or give an uninformative response" (Hunt et al., 1995).

What Do You Do . . . ? Questions

Responding to a question such as "What do you do after school?" presents a major challenge to a young child. Young children do not have good temporal organizational skills, so "after school" may be difficult to understand. The "What do you do . . . ?" format requires young children to draw from a broader field of experiences that may be hard for them to organize and form into a specific response.

It is important, then, to be very careful of restatements of young children's statements, as they will not correct you and they may agree to a faulty answer. It is the interviewer's job to be sure the child is on track with such issues, as young children do not monitor others or their own truth or accuracy in understanding.

Forced-Choice Questions

When asking forced-choice questions, 2- to 4-year-olds are likely to select one of your choices, as they do not evaluate your choices and generate a choice of their own. When asking questions, vary the order of the choices offered and reintroduce the question with a different order of choices to accurately track the child's response accuracy.

Broad Choice Questions

Young children do not survey a large body of information and distill a response, so instead of asking "What did you do that day?" you might ask, "Did you go to the store?" "Did you play?" and so on. This is where a good history can help you understand what the child's experiential background is and then you can more readily monitor the response quality.

There is a body of research that considers the way we ask questions of children; it is especially pertinent when questioning young children. Knowing the research and following it in interviews is a challenging task for any interviewer.

CONTENT-BASED CRITERIA
ANALYSIS (CBCA)

The CBCA (Steller & Koehnken, 1989) is an application of the Undeutsch theory (Undeutsch, 1989) that argues that persons who have actually experienced an event will report it in a manner different from those who have just heard about it. Developed to help determine false or programmed allegations, the CBCA (also referred to as Statement Validity Analysis, or SVA) is not a specific interview format; rather, it is a method of analyzing statements made in an interview or disclosure. It consists of 19 criteria used to score an interview and determine its validity as an actual experience versus something fabricated or overheard. It is mentioned here because it is sometimes used to analyze the statements of preschool children. Application of the 19 criteria used to determine the veracity of a child's statement (Steller & Koehnken, 1989) is problematic when applied to preschool children. The 19 criteria are divided into five groupings:

General Characteristics
  1. Logical Structure
  2. Unstructured Production
  3. Quantity of Details
Specific Contents
  4. Contextual Embedding
  5. Description of Interactions
  6. Reproduction of Conversation
  7. Unexpected Complications
Peculiarities of Content
  8. Unusual Details
  9. Superfluous Details
  10. Details Not Understood
  11. External Associations
  12. Subjective Mental State
  13. Perpetrator's Mental State
Motivation-Related Contents
  14. Spontaneous Corrections
  15. Admitting Lack of Memory
  16. Doubting Own Testimony
  17. Self-Deprecation

18. Pardoning the Perpetrator

Offense-Specific Elements

19. Characteristic Details

Recalling our discussion in Chapters 3 and 4, it is easy to see why this method is not appropriate for young children. Preschool children do not think about their own thinking or evaluate the quality of others' understandings of their reports. Determining a deficit in the child's report because there is no "spontaneous correction, admission of lack of memory, doubting of own testimony, self-deprecation, or specific reproductions of conversation or description of interactions" does not render a young child's disclosure inaccurate. Furthermore, accounts in the developmental literature about children's memory do not find fluency in describing conversations or detailed descriptions of interactions. Because a statement is determined invalid by its lack of scoring across a variety of criteria, young children's statements are open to misinterpretation and false rejections. The use of the CBCA with preschool children's statements is inappropriate and, even more important, it may cause harm to young children by minimizing their reports and thus failing to offer needed protection or supervision. Lamb et al. (1997), in their recent analysis of the CBCA, state, "the level of precision clearly remains too poor to permit the designation of CBCA as a reliable and valid test suitable for use in the courtroom . . . CBCA scores should not yet—and perhaps should never—be used in forensic contexts to evaluate individual statements" (pp. 262-263).

ANATOMICALLY CORRECT (AC) DOLLS

Young children lack the vocabulary, the experience, or both, necessary to understand sexual acts, and it is hard for them to explain abusive acts. Young children are often better at showing than telling about their experiences. Sexually anatomically correct dolls seem a very logical and natural solution to the problem of understanding what kind of sexual abuse has happened to a young child. In the last 6 years, the use of AC dolls has come under attack—an attack so strong that many professionals are now reluctant to use the dolls. What about this controversy?

Initially, questions were raised about the dolls being used as a test for sexual abuse. Defense experts argued that the doll interviews constituted using the dolls as a test, even though there was no establishment of the dolls as a valid or reliable test. Others argued that exposing genitals on a doll was a sexually stimulating experience for a child and led to accounts of abuse. Following these attacks, the American Professional Society on the Abuse of Children (APSAC) created a task force to look at these concerns and develop practice guidelines for use of the dolls. *Use of Anatomical Dolls in Child Sexual Abuse Assessments* (APSAC, 1995) lists five appropriate ways the dolls can be used as part of the assessment process (these uses are discussed more fully in Everson & Boat, 1994): anatomical model, demonstration aid, memory stimulus, screening tool, and/or icebreaker. The dolls have been criticized as overstimulating and suggestive, but data from multiple studies have not supported this criticism (Boat & Everson, 1993; Everson & Boat, 1990; Jampole & Weber, 1987; Sivan, Schor, Koeppl, & Noble, 1988). Data exist that compare the interactions of abused and nonabused children. Various studies find that touching and exploration of the doll's genitals is fairly common, but sexually abused children are more likely than nonabused children to play and interact with the dolls in sexual ways, that is, enact sexual intercourse or other sexual activities (Boat & Everson, 1993, 1996; Everson & Boat, 1990; Sivan et al., 1988). Guidelines published by both APSAC (1995) and the American Psychological Association (Koocher et al., 1995) endorse the use of the dolls as a demonstration aid or props to help children show what has happened to them.

The appropriate age for use of the dolls has been explored by several child development researchers. Goodman & Aman (1990) found that 3-year-olds' delivery of their experiences was not enhanced by use of dolls to demonstrate self-experiences. When the child is a very young 3-year-old, Bruck, Ceci, Francoeur, and Renick (1995) report that using the dolls as representations for the child's self can lead to misinformation and misinterpretation. They also report that when immaturity is coupled with leading and suggestive questions, the dolls can provide false information. Bruck, Ceci, Francoeur, and Renick asked young 3-year-olds to use an AC doll to demonstrate an exam by their pediatrician. They report, "The dolls increased inaccurate reporting because some children falsely showed that the doctor had inserted a finger into the anal or genital cavity." Bruck, Ceci, Francoeur, and Renick conclude that AC dolls "should not be used in forensic or therapeutic interviewing with 3-year-old children" (p. 95), and Ceci (1994) has expressed concern about the use of the dolls, "Use these dolls with extreme caution, if at all. No one ought to be glib about the error rates with these dolls and error rates in the studies."

In evaluating these conclusions, it is important to understand that the children in this sample had a mean age of 35 months. What do we know about representation of self and its developmental emergence? Chapter 3 detailed research indicating that representation of self emerges between the age of 3 years and 2 months and 3 years and 6 months in white, middle-class children. The Bruck, Ceci, Francoeur, and Renick study is constructed to take place during the months immediately preceding this skill's emergence. The study's findings are not generalizable for all 3-year-olds or for older children, just very young children who do not have representation of self. This conclusion frames the breadth of the article's argument much differently.

The dolls in the Bruck, Ceci, Francoeur, and Renick study were also used as demonstration aids, which Boat and Everson (1996) specifically state is not recommended for children under age 3½. APSAC guidelines specifically caution against using the dolls as a diagnostic tool. Thus, in this study, the dolls are used in a manner not supported by guidelines in the field. Using dolls for representation of self is inappropriate with young 3-year-olds, and possibly with older 3-year-olds and some 4-year-olds coming from more impoverished backgrounds. But if a child has shown the presence of self-representational skills, the dolls are then appropriate for use as a demonstration aid.

DeLoache (1987, 1989) has looked at young children's ability to use a scale model of a room as a symbol for a larger room and she has found that 2½- to 3-year-old children often do not realize the two are related. In DeLoache and Marzolf (1995), two problems in using symbols with young children are discussed. First, "the ability to use a real-object symbol, such as a scale model or doll, requires dual representation: The child must think about the symbolic object both as the object that it is and a representation of something other than itself. . . . Furthermore, even if children could appreciate a self-doll relation, they may still have difficulty mapping from one to the other" (p. 158). DeLoache and Marzolf specifically designed a study to look at three groups of young children (ages 2½, 3, and 4) and their use of dolls to recount a recent experience. They found that the 2½- and 3-year-olds had difficulty mapping a sticker placement on their body to a sticker placement on the doll. The 4-year-olds could successfully perform this task. The youngest group also had difficulty mapping sticker placement from the doll to self. In addition, the younger children did not naturally use the doll for demonstration purposes; instead, they used the dolls only at the interviewer's request. Their direct responses to the interviewer's questions were more informative than doll demonstrations. DeLoache and Marzolf report that "the problems we document for 2½- and 3-year-old children's use of a doll as a self-representation should not be overgeneralized: they would be less of an issue for older children" (p. 171). In a replication of this work across a series of studies, DeLoache, Anderson, and Smith (1995) find support for the difficulty of mapping between self and dolls. They conclude that "very young children do not fully appreciate the intended self-doll relation or they have difficulty mapping from themselves to a doll, or both" (p. 8).

DeLoache and colleagues do not, however, disregard the use of dolls with young abused children. They go on to state,

> Our results speak specifically to using a doll in a directed interview; they are not necessarily applicable to using AD [anatomically detailed] dolls in unstructured observations of free play. In the interview situation, children are more or less explicitly instructed to use a doll as a representation of themselves, and they are asked to use the doll to show or enact specific experiences. Our results and those of other investigations indicate no benefit for very young children from the presence of a doll in this situation. In free play, there are no specific correspondences being imposed on the children, and their general, rather than specific, knowledge can be represented in their play. Thus, the representational issues relevant to using dolls in free play may be less problematic. . . .
>
> We found that 2½-year-olds were quite unsuccessful when asked simply to map between their own body and a doll. Neither the 2½- nor the 3-year-olds were very good at using the doll to demonstrate what they had already reported. (DeLoache et al., 1995, pp. 171-172)

Knowing when use of dolls as a representation of the self is appropriate is a key component in successfully interviewing preschoolers. There is a growing body of research that supports the use of dolls with children ages 4 and older. The dolls are, in fact, an important aid in the assessment of abuse allegations with children.

*   *   *

The purpose of this chapter has not been to criticize or devalue the various interview formats presented, unless the format was shown to be specifically inappropriate. In fact, these formats were selected because most of them are commonly used interview forms and often serve as models for other, adapted interview formats. They are cited to emphasize that one format for interviewing does not fit all children, especially very young children with rapidly changing developmental needs and structures.

7

The Touch Survey: Systematic Screening for Child Abuse

There are many ways to interview children about sexual abuse (Boat & Everson, 1986, 1996; Davies et al., 1996; Doris, 1991; Faller, 1995; Jones & McQuiston, 1986; Levitt, 1993; MacFarlane & Waterman, 1986; Morgan, 1995; Saywitz, 1992; Saywitz, Snyder, & Lamphear, 1996; Steward, 1992; White & Santilli, 1988; Yuille, 1996). In addition to published techniques, there are special protocols used by the more than 300 centers affiliated or associated with the National Children's Advocacy Center Network. Different interviewers incorporate different techniques: the use of drawings, the discussion of body parts and touching, the addition of anatomically correct dolls (AC dolls), questioning during medical examination, structured questions around

AUTHOR'S NOTE: Originally published by S. K. Hewitt and A. A. Arrowood (1994), Systematic Touch Exploration as a Screening Procedure for Child Abuse: A Pilot Study, *Journal of Child Sexual Abuse, 3*(2), 31-43.

memory retrieval cues, and even an interactive computerized model (Faller, 1995). Most interviews involve some rapport building, an exploration of the child's world, a review of body parts, and non-leading questioning about possible genital touch.

The best interview formats combine a comfortable style for the interviewer, a forensically defensible structure, questions that are appropriate to the needs and developmental status of the child, and a nonbiasing exploration of the information sought. Children's willingness to respond to an interviewer and an interview format is a significant variable in effective assessment. The best information comes when there is a good match between the interviewer and the child; it also depends on the quality of rapport and communication they are able to develop and the appropriateness of the interview questions.

Not all interview formats are constructed to meet the needs of the preschool child. The Touch Survey, the focus of this chapter, was developed in the early 1980s when, as a school psychologist, I had to screen Head Start children for possible abuse issues. The conceptual model for this touch screening grew from the idea of a continuum of touch: touch that was good, bad, and neutral (Anderson, 1977). Integrating the idea of screening positive, negative, and touch absence into a standardized assessment finally combined to give birth to the Touch Survey.

The Touch Survey screens for possible abuse in several areas: physical abuse, sexual abuse, and emotional abuse or neglect. Physical abuse is screened by looking at spanking, hitting, or pinching; sexual abuse by asking about genital touches; and emotional abuse or neglect by asking about hugging and kissing. Because most abuse does not occur in isolation (Belsky, 1993), it is important to screen for multiple forms of abuse. Emotional abuse is also rarely included in screening. This measure, by exploring physical contact that is usually positive and nurturing, can also screen for an absence of nurturing and affectionate touch.

The Touch Survey requires that a child be able to use drawings as a representation of him- or herself. Because self-representation is frequently not well developed until age 4, the Touch Survey is suggested for use with children age 4 and above. Some older 3-year-olds who have come from stable and enriching backgrounds may have self-representational skills, but they also need to sustain sufficient attention to interview. A warm-up exercise is included in the Touch Survey protocol to assess the child's skill level before administration of this survey. Although not recommended for children under 4 years, the Touch Survey can be adapted to the unique needs of 2- and 3-year-olds, a technique that is detailed later in this chapter.

The Touch Survey uses a paper-and-pencil format. This format shifts the focus from an emotionally more intense face-to-face questioning to a less intense disclosure modality: writing. A paper-and- pencil format also provides a concrete record for the child's statements and drawings. The Touch Survey has been accepted as evidence during testimony in Minnesota courts. Originally this measure was developed to be used at the end of a formal psychological status evaluation, where previous work with the child had helped to create good rapport and a comfortable environment. This measure can also be used as part of an initial, single-session interview, as required by police or child protection, when combined with initial rapport building and screening. My clinical experience has found that richer responses come from stronger relationships.

The use of the Touch Survey without the development of relationship—the kind that can be fostered over the initial evaluation period—may result in lower levels of responding and some missed information. Spending time with the Feeling Faces technique that follows is a quick way to establish a relationship. You could also have the child draw his or her family or use some of the prescreening ideas from Chapter 5.

Before detailing the administration of the Touch Survey, one important assessment issue must be addressed. The Touch Survey screening directly asks children if they have experienced genital touch. Some might argue that presentation of such a direct question could be leading or suggestive. There are several arguments to refute this concern. First, all previous questioning about positive as well as neutral or negative touch (i.e., spanking, hitting, pinching, kicking) has been done in exactly the same format, so questions about genital touch follow a preestablished format that is practiced across all categories. Second, the research cited in Chapter 3 clearly documents the need that young children have for external structure or "scaffolding" to help them present what they know. Most young children do not give elaborate, spontaneous, well-constructed, narrative explanations of their abuse. The Touch Survey format directly asks if anyone has touched them, "in the front or the back, where you go to the bathroom." This question is direct but it is not leading and suggestive. The act of asking this question does not create an abuse narrative if nothing has happened. Third, there is no evidence from the initial research with this protocol (which is documented at the end of the instruction section) that simply asking a child if there has been touching in the genital area results in false positive statements.

❏ Method of Administration

Materials used for the Touch Survey procedure include two pencils or markers, one of them pink or red, and sheets of $8\frac{1}{2}$- × 11-inch paper. You may use one pencil and offer the child a pink or red one as needed. The Touch Survey has two parts, a warm-up exercise for children 8 years and younger and the actual Touch Survey. The warm-up procedure, or Feeling Faces, reviews various faces and feelings to develop rapport, learn about the child's emotional environment, check on self-representational skills, attention span, and the child's ability to work on a paper-and-pencil task. It also ensures a working knowledge of different feeling states, which is applied in part two. The Feeling Faces exercise is also beneficial to use for children older than 8 years of age for whom there is a need to build rapport.

The second part of the Touch Survey, touch exploration, is designed to explore areas in which abuse might occur.

FEELING FACES

Begin by using a marker to divide a sheet of paper into four boxes. Then, while the child watches, create four faces, one per box, showing happy, sad, mad, and scared expressions (see Figure 7.1). Then point to each face and ask the child what feeling is on the face. Write the child's label under the face. Some children have no labels for their feelings. This is important, especially if they are later asked to state their feelings about a type of touching. You may provide a feeling name

happy

sad

angry

scared

Figure 7.1. Feeling Faces

to the child, but recognize that the child may not be reliable in later responses to questions about feeling states on the Touch Survey.

After you have labeled each of the faces, ask the child to identify which of the four faces he or she has the most often. Put a number one in that box. Then help the child to continue to identify facial expressions and produce a rank order of the faces, according to how often the child has those faces or feelings. Finally, go back to each face, starting with number one, and ask: "What makes you feel (happy, sad, etc.)?" [Write the child's response at the right side of the box.]

This warm-up procedure for the Touch Survey is nonthreatening, creates a comfortable focused rapport, sets the stage for the paper-and-pencil format to follow, and provides information about the affective state of the child.

TOUCH SURVEY

Using a pencil or pen, divide a blank sheet of paper into six boxes. Then say to the child:

"I want to talk with you about different kinds of touching that could happen with kids. But first, I want to make a picture of a kid—let's make it you." [Now draw a simple stick figure in the upper left-hand corner and add details that might be specific to the child, such as their hair style, ribbons, bows, earrings, and so on. *Do not* add the mouth to this figure yet.]

This procedure is shown in Figure 7.2.

Continue by saying to the child:

"The first kind of touch I want to talk about is hugging." [Write "hugging" under the figure in the upper left-hand box.] "Have you ever been hugged?" [Record "yes" or "no" inside the top right-hand side of the box.] "Did you like to be hugged?" [Record this "yes" or "no" response below the first response.] "Now, I'd like you to make the feeling on your face that you have when you have been hugged." [Offer the child a pink or red pencil or marker and have the child draw in the mouth, showing his or her expression. For very young or very impulsive children, be sure to take the marker or pencil from the child at the end of each drawing as some children will use their markers to spontaneously draw in other places across the protocol.]

Next, ask the child to verbalize the feeling that her or she has just drawn and note it opposite the face. Continue with two additional questions:

"Who hugs you?" [Record all the persons the child lists on the right-hand side of the box. If the child proceeds to list more than four or five people, you can limit the number of people the child lists or, for clinical reasons, you may decide to list all the people but may not follow up with the entire list for the next step.] "Where does [the first name] hug you?" [Record with arrows from the name of the person to the circles on the area of the body parts that are touched.]

Proceed to the next box. Draw the figure of the child again, and ask about tickling. The same procedure that was used for hugging is also used for documenting and illustrating tickling. Tickling can be viewed as positive or negative by the child. Tickling that is negative most often

Figure 7.2. Beginning the Touch Survey

ignores the child's boundaries when the child has asked that it stop. Disregard of a child's wishes and boundaries is important information to know. Such information can be part of an abusive form of inter-action.

For the next three boxes, repeat the same format, asking about spanking, kissing, or hitting, kicking, and pinching. Here are some guidelines that I have found helpful in asking about each of these actions. When asking about kissing, it can be helpful to ask whether anyone "tastes" them (i.e., puts their tongue into the child's mouth). In some states, this is a form of penetration that is illegal. When asking about spanking, it is helpful to ask about what is used to spank (hand, belt, etc.) and how often spanking occurs. Some kids can provide information on how hard they are hit and if marks or bruises are left. Hitting, kicking, pinching is explored in the same way as spanking. Very often, sibling or peer contact is recorded in these forms of touch-ing and this can provide important information. This allows you to assess the level of family control for intersibling abuse as well as intimidation.

Sibling abuse is one of the more frequent but less well documented forms of abuse. Terrorizing by an older sibling can have major effects on a younger child. New information about physical abuse may also surface here. Be careful to ask about what kind (e.g., "What do you get hit with?"), and ask if marks are left or if the child has any marks left now. If there are marks, this information needs to be reported and investigated. A real lack of affectionate touch may reflect emotional dynamics such as isolating, ignoring, or rejecting/spurning of the child, which are all forms of emotional abuse (Garbarino, Guttman, & Seeley, 1986; Hart & Brassard, 1987).

Some children immediately volunteer repeated instances of physically abusive touch (i.e., hitting, kicking, punching, slapping, etc.) When this occurs, the presence of physical abuse must be considered and appropriate questions asked and followed as the entire measure is completed. Kids who avoid volunteering any kind of touch information, or who seem very repressed and reluctant to discuss touch on paper, need to be watched closely. Clinically based experience with this technique has shown that additional examination of psychological status should be conducted to determine the source of the child's constricted affect. Time in therapy can also help make a child's reasons for repression more understandable.

The sixth box on the sheet of paper used in part two of the Touch Survey procedure is for sexual touch exploration. The sixth box is introduced by saying:

"And now I want to ask you about another kind of touch." [Point to the crotch area of the drawing.] "Has someone ever tickled you here, where you go potty, or in the back on your butt?" [Follow this with] "Has someone ever hurt you here, where you go potty, or in the back on your butt?" [Note: For older children, the word "touch" may be used in place of "hurt" or "tickle," but preschool children may not have good differentiation of this more conceptually based word, and concrete action words such as "hurt" or "tickle" may capture both positive and negative touching in this area. Second, young children may not understand the concepts of "in front" or "in back." You can clarify this concept by asking the child if they have a butt and ask them to point to it, thus specifying the location.]

If the child says "no," indicating that sexual touching has not been experienced, then ask the child to put on the drawing a face that shows how he or she *would* feel *if* it happened. These responses are recorded (see Figure 7.3 for an example of a sexually abused child's responses). Clinical experience with this measure has shown that some children 5 years of age and older who have *not* experienced sexual abuse often respond to questions about genital touch with a "You've got to be kidding!" manner or by being embarrassed, as well as simply denying the experience of such touch. Some sexually abused children acknowledge the touch directly and can clearly tell who touched them and in what ways.

If the child says "yes," genital touch has happened, then complete the box in the same format used for the boxes above, with the child listing the type of feeling they have about that touching and the person or persons who may have touched them in that area. When a child responds that abuse has happened, it is often very effective to give children the marker or pencil they used for completing their facial expression and have them draw a mark starting at the name of the alleged offender and moving to directly point to the place where abuse has happened. *It is important, because this drawing is one dimensional, to clearly label whether the child is referring to touch in the front or in the back.* If more specific information is needed, then the child can be asked to provide a name ("What do you call this part in front? In the back?"). You can now follow up using the child's term and ask about specific touching in that area. Be sure to differentiate any appropriate toileting or bathing touch from abuse.

With children who have been censured, you can ask the child what would happen *if* a child were to disclose abuse. Clinical experience again has shown that some young children respond, "My dad goes to jail." Children often feel that they too might go to jail. With preschool children, as with all children, it is important to be straightforward and honest in your answers about the consequences of child abuse for perpetrators; however, information may need to be developmentally adapted. Again, in my clinical experience I have found that explaining to children that grown-ups might need a "time-out," without using jail or prison as terms, can help a child understand that if grown-ups have done something wrong, then they need a time-out just as children do.

Figure 7.3. Completed Touch Survey With Sexual Abuse Indicated

Children who have been previously sensitized to questioning about their genital area may shut down when asked to label genital parts, especially when that focus is part of a more directed interview format. The highly structured nature of the Touch Survey used here minimizes this avoidance because it questions, in a repetitive, familiar pattern; thus, the Touch Survey's pattern of direct questioning across touches may mute warnings to not talk about genital touch.

AC dolls can now be used as a follow-up for demonstration of the information offered here verbally or in drawings. With AC dolls, the child can directly show you what kinds of touches have happened.

When you move to a demonstration model such as the AC dolls, it is very easy to forget to complete the protocol portion that screens for a child's touching of a perpetrator's body. Don't forget to go back and complete the protocol to screen for touching a child may have had to do to a perpetrator. If you forget this step, it can be followed up on a separate occasion by reviewing the previous productions—if the child will allow this—and then moving to the final screening of a child's touch to others.

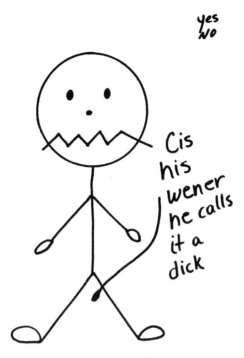

Figure 7.4. Completing the Touch Survey: Assessing Touch of Others

When children become evasive or anxious here (changing the sub-ject, refusing to respond, or ignoring your questions), then you need to take careful note. These reactions suggest the need to follow up. Some young kids, when I have asked them how they would feel *if* such things happened, have given inadvertent admissions, such as, "I felt mad when he did that." You can follow up with an affirmation of the kid's difficulty in discussing this type of touch and also ask a question like, "What makes it so hard to talk about this kind of touching?" You should be alert for descriptions of threats or other forms of censure.

The last step in the Touch Survey involves turning the paper over and drawing one large stick figure with eyes and nose only. The hair and mouth are omitted so the figure is to be neutral in shape and expression. Then say, "Sometimes adults (or big kids) want kids to touch their bodies. Is there somebody who wants *you* to touch their body?" You record the child's responses as you did before, indicating who wanted such touching and where on the body the touch occurred.

Many times kids will just say "no" to your initial questions, but you can follow up by asking if there are any grown-ups or big kids that like the child to hug them or give them a kiss or hold their hand. Frequently, children acknowledge that parental figures or other close figures ask for such touch. After the child is engaged in a discussion about touching of others, then the final genital touch question for this drawing can be asked. It is asked in a parallel form to all the other questions previously asked. To ask this question again, point to the crotch area and ask the child if there is someone who wants them to touch their body in private places. Be alert, as in previous steps, to realize that some children who have been abused may not have had their genitals touched, yet they may have been asked to sexually touch someone else. If the child does not acknowledge any abuse but seems specifically troubled, evasive or elusive—for example, "I can't say for sure"— then the education and reassurance that the child is not to blame is critical.

When you have completed the protocol to this point, children who indicated they have not experienced sexually abusive touch will often fall into two groups: (1) children who are forthright and comfortable in indicating no genital touch, or (2) children who appear uncomfortable or distressed with questions about genital touching. Children who have case histories strongly supporting the possibility of abuse can profit from some additional questioning. (This follow-up questioning was not included in the experimental sample whose statistics are reported at the end of this narrative.)

For this second group of children, I return to the box with the private parts focus; I point to the child figure and say, "One time, when you were little, did somebody touch you here?" and I point to the genital area in the drawing. I have found that distancing an act in time lessens its threat and, with this simple question, I have frequently had children tell me of their past abuse. Both groups of children, those comfortable and uncomfortable, can benefit from completing the Touch Survey by moving into prevention education material.

The final component of the Touch Survey is to offer prevention education training. You can ask the child, "Do you know what the rules are for touching children in private parts?" (or an alternate, more simple way to state this is "where you go potty?"). If the child indicates they are aware of rules, you can then ask them what these rules are and let the child articulate his or her understanding. Otherwise, you can work within a traditional prevention education model outlining good and bad touch and steps for children's disclosure.

If there are elements in a case that make it particular high risk, then you may also help the child formulate a safety plan or a strategy in case of future disclosures. For example, "If somebody did touch you in private places and you wanted to tell someone, who would you tell? How would you tell?" Discussing and planning this concern with children can facilitate their later disclosure.

Not all cases of abuse respond to single-session interviews and some children disclose over time, in a piecemeal fashion (Sorenson & Snow, 1991). Often a child's fearful, evasive, or conflicting responses on the Touch Survey indicate a need for follow-up. Psychosocial evaluations (see APSAC, 1997) can be initiated. This extended evaluation helps determine a child's overall status, develop a closer relationship, and put the child's remarks and reactions into the context of their history and current status. If your role allows, you may choose to see the child again for a more thorough emotional-status evaluation or to develop more trust in the relationship with the child. Later, you could again explore abuse issues, but as always, avoiding leading or suggestive questioning. If your role or your time schedule does not permit repeated contact, you might ask the child to say who at home or at school he or she could trust and would be able to talk to about any abuse. You might then try to arrange regular contact for the child with this person (teacher, social worker, counselor) and, with proper releases, inform that professional of the abuse concerns. You should check to be sure the professional has an adequate understanding of child sexual abuse, is willing to listen to the child, and knows what to do to help children. You must remain clear, however, about the differences in, and conflicts between, the assessor and therapist roles.

If a child does not seem to have any unusual reactions to the various touch examples, the review of boundaries can, in itself, afford a child appropriate information to allow him or her to report, should abusive touch occur, and thus shorten the length of time it might continue. This information might also allow a child to be helpful to a classmate or friend who discloses abuse.

❏ Research on the Touch Survey

Few child abuse interview formats have been assessed for validity. Results obtained from systematic touch exploration have been compared to results of the complete case investigation in a pilot study. Subjects in this study were 42 children 4 to 8 years of age. These children were referred to five psychologists for evaluation at the Midwest Children's Resource Center (MCRC), a specialty child abuse service of Children's Health Care, St. Paul, Minnesota. The sample was drawn from a population of all children seen during a 12-month period at MCRC with fully completed protocols. Forty percent of the children were female and 60% were male, with most of the children from families of lower socioeconomic status.

To investigate the efficacy of the Touch Survey as a screener for child sexual abuse, the initial results obtained on the Touch Survey were compared to the final case conclusions. The latter conclusions were drawn after completing a full-scale evaluation that included psychological testing, parent or guardian interviews, review of police, child protection or medical data, interviewing information from collateral resources, and a final staff review for consensus on case determination. Initial determination of abuse was made by child protective services, but final MCRC conclusions were made by the whole staff team, including the member who initially administered the Touch Survey. Results of this research are detailed in the *Journal of Child Sexual Abuse*, 1994, in an article by Hewitt and Arrowood, titled "Systematic Touch Exploration as a Screening Procedure for Child Abuse: A Pilot Study." Table 7.1 reflects a summary of the findings of that pilot study.

It is clear from the results presented in the table that false positives were not found. In other words, during the screening procedure no child fabricated that abuse had occurred when the full evaluation determined it had not. Accurate findings (valid positives and valid negatives) accounted for 55% of the cases. Table 7.1 also shows that 16% of the cases were determined to be inconclusive and consistent with the "don't know" response on the Touch Survey. The finding that the Touch Survey procedure indicated no abuse for 29% of the cases, even though the full evaluation indicated that abuse had occurred, suggests that the screening procedure has a bias toward children underreporting. Such bias is important to recognize in using this

Table 7.1 Endorsement Percentages on the Touch Survey (*N* = 42)

Response Consistent With Overall Conclusion: Abuse verified (Valid Yes)	31
Response Consistent With Overall Conclusion: Abuse not determined (Valid No)	24
Abuse Determined, Touch Survey Indicates No Abuse (False No)	29
Abuse Not Determined, Touch Survey Indicates Abuse (Fabrication)	0
Indeterminate Response	16

screening procedure, but is also not unlike other forms of initial under-reporting. These results are consistent with the literature, which finds children often underreport (Jones & McGraw, 1987), and that initial screening results may provide only partial disclosure (Sorenson & Snow, 1991).

In this study, the Touch Survey was administered after formal psychological testing by the same examiner who did the testing. Nonthreatening contact before abuse interviewing can help reduce anxiety about the interview material. It is possible that administration of the Touch Survey without good rapport could further elevate the false negative bias of this interview. Research needs to be done to compare disclosure outcome rates with single-session interviews versus the rates found when the Touch Survey is used at the end of a formal evaluation.

While the Touch Survey is not a psychometrically based test with norms and standards, the results of the present pilot study indicate that the procedure is a useful tool for screening in cases in which child sexual or physical abuse is suspected. One limitation of the study's design is that the full evaluation results were not completed independent of the findings on the Touch Survey, although the full evaluation at times did reach a conclusion that differed with the results of the Touch Survey (i.e., abuse had occurred despite the no-abuse entry found on the survey). This procedure is clearly one that needs to be subjected to further study. Replication of this research with other populations should be undertaken, clearer separation of this screening instrument and the final conclusions would be helpful, additional work with physical and emotional abuse could be done, and tracking the use of the survey in court cases would be helpful.

❑ Simplification of the Touch Survey

Use of drawings as representations of self for young children is not safely recommended for children under the age of 4 years. (Remember the earlier discussion about this skill in Chapter 5? This skill is emerging between 3 and 4 years. Children from lower socioeconomic status homes may have some skill lags.) A review of videotaped interviews with 2-year-olds and young 3-year-olds shows that these children more frequently use their own bodies to demonstrate the things that have happened to them; they are not good at using abstract props or symbols. Research with young children's use of anatomical dolls indicates that the disclosures of 3-year-olds are not facilitated by the use of such props (DeLoache & Marzolf, 1995; Goodman & Aman, 1990).

If 2- and 3-year-old children cannot use drawings or symbols very well but they can verbally relate some of their experiences, is it possible to construct a brief interview that might still be appropriate? There are stages of interview complexity. A very primitive and concrete interview example (identifying body parts on a child and then asking about specific genital touch) is outlined in Chapter 3. This very first level of interviewing, probably suitable for 2- to young 3-year-olds, does not allow for much questioning or exploration of context, specifics of the abuse, or frequency and time of the abuse. Very young children have greatly limited ability to respond to such topics, and additional information about possible abuse must be inferred from behavioral sequelae and other collateral sources, over time and across locations.

Three-year-olds are more sophisticated than 2-year-olds, and they can participate in a more detailed interview, although they are still not good interviewees. A second level of interviewing, appropriate for some 3-year-olds, involves a downward adaptation or simplification of the Touch Survey. This adaptation has been used clinically, but it does not yet have research documentation. The interview format provides a simple, concrete, structured assessment of the child's touching relationships, appropriate for the child too immature for the written touch exploration. This procedure offers 3-year-olds, or some delayed 4-year-olds, the kind of "scaffolding" needed by young children as it proceeds in a nonleading or nonsuggestive manner.

Cautions still apply, however. Three-year-olds are not able to do a thorough exploration of location, duration, chronological order, and

types and variations of abuse, nor are they able to give good spontaneous narrative descriptions of their experiences. This interview adaptation provides one vehicle for assessing a young child, but it should
not be interpreted without history, background, current status, and
good objective data on behavior and adjustment. Even then it is difficult to "prove" abuse with this age group. A case can be considered
high risk and protection sought when a collection of information is
brought together that matches cases of known abuse.

I talk with the child, establish rapport, and screen for interview
capabilities before I begin the modified interview. To begin this format,
I ask the parent, at the intake session, to provide a physical description
of the alleged abuser and to provide the name and description of
another major caretaker. Then, when I meet with the child, I ask him
or her to select dolls from a large assortment of small dolls that are of
mixed sexes, ages, and racial backgrounds, a doll that looks like their
primary caretaker, one that looks like a second caretaker, and one that
looks like the alleged abuser. I ask, "Can you find a doll that looks like
your daddy?" "Now, can you find one that looks like your mommy?"
"Can you find one that looks like Jimmy, your babysitter?" (Note the
risks here. Young children cannot work with a large number of dolls
so you need to limit your query to a small number of subjects, but in
doing this you are also limiting the perpetrator possibilities. Simply
asking questions about genital touch does not create allegations of
abuse, but in this format you are clearly limiting the choices. It is best
to use this approach only when there are other, clear indications that a
specific person is implicated as a possible perpetrator. This same short
inquiry can also be repeated with another alleged perpetrator figure.)

After the child has picked the three dolls, I add one small doll, the
same sex as the child.

*Here I also use the multicultural, bendable dollhouse families distributed by
Kidsrights that I mentioned in Chapters 4 and 5. I like the small molded genitals
on these dolls; they provide anatomical parts, yet they are not prominent
features of the dolls.*

Now I present the primary caretaker doll to the child and say, for
example, "I have a daddy doll here." "Do you have a daddy?" "Let's
have this be the daddy doll." Then I present the secondary caretaker
doll to the child and say, for example, "I have a mommy doll here."

"Do you have a mommy?" "Let's have this be the mommy doll." Then
I ask the child about her alleged perpetrator in terms of the function of
that person in the child's life, for example, "Do you have a babysitter?
What's your babysitter's name? Do we have a doll for Jimmy? Let's
have this doll be the Jimmy doll." Most 3-year-old children will readily
accept these dolls and begin to play with them.

> It is important to recognize that very often we are not clear who the perpetrator
> might be. In some cases it has turned out to be an unsuspected family member.
> One can never make assumptions that an alleged abuser is actually a child's
> abuser. Also, take care that the supposedly neutral dolls are not presented in
> any way that is biased toward possibly not representing perpetrators as well.

Next, I watch how the child uses the dolls in free play.

> One 3-year-old child set up a table and had the mom and her sister (the second
> family member we chose) come to eat. The child was the cook and served them
> breakfast. She put the alleged abuser doll in the bedroom alone and did not
> include him in the play. She was clearly able to use dolls representationally, but
> she did not have self-representational skills.

If the child is not comfortable with the dolls and does not use them
in an appropriately representational way, do not use this interview
strategy. Instead, return to the assessment procedures for nonverbal
children given in Chapter 4 and develop the information there.

> Other children, when presented with an alleged abuser, have thrown the doll
> away or refused to play with it. One young child took all my dollhouse furniture
> and barricaded the alleged perpetrator doll at the back of one room. This act
> spoke more loudly than any of his words about the quality of the relationship
> between the child and this man.

> None of these play examples prove sexual abuse has occurred; the play is only
> an expression of the relationship. Additional work is needed to clarify the
> reasons for the relationship problem.

After the free play observation, the dolls are used in a concrete,
adapted touch exploration format. No more than four dolls are recommended for presentation, and the dolls are presented with the least

likely abuser first, the alleged abuser in the middle of the series, and another family member or an unlikely abuser at the end.

Clinical experience has vividly demonstrated that a clinician's choice of least likely offender doll may not always be accurate. Sometimes I've had the initial person I presented turn out to be the offender!

The child's play is interrupted with the dolls, and the primary caretaker doll is picked up. Then I say to the child, "Here's the daddy. Does your daddy hug you?" I wait for the child to answer. If she says "yes," then I hold the daddy doll out toward her and say, "Show me how your daddy hugs you." Most 3-year-olds reach for the doll, pull it close, and hug it. Then I ask the child if her daddy kisses her. If she says "yes," I ask her to show me, on her body, where her daddy kisses her. I continue with this format to screen for "tickle" and "spank" with this first doll.

Private part touching is harder to demonstrate. I continue to hold the first doll while I ask the child if he has a _____(the name his caretaker has told me is used for genitals)? I ask him where his_____(name of private part) is, could he show me where that is. After he shows me, I ask, "Does your daddy (and I point to the daddy) tickle your (the name for genitals)?" In asking this question, I also point to the general area of the genitals." "Does your daddy (and I point to the daddy) hurt your (his name for genitals)?" Again I point to the general area of his genitals. (If sodomy is suspected, the child could also be asked for the name they call their bottom, and that name is presented).

I repeat this questioning for the other family member and the alleged perpetrator. Some children have very short attention spans, but usually they will cooperate with this format. Occasionally, I may have to shorten the Touch Survey to hugging, kissing, spanking and private parts, or other combinations that may be relevant for the case. Interviewing with 3-year-olds must be very flexible and it requires care and attention to be sure the child is on task with you. Cross-validation of information from behavioral repertoire, and so on is essential. Again, the constraints and concerns noted above in the information about interviewing 2- and 3-year-old children should be kept in mind during the process of this adapted interview.

This downward extension has also been used with children who have educational handicaps, causing lower ability and more concrete skill levels.

* * *

Exploring touch with children through the use of the Touch Survey does not guarantee that abuse will be uncovered or documented. This screening does, however, provide an informal, comfortable format from which trained assessors or mental health professionals can approach this important area.

8

When Abuse Is Not Proven: Managing High-Risk Cases

The law makes a black-and-white decision when someone has been accused of sexually abusing a young child. That person is either found guilty or not guilty. Many of the allegations of sexual abuse toward those in a preschool population, however, are classified as "don't know" or "not determined." (U.S. Department of Health and Human Services, The National Center for Child Abuse and Neglect [NCCAN], 1996, Thoennes & Tjaden, 1990). These cases contain varying degrees of gray, some showing minimal risk factors for future abuse and others having multiple indicators of a strong probability for new abuse. Concerns rise sharply when the rules of the justice system cannot prove that abuse has occurred and young children are abruptly ordered to

AUTHOR'S NOTE: Portions of this chapter were originally published in S. K. Hewitt (1991b), Therapeutic Management of Preschool Cases of Alleged But Unsubstantiated Sexual Abuse, *Child Welfare, 70*(1), 59-68. Used with permission.

resume prior levels of contact with an alleged abuser. Although it is not at the threshold to legally prove abuse, the originating evidence does not vanish with the court's decision. Neither are there fail-safe formulas available to protect young children as they enter potentially threatening situations. What can be done to allow the court-ordered contact while still protecting such children—those least able to protect themselves?

Little has been written about this topic, and most work on reunification (restoring contact between alleged abusers and children) after allegations deals with cases of *determined* abuse when both the offender and the victim are in therapy. Awad and McDonough (1991) detail a therapeutically managed case with sexual abuse allegations in a custody and visitation dispute. They argue that it is better to work with the parents and children over a period of time than to focus on getting convincing disclosures from children.

❑ Factors Affecting Reunification in Unsubstantiated Cases

When allegations are unsubstantiated, most often there are issues of reunification with a parent or other significant caretaker. These cases draw attention to three areas of concern: the risk that the alleged perpetrator may offend, the resistance of the custodial parent to reunification efforts, and the vulnerabilities of the child. Each of these areas will be reviewed before considering the idea of a structured, therapeutically moderated program for reunification that seeks to minimize the possibility of abuse while working to maximize safety factors for the child.

OFFENDER POTENTIAL FOR ABUSE

(Note: I am indebted to Mary Kenning, Ph.D. for contributing the following review of risk factors in sexual perpetrators.)

One of the most pressing questions for reunification is how likely is it that the alleged offender will repeat the allegedly abusive behavior. Nonoffending parents may be convinced that the alleged offender is at high risk to reoffend, but it is important to remember that not all offenders reoffend. This is not to minimize the need for assessment of risk but to place it in context.

There is agreement in the field of sex offender research that incest offenders reoffend (recidivate) at a lower rate than do other types of child molesters. One of the most rigorous studies to examine recidivism rates was conducted by Barbaree and Marshall (1988). The authors examined not only arrest records of 64 child molesters but also those of social service and others for any reports of sexual abuse that might not have been chargeable offenses. By applying this knowledge to new offenses, Marshall and Barbaree found recidivism rates of 32% and 14% for the untreated and treated group, respectively, over a 5-year period. These are group data and do not predict individual situations. This study does, however, give cause for hope that it is more unlikely than likely that the child who is reunifying will suffer further abuse. Obviously, the hope that a particular child is not at risk for reoffense is not sufficient. In the past 10 years, there have been significant advances in the field of sex offender research that allow better assessment of high-risk offenders. Recently, Quinsey, Lalumiere, Rice, and Harris (1995) noted that there now exist data from their studies and others to reliably demonstrate the variables related to recidivism. One way of predicting risk using quantitative data and formulas is called the *actuarial method.* It uses base rate information to calculate predictions, systematically maneuvering large amounts of data for precise outcomes. Quinsey's group has suggested that recent actuarial data can be used to anchor clinical judgments. Clinicians could start with an actuarial assessment of risk of recidivism and then alter it as necessary with additional clinical information. In this approach, actuarial information is key to the case, rather than just another piece of data in the evaluation process.

Several recent studies offer conclusions about those variables most likely to predict sexual recidivism. Quinsey, Rice, and Harris (1995) and Marshall (1994) both drew data from incarcerated sex offenders. They found several empirically derived factors reliably related to recidivism:

Past criminal offenses (both sexual and nonsexual)

Past violent offenses (including the immediate offense)

Number and age of current victims(s)

Younger versus older age

Unstable employment history

History of sexual victimization

Deviant sexual interests or arousal

Psychopathy (as measured by the Hare Psychopathy Checklist)

Unstable history of adult romantic relationships

Substance abuse

Lower intelligence

Refusal of admission for the current offense

In Washington state, decisions made by courts about sex offenders have led researchers to identify better community probation risks. Those who are older, married, employed, were not sexually abused themselves, have younger victims or a single victim, used no force in their offense, have no prior adult or juvenile criminal convictions, and admit the offense are shown to be at lowest risk. (Berliner, Schram, Miller, & Milloy, 1995).

Using these guidelines, those at lowest risk to reoffend would be those who

Had no prior criminal record

Had a single young child victim

Used no force in the offense

Had adequate romantic relationships or close friendships in the past or currently

Had no substance use problems

Had not been a sexual abuse victim themselves

Would be in their late 20s or older

Are not psychopathic

Are employed or have a stable employment history

Are of at least average intelligence

Show no deviant arousal patterns

Are among those who admit to their offense

Marques (1995) also found in her survey of sex offender recidivism, that offenders who were married, did not have a history of being physically abused as a child, or had been unemployed at the time of their offenses responded better to treatment.

It is clear that some risk factors are rather easily assessed and others more difficult to ascertain. Some of this information is static (i.e., unchangeable), whereas other predictors are more dynamic or open to intervention. Thus, a person's level of risk might change on the basis of the present situation and, at least in theory, on the basis of treatment or other intervention. In this way, actuarial information forms the basis for prediction of risk, but clinical information and methods contribute significantly to judgments about whether certain factors can be modified in a given case. For example, in a sexual offense, the gravity of a misdemeanor assault of a male peer 5 years ago does not have the same effect on predicting risk of recidivism as does a recent beating by the offender of the mother of his child victim. Knowing the circumstances surrounding either event could contribute important information about the person's potential to modify his sexually aggressive behavior.

Finally, it is important to carefully evaluate the issue of denial of the offense on the part of the alleged offender. In the past, denial of sexually aggressive behavior was considered a significant predictor of the risk of recidivism. No studies have validated this assumption, however. The Berliner et al. (1995) study showed that those who admitted their offenses were more likely to be given community probation than those who did not. Denial of the offense was associated with greater likelihood of committing another felony—but not a sex crime. In addition, being young, being single, having committed violent offenses, and having committed other offenses were also associated with general recidivism.

Other authors such as McGrath (1993) have suggested that denial indirectly increases the risk of reoffense because it usually prevents an alleged offender from entering sex offender treatment programs. There are well-documented higher risks of recidivism associated with lack of treatment. However, Schlank and Shaw (1996) as well as Barbaree (1991) have shown that it is possible to effectively treat many sex offenders who deny their crime. Kennedy and Grubin (1992), in their study of 102 incarcerated sex offenders, found that men who denied their offenses at the outset of treatment had lower recidivism rates than did men who admitted but rationalized their molesting behavior. Some sex offender researchers (Rogers & Dickey, 1991) have concluded that denial itself does not make an offender "bad" and note that it probably represents an attempt to cope with a highly adversarial situation with far-reaching, life-changing consequences. These authors point out that not even supposedly normal adults in a community sample are willing to disclose all their sexual experiences, even when there are no consequences for doing so (Snell, Belk, Papini, & Clark, 1989). None of this information is meant to excuse or justify the behavior of the allegedly offending parent. Instead, it provides a way to anchor clinical decision making and must be used in combination with data from observation of the alleged offender and the child to help determine the specific individual risk factors present. Nonoffending parents can be provided with this information as a way to help reassure them without dismissing or negating their information about the situation.

Many of the above studies were conducted with convicted or incarcerated sex offenders. Clinical experience has found that often, alleged perpetrators in the therapeutic management cases present a "milder" profile than the incarcerated offenders. The former may have a history of sexual harassment allegations, or "bad boundaries" (e.g., walking around the house with their bathrobe open to expose their genitals, wearing baggy boxer shorts so that when they sit down they expose their genitals to others), an insensitivity or disregard for other persons' feelings and preferences, difficulty with empathy or role taking, a history of stalking or threatening, a history of poorly controlled anger or acts of revenge, and, at times, an ongoing problem of alcohol or chemical abuse. It is difficult to conduct research on a group of alleged offenders as, having been convicted of no crime, they are reluctant to participate in any research, and their histories are rarely researched. Therefore, the factors that are active in the convicted offender population are the best information we have to help assess the risks associated with reoffending.

CUSTODIAL PARENT'S RESISTANCE

In cases in which there is animosity between divorcing parents and where allegations of abuse surface, the tension between parents can be intense. The custodial parent may become very resistant to any form of contact between the child and former spouse. His or her actions may stem from intimate knowledge of the alleged perpetrator and the fear of his or her actions, especially if there has been a history of domestic violence or drug abuse. These actions may also be fueled by fears from one's own unresolved abuse history, intense dislike of, and anger at, the former spouse, or improper questioning that has resulted in allegations that cannot be substantiated. Despite thorough investigation, the custodial spouse may still maintain an unshakable belief that a child was abused.

These cases are also ripe for false allegations. Richard Gardner first wrote about visitation interference after divorce, which involved an attempt by one parent to alienate a child or children from another parent. He called this dynamic the Parental Alienation Syndrome (PAS; Gardner, 1985). The alienation may be the result of subtle or covert acts (not telling a child the other parent has called) or more direct influence (leading the child to believe the other parent is a drug abuser, unfaithful, violent, etc.). Myers (1997) writes about the PAS:

> Gardner's parental alienation syndrome has not, to my knowledge, been subjected to empirical study, research, or testing. . . . It's clear that the syndrome is not accepted as a scientifically reliable way of telling whether an allegation of sexual abuse is true or false. Moreover, in my opinion, much of Gardner's writing, including his discussion of his parental alienation syndrome, is biased against women. . . . In the final analysis, parental alienation syndrome is little more than a scientific-sounding label for conduct that judges and lawyers have known about for years. . . . The wiser course would be to discard the syndrome and confront unethical behavior head on. (pp. 136-137)

Divorce and custody literature has considered the issue of parental tension manifesting itself in allegations of sexual abuse (Cartwright, 1993; Dunne & Hedrick, 1994; Palmer, 1988). It notes that alleging sexual abuse by a visiting parent usually leads to a cessation of visitation as the allegations are investigated. Then, if the allegations are not substantiated, resumption of visitation between the child and the estranged parent requires careful guidance. They also note that resistance from the child, fostered by subtle or more overt messages from the custodial parent, can interfere with the child's ability to develop a relationship with the other parent.

CHILD RISK FACTORS

Little research exists about the risk factors young children have for abuse in a reunification setting. Most risk factors for children are embedded in their families and their surroundings (see DePanfilis, Daro, & Wells, 1995, for a special issue of *The APSAC Advisor*, which provides an excellent review of the risk assessment process). Clinical experience with therapeutic management has shown that children who are verbal, assertive, clear about appropriate boundaries, have no prior history of sexual abuse, are knowledgable about body part identification, have a history of appropriate and reliable nurturing, and have a caretaker with whom they can freely share information are at less risk for abuse.

High-risk young children are more associated with passive, dependent, verbally limited, isolated children who have a history of poor caretaking (which results in a level of need for human contact without regard for its quality), have poor information about body boundaries and rules for touching, have a history of prior sexual abuse, do not have labels for their body parts, and do not have a primary caretaker with whom they can freely share information.

Is there a way for court-ordered reunification cases to be handled that balances the child's needs for safety, the rights of a parent to have contact with the child, and the fears or anger of a custodial parent?

None of the literature reviewed above provides a step-by-step, preschool-focused procedure for reunification after unsubstantiated allegations of abuse. In 1991, an article I wrote, "Therapeutic Management of High Risk Cases of Alleged but Unfounded Preschool Sexual Abuse," was published in the *Journal of Child Welfare*. This article has received some attention for its provision of an alternative that transitions children into visits with an accused offender. The protocol attempts to minimize conditions that would allow for future abuse as it also promotes the safety of the child. Five years have passed since the publication of that article and continued clinical use of the protocol has revealed additional information. This chapter will outline a revised version of the earlier reunification protocol, followed by a discussion of the various issues that arise in applying the procedure.

This chapter is, more than others, about my role in controlling risks and promoting the safety of a child while juggling tensions among the adults as I push a process along. This is a more authoritarian position and the language and tone of the chapter will reflect my change of role.

❏ **Therapeutic Management of Reunification in Preschool Cases**

BEFORE YOU SEE THE CASE

Therapeutic management cases need to be court ordered. Both sides of the dispute must agree that they will allow one person to direct the process. Often, attorneys will encourage their clients to participate, seeing this process as one way to work toward a level of contact even when parties are antagonistic. Without joint agreement, it is difficult to use this protocol, and parties must seek other legal solutions. The specific act of court ordering also lends immunity to the therapist, as they are acting as an agent of the court and protected from undue interference with their duties (see Myers, in press, for a more thorough discussion of immunity issues). Immunity helps protect me when I need the authority and flexibility to act in a manner that, at some time or another in the process, will be disagreeable to each parent. Immunity will not, however, protect against bad practice. Regularly staffing these cases with reliable professionals helps support the grounds for actions taken.

All file materials and documents connected with the case should be reviewed before beginning the management process. It is important to know the risks and concerns that have brought the case into court. This knowledge can help you know what may be most threatening for the child.

THE PROCESS

Meet With the Nonoffending Parent

This meeting has several important components.

1. The process of therapeutic management is reviewed and any questions are answered.
2. A relationship with the parent is begun. The parent will need support going through this process, and the initial meeting addresses this.

3. Because the therapist's actions in the case will at times conflict with the custodial parents' wishes, it is important for the parent to know that he or she has good support built in. If not, parental anxiety and fear about the process can readily transfer to the child, and the work of reunification will generate yet another stress on the child. I often refer the parent for therapy in the following way: "You know, _____ , I think that this court-ordered reunification must be very difficult for you. I know that you worry about your child and that you fear for his/her safety. I cannot imagine a position more difficult than having to turn my child over for visitation with a man (woman) who is frightening to me. I think it is important for you to get some support to help you through this. For this reason, I want you to be in therapy, not because I think you are crazy or weird but because you need your own place for support. You know that I am under court order to work on reunification between your child and your ex-husband (-wife), and I will do that the best I can, but my primary concern will be with your child and his/her safety. I will not be on your side or your ex-husband's (-wife's) side. I know from experience there will be times I will push ahead when you don't agree and other times when you might not like my recommendations. It is important that you have a place, just for you, to talk about what this is like for you. Do you need help with a referral?"

When a nonoffending parent's anxiety is discussed openly and solution-oriented problem solving is facilitated, the caretaker's anxiety and fear are less likely to be transferred to the child. Therapy work can also help the nonoffending parent to separate personal issues from the child's needs, especially if the issues stem from a personal background of sexual abuse, whether that is fully disclosed or not. (Remember the research cited above that found the maternal history of child sexual abuse related to probable abuse in a group of 2-year-olds?) There are some cases in which the custodial parent refuses to be in therapy, despite the fact that their own issues are creating problems. This is when it is important to be court ordered. On occasion, I have written to the judge and asked to have the parent ordered to be in therapy or I cannot proceed to fulfill the order of the court. In some cases, when a background of abuse has been suspected but always denied, the therapy referral has been one of the most significant interventions in facilitating case progress.

In addition to relationship building, an ability to work with the caretaker is important to allow access to the child. Preschool children's natural dependency on adults requires that they maintain a relationship with their primary caretaker. The custodial parent therefore becomes an essential component of any therapeutic work that is to be done with the child.

4. A good history for the child is taken. This interview explores developmental background, the child's experiences, the history of the allegations, and the child's current status.

5. The meeting reframes the custodial parent's role because the parent is specifically removed from the investigative procedure. I talk to the parent like this: "_____, I know you have made (x number) of reports to child protection with your concerns about your son/daughter. The court has looked at all of them, it has not substantiated them, and now visitation is ordered. If you report another allegation, how much credibility do you think the report will have? The focus here is the safety of your child. I need to remove you from the job of investigator and reporter. Your job is now to focus on being (the child's) parent. If you suspect problems or abuse in the visits, I want you to report them to me immediately. I will follow up. You are to no longer investigate the statements your child may make that could indicate abuse; rather, you are to only listen carefully to these concerns, thank your child for telling you, write the statements or actions down, and call me (or the child protection worker on the case, depending on what works best). If your child complains of soreness or there is any blood following a visitation, then you are to take the child directly to (specify an emergency room that is trained and equipped to handle child abuse reports). Are you clear about your new job? Do you understand why I need to do this?"

I often practice "active listening" (Gordon, 1975, pp. 49-61) with parents so they know how to listen without investigating. Active listening refers to a process of listening in which the listener accepts and reflects what the speaker says, they do not enter their own thoughts or feelings into the interchange. This is a difficult position for custodial parents, and also a measure of their ability to separate their own issues from those of the child.

6. Create a list of the kinds of touching that you feel are OK, that you like, with your child and touching that is not OK, or touching that you don't like.

The work described in this chapter often takes more than one session to complete. The order of work in a session may also change, depending on the issues of the various participants. The work should, however, follow the basic topic flow across the various participants.

Meet With the Child

This meeting, too, has multiple components.

1. The child is informed about the therapeutic process and the therapist's role to be present during the visits and to help create safety rules. The child's safety is the focus in this process.

2. The child is also told that there will be no more inquiry about abuse and who did what. The focus will now be on what kind of touching the child

likes—and doesn't like—with the other parent, what rules are needed for the meetings, and what things the child wants to do in the visits.

3. A relationship is developed with the child.

4. After sufficient rapport has been established, the child is encouraged to create a list of the kinds of touching he or she likes and doesn't like with the custodial parent as well as the noncustodial parent. When I am doing this with 3- or 4-year-olds (I do not use it for children any younger than this), I structure the inquiry about the kinds of touches they like (e.g., do you like to be hugged, tickled, etc.), and I write them down for these younger children as well as the older children who cannot yet write.

Meet With the Custodial Parent and Child

1. At this meeting, the relationship between the nonoffending parent and child can be observed, and attempts to enhance the bond and relationship between them can be identified.

2. The custodial parent is encouraged to offer the support to the child in proceeding with these visitations, indicating that the parent is not mad at the child for going on visits, still loves the child, and the child has the parent's support to go forward in the reunification. Often this is a difficult piece for the custodial parent to offer the child, but with therapeutic work the parent can come to a more acute recognition that the child has no choice but to participate and that one of the strongest roles the parent can adopt is to provide permission and support for the child.

3. When some parents cannot give this permission without feeling as if they are lying, some have told their child that although they are no longer friends with the other parent and they do not want to see him or her, they know the child has to see the other parent. They have also worked hard to help keep the visits as safe as they can be. They have their own person to talk to about their feelings and the child should go ahead with the visits.

4. In addition to discussing the upcoming visitation, the custodial parent and child are encouraged to share their lists of touch with one another. This sharing and signing off on an agreement of touch between them can act as a practice session for the same process with the alleged offender.

Meet With the Alleged Abuser

1. The process of therapeutic management is explained and questions answered.

2. It is important to hear the alleged abuser's version of the allegations, his or her history, and the concerns he or she has for the forthcoming process. Explore the feelings about his or her child and the allegations

made, especially deal with any anger they might have toward the child's part in the allegations.

3. In addition, the alleged abuser can be referred for therapy to help deal with anxiety or individual concerns about the process. Experience has shown, however, few follow up on this referral; most are interested only in rapid reunification.

4. The alleged abuser is then asked to draft a list of the touching that is OK and not OK with the child. This kind of touching is reviewed for its appropriateness and is then compared with the lists the child has made. Discrepancies between the two lists are discussed.

5. The alleged offender is asked to sign off on the child's preferred touching list as a way of indicating his or her approval of the child's choices.

6. A plan is made for the upcoming meeting. Arrival and departure times are both carefully scripted so there is no chance of an unscheduled meeting in the parking lot, hallway, or elevator. I ask the custodial parent and child to come 10 minutes before the appointment time and wait in my waiting room. When I am free, I move them to my office where they wait until the other parent arrives. I ask the noncustodial parent to arrive 10 minutes after the time of the appointment and come to my waiting room. I then have the custodial parent leave the child in my room and wait in a separate room away from the other parent's view. I move the reunifying parent to my office and remain with them and the child for the entire session. The custodial parent may wait in the waiting room or return at 10 minutes before the end of the hour. At the end of the session, I transition the child to the custodial parent who is instructed to leave the premises while I spend the last 10 minutes debriefing with the reunifying parent. (I am very clear to all parties that any violation of this time schedule will result in my reporting a lack of cooperation to the court.)

The reunifying parent is told that the allegations will be openly discussed at the meeting with the child, that they will be asked to tell the child that they are not angry with them and they do not hold them responsible for the allegations. Most reunifying parents are willing to do this without any problems, but if there are difficulties with this, it is an important issue to process.

The parent is also told that he or she will be asked to share the touch lists he or she has made and later he or she will be in charge of telling the child the rules for improper sexual touch and of letting the child know that no one should do such touching.

Most parents who have not had contact with their children for a long time want to bring presents to these first sessions. It is important that the sessions focus on the work that is to be done here and not on delayed holidays. Explain that gifts can wait for future meetings—they are not allowed until the work is done—and that they can be planned as part of the future process.

The parent should be directed to not ask for any physical contact, nor take a position to prompt such contact (i.e., kneeling on the floor with arms open). The parent is to follow the child's cues and respond only as the child directs.

Meet With the Child to Prepare for the Visit

1. The child is informed when the visit will take place and is enlisted to help set the rules for the meeting and to plan the session events. Actively involving the child in planning the meeting helps him or her feel a sense of empowerment and some control over what may be a frightening situation.

2. The child's rules for the meeting often range beyond rules for touch. Frequently, he or she will specify no yelling, no hitting, and no fighting as the most important rules. I agree to tell the visiting parent these rules before the visit. For some children, I take the list of meeting rules they want and have the alleged offender sign this list to indicate his/her cooperation with the rules.

3. Especially important to script as rules for the meeting are the kinds of touching that happen at the beginning and ending of the meeting. Does the child want to say hello with just words, or a handshake, or a hug? How does the child want to say goodbye? Next the child can help plan the activities of the meeting (e.g., play a game, have a snack, build with blocks). Often these sessions are coming after a substantial break in the child-parent contact and reunification behavior is important to specify.

4. The child and therapist should go over the two lists of touching that the alleged offender created and discuss these lists. They should also review the alleged offender's approval of his or her own list.

5. Occasionally, new, or clearer, allegations of abuse surface during this meeting. These may be prompted by the proximity of the visit or by the support the child has been given. Report all new allegations and await determination of whether the sessions should go forward.

HOLD THE INITIAL MEETING BETWEEN THE CHILD AND ALLEGED OFFENDER

1. After a carefully scripted arrival, the initial meeting should proceed with an announcement of the rules for the meeting by the therapist and encouragement for the child to go ahead with the planned activities. Often the alleged abuser and the child need time for reacquaintance.

2. After a comfort level has been established, the work of the session begins. The alleged offender should at this time tell the child they are not angry with him or her for the allegations, the alleged offender is interested in working with the child, and there will be no retribution for the allegations. Often children are afraid the alleged offender will be mad, so careful discussion and monitoring of this behavior is important.

   The child and the alleged offender review the lists of touches they have both created, and cooperate in creating a list of touching that is OK and not OK. This will form the rules for any future touching between the two of them.

   This next part of the procedure is very important. The alleged abuser should take the lead in explaining to the child what is OK and not OK touching and that no one should touch them inappropriately. The alleged abuser should also say to the child that it is wrong to tell a child to not talk about touching people. No one should do that and if someone ever does, the child should tell a grown-up he or she can trust. If needed, the alleged perpetrator can tell the child that he or she would not be mad at the child if the child were to discuss any inappropriate touching with a trusted grown-up. This "double bind" for the alleged offender helps undermine any attempts at touching that are inappropriate, and it also undermines the secrecy that can be part of sexual abuse.

   Both the child and the alleged abuser should sign off on the joint list of rules that they have made. This formalizes an agreement that these rules are understood and will be followed.

3. Carefully watch the end of the meeting, because some children will disregard the initial rule they set for no touching and spontaneously hug the parent. Sometimes the hug is clearly child generated, but other times it is prompted by the parent. Sometimes the hugging happens so quickly it is hard to stop. In any case, the change in the rules should be discussed, and further changes should be decided in advance, not spontaneously altered.

Follow Up With the Child

1. Ask the custodial parent to carefully document any behavior problem of the child (both overt problems or internalized problems, such as sleep or eating problems, increased anxiety or depression) both before and after the meeting with the alleged offender. Check in with the custodial parent about his or her feelings and concerns.

2. Meet with the child to discuss his or her perceptions. Discuss what the child liked and did not like. Some children are capable of tolerating follow-up sessions rather quickly, whereas other children may begin to develop problems in the face of contact. Future meetings are paced to the child's ability to tolerate the contact and to the reunifying parent's ability to follow rules and behave appropriately.

There are many pathways a case might take after this structured, formal part of the protocol. After this point, each case determines its own path.

❏ After the Structured Sessions Have Been Completed

Therapeutic management is not a guarantee that future abuse won't occur, nor is it a magic cure for difficult cases. It is a structured approach to reunification that helps preserve the child's limits and power, and attempts to minimize future forms of abuse. Ongoing work with the cases can take many forms.

MOVE DIRECTLY TO REUNIFICATION

An alleged abuser and child may quickly and comfortably re-create a relationship, and the issue of boundaries and possible abuse are discussed openly and freely. A good relationship appears to be in the making. In this case, with support of the custodial parent, reunification can often be accomplished within 6 weeks to 3 months. It may be necessary to pace out some visitation, but if the noncustodial parent is seen to have safe behavior with the child, is responsive to the child's limits, encouraging of the child's autonomy, and supportive of the child's preferences, then the contact that was initially in place is reinstated. Follow up to monitor the child's status and safety.

Transition the Contact to a Supervised Setting

When parent-child problems are noted in the structured sessions and the parent does not respond to suggestions or interventions and the child is responding well to the contact, then alternatives other than resumption of unsupervised contact must be considered. One option that has proven useful is to move the case to a supervised visitation center such as the Children's Safety Centers Network, Inc., created in St. Paul, Minnesota (Cardelli, 1996). The Centers were created to provide a safe, supervised environment for high-risk or problematic visitation cases between parents and their children. The Centers are staffed by volunteer personnel who are trained and supervised by professionals. These observers are always with the child and parent and they chart their observations. Most visits are between one and two hours, once a week. The Centers charge for their services, and most cases are court ordered. The Centers require that the visiting parent sign an agreement for rules of conduct during the session and for leaving and pick-up procedures. The staff will intervene if inappropriate behavior is observed, and they have the authority to stop a session if necessary. Staff notes can be used as important feedback for therapeutic work or for court documentation of problems. If visitation needs to be halted, the Center's notes provide documentation of the problems which precipitated the suspension. The Safety Center does no therapy and no intervention, but it does provide a safe and secure environment for parents to meet and play with their children.

When a parent is unwilling to work on a relationship in additional therapy and problems continue to be noticed in the parent-child relationship, the case reunification may go no farther than visits within the supervised context of the Safety Centers. If problems persist, the Center's documentation is used to create a letter to the court indicating that reunification is not proceeding well. The court-ordered reunification may then change to infrequent visitation or a suspension of visits until the parent has completed the necessary changes.

When a parent agrees to work in therapy in conjunction with the Safety Center visits or in place of such visits, the therapist, working with a parent and child, can deal with some of the problems in the relationship. This may involve basic child development understanding, management procedures, communication, or boundaries.

A case that demonstrates this step is as follows: A young father, who had been accused of molesting his 2-year-old daughter, was referred for therapeutic management. In the initial sessions, the child had difficulty creating a list of touches, but I could get a list from the father and an agreement about touching rules. When meetings started, his daughter was avoidant of him because he was a stranger, but as time progressed and he was no longer a stranger, she still continued to be avoidant. The reasons for her avoidance were clear. He was very controlling with her and continually intruded on her play. He brought items that were developmentally inappropriate for her interests, and he did not respect her needs for autonomy and her own exploration. With work, this young father was able to understand his child's developmental level and see her as a separate individual who had needs for autonomy. He learned to follow, enrich, and expand her play (instead of control it). He also began to bring more appropriate toys to the sessions. As the father's skills improved, the child became friendly and sought more proximity. Eventually, she spontaneously came into the circle of her father's arm and leaned against him as she shared her toys with him. The father was ecstatic about the child's change, but he also recognized he had begun to see her in a different way. This father and daughter were transitioned out of therapy into outside visitations. The father's ex-wife stated that one of the reasons she left him was his control and domination of her, the same qualities she had seen in his interactions with their child, and she wanted to protect her daughter from this negative influence.

A videotape is often helpful in capturing behaviors that are problematic. Videotaping offers concrete examples of problematic interactions, and work with the reunifying parent on these behaviors is helpful. Parents can also be referred to parenting classes or early childhood family education work, but the younger the child, the more the focus is on the relationship. Simple parenting classes are not enough to change this essential shared element.

The above case portrays a therapist who manages and also does intervention. Not all cases will allow this dual role. Therapeutic management cases often come to the therapist who has been working with the child in ongoing therapy. There is a dilemma in this, however; therapeutic management proceeds at the directive of the court. Therapy proceeds at the directive of the child. These cases frequently create a conflict between the child's need to have his or her own individual timing and the timing of a court-ordered process. Over time, I have decided that therapeutic management is usually best done by a therapist who is not the child's individual therapist. The child keeps a therapist for his or her own support, and this therapist can help inform the reunifying therapist about the child's individual progress and needs. The reunifying therapist can share information about the child's reactions in the reunification sessions. This role separation keeps the child's therapist out of the position of recommending visitation schedules or changes, and allows him or her to freely work between the parents for the child's interests.

Progress to Visitation Outside
Supervised Sessions

If visits between the parent and child seem healthy and the contract has been followed, steps toward moving visitation outside the specific therapy session can be initiated. These can be visits to a park or to

McDonald's where the therapist accompanies the parent and child and observes their interaction in a more informal situation. If these visits go well, the next step may be to have visits supervised by another party that is jointly agreed to by both parents. Occasionally, a guardian *ad litem* may choose to supervise visitation.

It is essential that any external supervisor be informed of the issues involved in the allegations and be informed about the contract for touching that the parent and child have. Helpful guidelines for supervision of visits between parents and children have been organized by Toni C. Johnson (1997). These guidelines are not only for the supervisor but also for the alleged offender and the custodial parent. A simpler, shorter list is shared with the child as well so he or she understands what is to happen. Including the child is often overlooked, but it is very important for the child to be aware of the boundaries that are set and to feel a part of the process that sets and maintains the rules.

Follow-up contact after these outside supervised visits involves obtaining feedback from the outside supervisor plus an office visit with the child alone or the parent and child together. The therapist can discuss any issues or problems that have occurred during the visitation. If the visits continue to go well, then unsupervised visitation for a set period of time between the parent and child can be initiated. A therapy appointment at the end of the beginning unsupervised visits allows a chance for monitoring and, if needed, intervention for any problems that arise. As the case progresses, the visits can be followed-up on a more informal and less frequent basis. If visitation continues to go well, unsupervised visitations are set in place and follow-up is as needed.

SUSPENDING THE VISITATION

When the Reunifying Parent Is Uncooperative

There are some cases in which the therapeutic management process cannot move forward. For example, a parent may refuse to give the child the rules about inappropriate touching; a parent may be unable or unwilling to abide by the boundaries that are set regarding touch initiation; a parent may have trouble controlling his or her anger at the monitoring therapist or the child during the course of visitation; a parent may threaten or endanger the safety of the therapist, the visitation supervisor, or the child; and so on. At this point the therapist can inform the court that, because of violations of the therapeutic management contract, visitation is unable to go forward. The reunifying parent can be referred for additional evaluation (if that has not already been done in the course of the case) or individual therapy. The court must specify any changes required from the reunifying parent before visits can resume. The original court order for reunification may remain in place during this process because the process of reunification is not stopped but only suspended until sufficient changes have taken place. When these changes have been effectively made, then visits move forward again.

After conducting reunification cases for 15 years, I have come to appreciate the power of controlled, well-supervised visitation sessions in dealing with the problems children face in the aftermath of unproven abuse allegations. A parent may truly be a threatening and potentially damaging person in a child's life, but when the child has some form of controlled contact (perhaps as infrequently as once a year or not until the child is 7 or 8 years old), this child has the opportunity to see that the safety net around him or her can control and protect. Brief contact, even with a damaged parent, can help ground the myth or fantasy that may exist when a young child's last contact has been with a frightening parent. As the child gets older, controlled contact allows for a more mature appraisal of the reality of the parent's status. Nonetheless, not all case reunification is healthy for children. Cases which cannot be controlled and are not respectful of rules or reliable in following them (especially if visits bring threats of violence, evoke old trauma, or reinforce old censures) are not safe for children. The failure of a procedure to reunify can act as a document that supports the ongoing cessation of contact.

When the Child Develops Problems

Visits may be suspended for reasons other than problems with the reunifying parent; the child may become very upset and be unable to tolerate visits. Some children are afraid of visits at first and then they warm up, but there are other children who become even more frightened after visitation. Sleep disturbance, behavioral regression, withdrawal, aggression, or other forms of behavior problems are of concern. When this happens, the child should be seen for individual evaluation and therapy. The child may work for a period of time until the source of the anxiety can be more fully determined.

When the Custodial Parent Has Problems
That Interfere With the Reunification Process

Some custodial parents become hypervigilant about any sexualized behaviors their child might be displaying. Experience has shown that many such parents have their own undisclosed abuse histories and fears carried over from their own unprotected abuse. These "ghosts" can be significant factors in the child's reunification program. When the custodial parent's anxiety spills over to the child, or causes the child to be unable to move forward and create a relationship with the alleged offending parent, the court may need to order that parent into therapy.

If a child shows a history of warming up to the alleged offender during supervised sessions but returns to each subsequent appointment in a very regressed or fearful state and there is no explanation for the change, then the actions of the custodial caretaker need to be assessed. A child may pick up the anger of a primary parent and not reattach to the other parent, even though the child may want to. Betraying the loyalty of the primary caretaker is sometimes too costly for a dependent child.

In other cases, the custodial parent's belief that something sexual has happened results in repeated leading and suggestive questioning of the child. Biased questioning can lead the parent to false conclusions. When a parent strongly believes in the existence of abuse, they are frightened and angry at the reunification process. They attempt to subtly sabotage the process, feeling that their concerns protect the best interest of the child. This scenario has been common in therapeutic management cases.

Finally, either the more overt effort to negatively bias the child (deliberately telling the child negative things about the visiting parent, or denigrating them to others in the child's presence), or the more subtle effort (talking negatively about the visiting parent on the phone while the child can listen, or refusing to acknowledge any positive aspects of the other parent's caretaking or affection for the child) can interfere with the reunification process. This alienation process (discussed earlier) is important to address.

In cases in which it appears that one parent's issues are interfering with the process of court-ordered reunification, full psychological evaluation of *both* parents is recommended. Understanding the dynamics of the accused parent as well as the custodial parent creates a more balanced picture. In some cases, the ability of the custodial parent to fully caretake the child has to be reconsidered, and the issue of custody may need to be reassigned.

❏ Analyzing Risk Factors in Projecting Reunification Outcome

Each child and each alleged offender bring to a case both strengths and weaknesses. By looking at these factors and considering all risk factors for abuse, the therapist begins to assess case vulnerability.

LOW-RISK PARENTS

Low-risk parents most often are

Fully cooperative
Respectful
Able to put the child's needs first
Aware of the child's reactions and emotional needs
Capable of empathy
Accepting of responsibility for their own behavior
Not controlling and dictatorial of the child
Able to wait for the child to lead
Aware of and respectful toward the touch rules that have been agreed to

HIGH-RISK PARENTS

On the other hand, high-risk parents most often

Minimize or deny their own involvement in the child's allegation
Project anger onto others
Accept no responsibility for their own behavior
Are domineering, insensitive, impulsive, explosive, angry, or demeaning

Display no empathy

Have an inability to give up a narcissistic focus

Have a history of antisocial behavior

Have an uncontrolled chemical dependency status

Consistently display poor boundaries relative to feelings or touch with the child

Have sexualized interactions with the child although no sexual abuse is seen specifically

Argue and are unable to control anger

Often create difficult situations with the therapeutic manager in the child's presence

Such cases are in need of intervention beyond therapeutic management. Careful documentation of the problems encountered in the therapeutic management process can stop visitation with a vulnerable child until such time as the alleged abuser has demonstrated significant change or the child is better able to protect him or herself.

LOW-RISK CHILDREN

A low-risk child is an older child who

Is clear about his or her own boundaries and capable of stating them

Has sufficient ability to verbalize

Is capable of recognizing problems and talking about them

Is assertive and confident in voicing his or her own views and concerns despite some adult opposition

HIGH-RISK CHILDREN

A high-risk child is a younger child, or an older child who is

Passive

Dependent

Withdrawn

Anxious

Fearful

Powerless

Unable to articulate concerns

Unable to recognize problem behavior, much less report it

You must remember these lists have been drawn from clinical experience; they are not the product of factor analysis coming from research. They may be modified pending the outcome of research.

Various cases of therapeutic management have involved different combinations of the above factors, and there is no one specific course that can be applied. This process seeks to maximize the safety of the child in reunification and it has a clear progression toward that end. Not all cases can be successfully reunited, however, and this protocol acknowledges the various problems in reunification. It also recognizes that some cases may fail, and that there is a provision for stopping the process when there is verification of a lack of cooperation, a refusal to remediate problems, or clear, destructive effects for the child to continue the process.

❏ Other Uses of Therapeutic Management

Therapeutic management has been used with parents who are contemplating divorce but have a concern for potential abuse by one parent or the other. Explicit discussion and documentation of forms of touch that are agreed to in contracts signed by the child and each of the parents can help minimize a parent's anxiety about the upcoming unsupervised contact between an ex-spouse and the child as well as provide clear boundaries for the child. There is a need for additional research and follow-up to establish the best protocol for this context.

Therapeutic management can also be applied when abuse has been proven and, after individual therapy, a parent and child are being reunified. In this case, an important precondition for the protocol is the offender's acknowledgment of the abuse to the child, his or her apology, and his or her acceptance of the responsibility for the abuse. The alleged offender must be willing to hear the child's comments, concerns, and feelings about his or her abuse experience. The alleged offender must also inform the child of the nature of the abuse problem, the kind of help the parent has received, and specific trigger situations that are to be avoided to help ensure that abuse does not recur. Another important precondition here is that both the child and the offender have done their work in individual therapy before the reunification piece is attempted. Again, additional research with this application of the protocol is needed.

❏ Commonly Asked Questions About Therapeutic Management

HOW LONG DOES IT TAKE?

This depends on the case. I have had some cases complete the process safely within 6 weeks to 3 months and there have been no new allegations of abuse. Most often these cases have had low-risk reunifying parents and low-risk children. On the other hand, cases with very young children and especially disturbing allegations have needed supervision for 3 or 4 years. This does not mean that I see the cases weekly. They often move to Safety Center visitation, or sometimes to supervised visitation with relatives, but I still monitor and check in with the child periodically. By about 7 or 8 years of age, I have had some children tell me, "I think it's OK to visit my dad at his place now. I know what he's not supposed to do, and I can tell people if he does anything that's not OK." Children have a better ability to report on problems if they have support, although they are still not old enough to be responsible for their own protection. Generally, the long-term cases involve both high-risk reunifying parents and high-risk children.

WHO PAYS FOR THIS?

Most of the parent-child sessions are paid for by insurance or medical assistance and viewed as family or joint therapy. Be careful not to assume that because the case is court ordered, the court will pay for the work!

❏ Issues Raised in the Process of Therapeutic Management

The task of reunification after abuse allegations raises several serious questions about the ethics of reunification.

CHILDREN'S RIGHTS OR ADULTS' RIGHTS?

At what point does a child's right to a peaceful and secure childhood have precedence over an adult's rights to have continued contact with the child? What level of psychopathology is a parent allowed before it is considered damaging to the child? When does the burden of contact outweigh the benefits? Is there a point at which the child can be granted release from an ongoing disruptive and stressful relationship?

Both a parent's degree of danger and the child's ability to tolerate the contact determine what is safe. When there is an inability to abide by the contract, or the child appears to suffer reactions that impede development, therapeutic management and visitation may be suspended or referred back to the court for formal cessation.

Children of different ages show different reactions to the stresses of reunification, but when these reactions threaten the child's ability to develop appropriately, the contact must be reevaluated. For example, a very young child who returns from 1-hour visits and who experiences repeated sleep disturbance; regresses in speech or language, toileting, or socialized behaviors; and is clingy and develops problems in separation from the caretaker, is indicating an inability to handle the contact. Careful analysis of the primary parent's role in caretaking the child and screening for any problematic care, plus behavioral charting of the child's reactions to the contact, can be helpful in sorting out elements in the child's disturbed response.

Orders for reunification that allow the therapist to develop timetables around the child's needs and the alleged offending parent's ability to respond appropriately provide maximum flexibility in protecting the child. Sometimes difficult visitations can be managed by spreading out the length between contacts; this can allow both parties to regroup and recuperate.

Because early years are so critical for later development, it is essential that they be guarded and that the child be allowed to develop a strong foundation of healthy emotional development. Research needs to be done regarding the costs and benefits of pursuing a high-risk reunification on the long-term adjustment of the child. Additional research is also needed to look at the effects on children who are involved in a therapeutic management process versus those children who are simply court ordered into visitation without any transitioning.

WHEN THINGS GO WRONG

If reunification is court ordered, what happens when things go wrong (e.g., the alleged offender refuses to cooperate, the child shows signs of increasing dysfunction). Can visitation be changed or stopped if it is court ordered?

Suspending contact until a child can regroup or an alleged abuser has changed problematic behavior does not have to be seen as disregard of the court order for visitation. An order can still stand and be addressed at a later time when the child is less vulnerable or the parent less problematic, and both are more able to tolerate a renewal of the reunification process.

Cases may need to return to court to be heard again if they are to be halted or suspended for a significant period of time. Careful documentation of the process in the case, and good behavioral logging of the interactions noted between the child and parent, as well as the child's reactions after the contact, can be important information for the court in deciding whether to grant a formal suspension of visitation.

CAN TREATMENT BE ORDERED?

Can we force a nonoffending parent into treatment if his or her behavior is inappropriate? A nonoffending parent who has not been convicted of abuse has a right to refuse treatment. However, if their behavior appears to be significantly deviant in the course of this reunification process, then a petition can be made to the court for the alleged offending parent to enter a treatment program that deals with offender dynamics. Many adult treatment programs for sex offenders now offer services to "deniers." This may involve education and small group work, but it does not require admission of guilt. Issues that present themselves in the supervised visitation can then be addressed and additional visitation made contingent on the capacity of the nonoffending parent to bring behavior into alignment with the touch contracts.

WHEN THE CHILD REFUSES

If an older child does not want to continue with visitations, whose rights have precedence?

Again, a helpful guide to keep in mind is the child's ability to cope with the visits, the custodial parent's ability to allow the child to participate in visitation, and the alleged offender's ability to function in a healthy and appropriate way with the child. This intervention format will not make a child love someone, but it will allow a child and a parent to have contact and work on their relationship to the limits of their abilities.

WILL THIS PROCEDURE GUARANTEE A CHILD'S SAFETY?

No. There is no guarantee that the behaviors and practices initiated in the supervised settings will transfer into unsupervised visitation time. There is no guarantee that this procedure will prevent future abuse. Limited research has shown promise, but much more needs to be done. It is my hope that this procedure addresses the underlying issues that promote abuse (i.e., secrecy, no knowledge of the rules about touch, lack of a reporting resource, poor relationships with the nonoffending parent, manipulation of the nonoffending parents). When the alleged offending parent is double-binded by giving the child the rules for safe behavior and the child is encouraged to talk about any violations, the child will likely display unusual behaviors or concerns to indicate if abuse has been reinstated. There is, however, no guarantee that this procedure will fully protect the child.

❏ Research on Therapeutic Management

Only limited, clinically based follow-up has been done to date. My original article reported on 7 cases that were followed for 5 years. No additional allegations were made for any of the cases; but in one case, questionable behavior was observed. Continued clinical experience has shown a low level of reported allegations, but no formal study has been done. No procedure is foolproof, and therapeutic management is no exception. But so far it has helped provide a measure of safety and structure to reunification.

Additional research is needed to document outcome following the use of this protocol. What kinds of cases move quickly through the system? What kinds of cases have difficulty? What are the long- and short-term effects on children and both of their parents who have gone through this procedure? What is the response of the courts to this procedure? What is the long-term outcome of cases in which the nonoffending parent's issues impede the process of the case? What are the characteristics of cases in which subsequent abuse occurs?

Preschool children are among the most vulnerable for child sexual abuse. When the court orders children into a relationship that has been ruptured by allegations of abuse, the child also needs the court's support in transitioning that rupture. We have few provisions to suture the gaping holes created by abuse allegations, and we often send children into situations that even adults are unable to negotiate.

We need to actively work to protect children in transition to ordered visitation after abuse allegations. From my experience, implementation of therapeutic management techniques can help children bridge the chasms. When threats of possible abuse exist and reunification is still ordered, it is my hope that the therapeutic management protocol can "buy time" for these children until they are of such an age that they can actively help in their own protection by successfully identifying and reporting issues of abuse. Until that time, the management of their safety will remain in the hands of the courts and adults involved in the process with the child.

9

Where Do We Go From Here?

I'll share with you my private conceptualization of therapy, the one I don't share with my families when they come for treatment. The process of therapy is like the experience of the traveler who has come for help when she is having difficulty climbing a particularly steep hill in her path. Therapy helps give her new skills to climb the hill. When she is finally at the top of the hill, she is awed by a new awareness offered by her hard won vantage point. She can now see some of the hills ahead that she had not imagined before! Where we go from here is a little like that.

❑ **Toward Better Services**

This book is about how to better assess young abused children. The more we know about the importance of the early years of life, the more compelling becomes the need to do something to assist our interactions with this group of children. Once we seriously endorse the need for better assessment of abuse concerns, we face other, new challenges: How do we deliver services? How do we assess and intervene with the parents who have problems? How do these changes affect our current service delivery systems? What can we do for prevention?

HOW DO WE DELIVER SERVICES?

Young children must be treated in the context of their families; they cannot be treated alone. Life is about relationships, even for the very young. Healthy attachments buffer children from stresses (Gunnar, 1995) and they are probably at the heart of abuse prevention. How do we, as a society, help facilitate development in this critical arena?

Through programs like Hawaii Healthy Start and Healthy Families America, we are beginning to offer supportive relationships to new parents and their families, starting at or before the time of birth when new families are most vulnerable (Daro, 1996). These programs offer, in a fashion parallel to the way in which healthy families give to their children, a caring and concerned relationship, help when there are difficulties, and support in the job of learning new roles and responsibilities. These home visitors offer help in creating a family. The relationship develops in response to the parent and child needs and offers respect for the new parent's role. Presence of these programs has been shown to drop rates of child abuse and neglect. When parents have problems and they cannot use resources or they refuse assistance, child protection may be needed. Because the focus of service delivery in these programs is relationship based, it is in many ways the antithesis of child protection: a system that determines a parent has failed and that may remove the child. But intervention in this continuum of services is more than simply separation of the child from a caretaker who has trouble giving adequate care.

HOW DO WE ASSESS AND INTERVENE WITH THE FAMILIES WHO HAVE PROBLEMS?

The infant mental health work of people like Zeanah, Anders, Seifer, and Stern (1989) and Zeanah et al. (1997) recognizes that work with problematic families is more that just prescribing a curriculum that teaches parenting skills. Applying research-based techniques to the assessment of the emotional relationship between parent and child (Crowell & Fleischmann, 1993) gives new strength to assessing parent-child relationships. Dysfunction and healthy function are not a matter of skills alone but a matter of the heart. Any service to young children must address the attachment relationship and its strengths and weaknesses, and it must offer services to that end. Intervention to alter problem patterns of attachment, as well as other skill and environmental issues, is at the core of intervention with families who have problems.

We also recognize that individual children suffer specific sequelae in response to trauma, neglect, or other problematic experiences in early childhood. The *DSM-IV*, the new, revised edition of the *Diagnostic and Statistical Manual of Mental Disorders*, classifies forms of adult and child mental disorders, but it is inadequate for complete assessment of very young children. Zero to Three/National Center for Clinical Infant Programs has recently developed a diagnostic manual for disorders of infants and young children, *Diagnostic Classification: 0-3. Diagnostic Classification of Mental Health and Developmental Disorders of Infancy and Early Childhood* (Zero to Three/National Center for Clinical Infant Programs, 1994). Once diagnosed, the issue of treatment for these individual needs arises. How do we treat very young, nonverbal children who do not have good representational play skills, but who still very clearly suffer trauma? There may be possible interventions that come from the application of theory and research in early memory and cognition covered in Chapter 3 that hold clues to methods of intervention (Hewitt, 1995), as well as the current treatment that focuses on family-centered work.

HOW DO THESE CHANGES IMPACT OUR CURRENT DELIVERY SYSTEM?

When we document early abuse and supply family services as well as individual help for the child, we encounter problems in the systems we have that protect or serve children. As mentioned above, service delivery through early, home visiting programs appears to be a positive model for supplying early intervention. But what about the families that end up in the child protection network? We know that the effects of early neglect and emotional absence are some of the most damaging for young children (Erickson, Egeland, & Sroufe, 1985). Our child protection system is currently geared only to respond to "imminent danger" cases, and even at this level the system is straining against budgetary constraints. It is impossible to conceive of a child protection system that responds to neglect or maladaptive attachment issues as a priority; there is simply not enough money or personpower. We need to develop new ways of meeting this challenge.

Our current legal frame of reference emphasizes parental rights. There is a place for parental rights to be salient, but there is also a place for the needs of young children to be given precedence. Recent shifts from parents' rights to children's rights in some states have sought to put the needs of vulnerable children who cannot speak for themselves at the fore.

WHAT CAN WE DO FOR PREVENTION?

Most prevention programs are directed at the child, but preschool children have demonstrated difficulties with some aspects of prevention education. For very young children, prevention efforts must rest with the parents. Yet we know, from the research cited above, that the mother with an abuse history carries an increased risk of abuse for her child. Much more information is needed about what factors in a parent's history are active so early in the child's history that place them at risk, how these factors are active, and what we can do to more effectively intervene.

This book is about getting better at hearing small children's voices about abuse. It is also about giving children a voice. Young children need ears willing to hear, followed by hands and minds willing to act. When this happens, they will truly have been heard and they will truly have a voice.

Appendix A:
Assessment Outline for
Very Young Children

Developmental History
  pregnancy, birth, delivery
  a wanted child?
  medical problems
  developmental milestones
  early caretakers
  attachment and separation history
  early traumas

Current Status
  caretakers
  routines
  idiosyncratic names

genital names

Sexual History
  prior abuse
  exposure to sexual activities
  explicit sexual materials

Possible Risk Factors
  chemical abuse
  physical abuse
  boundaries
  sleep or bathe with the parent
  family nudity

278

mother and father history of
  sexual abuse
adult attachment history
social connectedness
custody battle
arrest history
marital sexual history

History of the Concerns
first incidence of concern
what, where, when
describe child's behaviors
describe child's statements
detail
precipitating stimulus

how was it handled?
anger
shame, blame
fear
falling apart
calm acceptance
what questions were asked?
what words were used?

*Prior Incidents of Concern, In Order
of Occurrence*
repeat above questions

Screening for Significant Behaviors
sleep problems
play quality
toileting
bathing
fears, phobias/compulsive
  behaviors
separation problems

Objective Measures
Child Behavior Inventory
Child Sexual Behavior Inventory
Child Behavior Checklist

Collateral Information
medical exam
day care
relatives
child protection investigation
  notes
police investigation

Observation of the Child
Observation of the child with
  the alleged perpetrator
  (optional)
rule-out hypothesis

B

Appendix B:
Assessment of Children 3 to 5:
Prescreening Outline

Language
  articulation, vocabulary, length of
    utterance

Concepts
  who, what, where

Attention Span

Memory
  narrative ability
  scaffolding necessary

Play
  use of symbols
  representation of self

Real and Pretend
  right and wrong

Truth and Lie

Suggestibility

Correct Me

References

Achenbach, T. M. (1991a). *Manual for the Child Behavior Checklist/2-3 and the 1991 Profile*. Burlington: University of Vermont, Department of Psychiatry.

Achenbach, T. M. (1991b). *Manual for the Child Behavior Checklist/4-18 and the 1991 Profile*. Burlington: University of Vermont, Department of Psychiatry.

Ainsworth, M., Blehar, M., Waters, E., & Wall, S. (1978). *Patterns of attachment*. Hillsdale, NJ: Lawrence Erlbaum.

Alexander, P. (1992). Application of attachment theory to the study of sexual abuse. *Journal of Clinical and Consulting Psychology, 60*, 185-195.

American Professional Society on the Abuse of Children. (1995a). *Psychosocial Evaluation of Suspected Psychological Maltreatment in Children and Adolescents*. Chicago: Author.

American Professional Society on the Abuse of Children. (1995b). *Use of anatomical dolls in child sexual abuse assessments*. Chicago: APSAC.

American Professional Society on the Abuse of Children. (1997). *Guidelines for psychosocial evaluation of suspected sexual abuse in children*. Chicago: APSAC.

Anderson, C. (1977). Sensibilities, Inc., 4405 Garfield Avenue South, Minneapolis, MN 55904.

Ashmead, D. H., & Perlmutter, M. (1980). Infant memory in everyday life. In M. Perlmutter (Ed.), *New directions in child development: Children's memory* (pp. 1-16). San Francisco: Jossey-Bass.

282 ASSESSING ALLEGATIONS OF SEXUAL ABUSE

Awad, G. A., & McDonough, H. (1991). Therapeutic management of sexual abuse allegations in custody and visitation disputes. *American Journal of Psychotherapy, 45*(1), 113-123.

Balban, M. (1995). Affective influences on startle in five-month-old infants: Reactions to facial expressions of emotion. *Child Development, 66,* 28-36.

Barbaree, H. E. (1991). Denial and minimization among sex offenders. Assessment and treatment outcome. *Forum on Corrections Research, 3,* 10-33.

Barbaree, H. E., & Marshall, W. L. (1988). Deviant sexual arousal, offense history, and demographic variables as predictors of reoffense among child molesters. *Behavioral Sciences and the Law, 6,* 267-280.

Bauer, P. J. (1996). What do infants recall of their lives? *American Psychologist, 51*(1), 29-41.

Bauer, P. J., & Dow, G. A. (1994). Episodic memory in 16- and 20-month-old children: Specifics are generalized, but not forgotten. *Developmental Psychology, 30,* 403-417.

Bauer, P. J., & Fivush, R. (1992). Constructing event representations: Building on a foundation of variation and enabling relations. *Cognitive Development, 7,* 381-401.

Bauer, P. J., & Hertsgaard, L. A. (1993). Increasing steps in recall of events: Factors facilitating immediate and long-term memory in 13.5- and 16.5-month-old children. *Child Development, 64,* 1204-1223.

Bauer, P. J., Hertsgaard, L. A., & Dow, G. A. (1994). After 8 months have passed: Long-term recall of events by 1- to 2-year-old children. *Memory, 2,* 353-382.

Bauer, P. J., & Wewerka, S. (1995). One- to two-year-olds' recall of events: The more expressed, the more impressed. *Journal of Experimental Child Psychology, 59,* 475-496.

Belsky, J. (1993). Etiology of child maltreatment: A developmental-ecological analysis. *Psychological Bulletin, 114*(3), 413-434.

Belsky, J., & Most, R. K. (1981). From exploration to play: A cross-sectional study of infant free play behavior. *Developmental Psychology, 17*(5), 630-639.

Berk, L. (1994). *Child development: Third edition.* Needham Heights, MA: Allyn & Bacon.

Berliner, L., Schram, D, Miller, L., & Milloy, C. (1995). Actuarial prediction of sexual recidivism. *Journal of Interpersonal Violence, 10,* 85-105.

Boat, B., & Everson, M. (1986). *Using anatomical dolls: Guidelines for interviewing young children in sexual abuse investigations.* Chapel Hill: University of North Carolina, Department of Psychiatry.

Boat, B., & Everson, M. (1993). The use of anatomical dolls in sexual abuse evaluations: Current research and practice. In G. Goodman & B. Bottoms (Eds.), *Child victims, child witnesses: Understanding and improving testimony* (pp. 47-69). New York: Guilford.

Boat, B., & Everson, M. (1996). Concerning practices of interviewers when using anatomical dolls in child protective services investigations. *Child Maltreatment, 1*(2), 96-104.

Boehm, A., & Weinberg, R. A. (1997). *The classroom observer* (3rd ed.). New York: Teacher's College Press.

Bottoms, B., Goodman, G., Schwartz-Kenney, B., Sachsenmaier, T., & Thomas, S. (1990, March). *Keeping secrets: Implications for children's testimony.* Paper presented at the American Psychology and Law Society Biennial Meeting, Williamsburg, VA.

Bowlby, J. (1982). *Attachment and loss (Vol. 1): Attachment.* New York: Basic Books.

Bowlby, J. (1983). *Attachment and loss (Vol. 2): Separation* (Rev. ed.). New York: Basic Books.

Browne, A., & Finkelnor, D. (1986). The impact of child sexual abuse: A review of the research. *Psychological Bulletin, 99,* 66-67.

Bruck, M., Ceci, S. J., Francoeur, E., & Barr, R. (1995). I hardly cried when I got my shot! Influencing children's reports about a visit to their pediatrician. *Child Development, 66*, 193-208.

Bruck, M., Ceci, S., Francoeur, E., & Renick, A. (1995). Anatomically detailed dolls do not facilitate preschoolers' reports of a pediatric examination involving genital touching. *Journal of Experimental Psychology: Applied, 1*(2), 95-109.

Bussey, K. (1992). Children's lying and truthfulness: Implications for children's testimony. In S. J. Ceci, M. D. Leichtman, & M. E. Putnick (Eds.), *Cognitive and social factors in early deception* (pp. 89-109). Hillsdale, NJ: Lawrence Erlbaum.

Cantlon, J., Payne, G., Erbaugh, C. (1996). Outcome based practice: Disclosure rates of child sexual abuse comparing allegation blind and allegation informed structured interviews. *Child Abuse and Neglect, 20*(11), 1113-1120.

Cardelli, K. (1996). *Establishing a children's safety center.* (Available from K. Cardelli, Visitation Creations, P.O. Box 55, Clarksville, MO 63336-0055. Phone: (573) 242-3778.) (This organization provides information on creating a center of Children's Safety Centers Network, Inc.)

Carlson, E. (1997). *A prospective longitudinal study of attachment disorganization/disorientation.* Unpublished manuscript, University of Minnesota.

Carlson, E. A., Jacobvitz, E., & Sroufe, L. A. (1995). A developmental investigation of inattentiveness and hyperactivity. *Child Development, 66*, 37-54.

Carlson, V., Cicchetti, D., Barnett, E., & Brainwald, K. (1989). Disorganized/disoriented attachment relationships in maltreated infants. *Developmental Psychology, 25*, 525-531.

Carnes, C., Wilson, C., & Nelson-Gardell, D. (1997). *Addressing challenges and controversies in child interviewing: The forensic evaluation protocol and research project.* Unpublished manuscript.

Cartwright, G. F. (1993). Expanding the parameters of parental alienation syndrome. *The American Journal of Family Therapy, 21*(3), 205-215.

Carver, L., Bauer, P., & Nelson, C. (1996, May). *Individual differences in recognition and recall among 9-month-old infants: Possible implications for research on neural and functional plasticity.* Paper presented at the NIMH Conference to Advise Research on Developmental Plasticity, Washington, DC.

Ceci, S., & Bruck, M. (1993). Suggestibility of the child witness: A historical review and synthesis. *Psychological Bulletin, 113*(3), 403-439.

Ceci, S., Crotteau, M., Smith, E., & Loftus, E. (1994). Repeatedly thinking about non-events. Source misattributions among preschoolers. *Consciousness and Cognition, 3*, 388-407.

Ceci, S., Loftus, E., Leichtman, M., & Bruck, M. (1994). The possible role of source misattributions in the creation of false beliefs among preschoolers. *The International Journal of Clinical and Experimental Hyphosis, XLII*(4), 304-320.

Ceci, S. J. (1994, July 28). Speech presented at conference on Responding to Allegations of Child Abuse, Minnesota State Bar Association, Continuing Legal Education.

Ceci, S. J., & Leichtman, M. D. (1992). I know that you know that I know that you broke the toy: A brief report of recursive awareness among 3-year-olds. In S. J. Ceci, M. D. Leichtman, & M. E. Putnick (Eds.), *Cognitive and social factors in early deception* (pp. 1-9). Hillsdale, NJ: Lawrence Erlbaum.

Children's Safety Centers Network, Inc., 1714 East Cope Avenue, Maplewood, MN 55104. Phone: 612/748-1052. (This organization provides information on running a center; cf. Cardelli, K.).

Cole, C., & Loftus, E. (1987). The memory of children. In S. J. Ceci, M. P. Toglia, & D. R. Ross (Eds.), *Children's eyewitness memory* (pp. 79-91). New York: Springer-Verlag.

Cole, P. M., & Putnam, F. W. (1992). Effect of incest on self and social functioning: A developmental psychopathology perspective. *Journal of Consulting and Clinical Psychology, 60,* 174-184.

Corrigan, R. (1987). A developmental sequence of actor-object pretend play in young children. *Merrill-Palmer Quarterly, 33*(1), 87-106.

Crowell, J. A., & Fleischmann, M. A. (1993). Use of structured research procedures in clinical assessments of infants. In C. H. Zeanah, Jr. (Ed.), *Handbook of infant mental health* (pp. 210-221). New York: Guilford.

Dahlenberg, C. (1996). Fantastic elements in child disclosure of abuse. *APSAC Advisor, 9*(2), 1, 5-10.

Daro, D. (1996). Preventing child abuse: A new national initiative. *The Child, Youth, and Family Services Quarterly, 16*(2), 9-11.

Davies, D., Cole, J., Albertella, G., McCulloch, L., Allen, K., & Kekevian, H. (1996). A model for conducting forensic interviews with child victims of abuse. *Child Maltreatment, 1*(3), 189-199.

DeCasper, A .J., & Spence, M. J. (1986). Prenatal maternal speech influences newborn's perception of speech sounds. *Infant Behavior and Development, 9,* 133-150.

DeLoache, J. S. (1987). Rapid change in the symbolic functioning of very young children. *Science, 238,* 1556-1557

DeLoache, J. S. (1989). The development of representation in young children. In H. W. Reese (Ed.), *Advances in child development and behavior: Vol. 22.* New York: Academic Press.

DeLoache, J. S. (1991). Symbolic functioning in very young children: Understanding of pictures and models. *Child Development, 62,* 736-752.

DeLoache, J. S., Anderson, K., & Smith, C. M. (1995, March). Interviewing children about real-life events. Paper presented at the meeting of the Society for Research in Child Development, Indianapolis, IN.

DeLoache, J. S., & Marzolf, D. P. (1993, March) *Young children's testimony may not be improved by using dolls to question them.* Paper presented at the meeting of the Society for Research in Child Development, New Orleans, LA.

DeLoache, J. S., & Marzolf, D. P. (1995). The use of dolls to interview young children: Issues of symbolic representation. *Journal of Experimental Child Psychology, 60,* 155-173.

DePanfilis, D., Daro, D., & Wells, S. (1995). Special issue of risk assessment. *The APSAC Advisor, 8*(4), 1-31.

DiLalla, L .F., & Watson, M. W. (1988). Differentiation of fantasy and reality: Preschoolers' reactions to interruptions in their play. *Developmental Psychology, 24*(2), 286-291.

Dorado, J. (1996). *Narrative elaboration: A test of the effectiveness of a recall improvement procedure with low-SES and middle-SES preschool children.* Final report to the National Center on Child Abuse and Neglect. (Grant No. 90CA1534).

Doris, J. (Ed.). (1991). *The suggestibility of children's recollections.* Washington, DC: American Psychological Association.

Dunne, J., & Hedrick, M. (1994). The parental alienation syndrome: An analysis of sixteen selected cases. *Journal of Divorce and Remarriage, 21*(3/4), 21-38.

Easterbrook, J. A. (1959). The effect of emotion on cue utilization and the organization of behavior. *Psychological Review, 66,* 183-201.

Egeland, B., Sroufe, L. A., & Erickson, M. F. (1983). The developmental consequences of different patterns of maltreatment. *Child Abuse & Neglect, 7,* 459-469.

Eisen, M. L., Goodman, G. S., Qin, J. and Davis, S. L. (1997). *Individual difference factors related to maltreated children's memory reports.* Symposium presented at the 105th annual meeting of the American Psychological Association, Chicago, IL.

Eisen, M. L., Goodman, G. S., Qin, J., & Davis, S. L. (1998). Memory and suggestibility in maltreated children: New research relevant to evaluating allegations of abuse. In S. J. Lynn (Ed.), *Truth in Memory.* New York: Guilford.

Eisen, M. L., Goodman, G. S., Qin, J., & Davis S. L. (1999). Individual differences in maltreated children's memory and suggestibility. In L. Williams (Ed.), *Trauma and memory* (pp. 31-46). Thousand Oaks, CA: Sage.

Eisen, M. L., Goodman, G. S., Qin, J., & Davis, S. L. (in review). Memory and suggestibility in maltreated children.

Ericksen, C., & Ericksen, M. (1988). *A monster is bigger than 9.* (Available from Mary Ericksen, 300 Division St., Northfield, MN. Phone (507) 645-9131)

Erickson, M. F., Egeland, B. E., & Sroufe, L. A. (1985). The relationship between quality of attachment and behavior problems in preschool in a high risk sample. In I. Bretherton and E. Waters (Eds.), *Growing points in attachment theory and research. Monographs of the Society for Research in Child Development, 50,* (1-2, Serial No. 209), pp. 147-186.

Erikson, E. H. (1950). *Childhood and society.* New York: Norton.

Everson, M. D. (1997). Understanding bizarre, improbable, and fantasy-like elements in children's accounts of abuse. *Journal of Child Maltreatment, 2*(2), 134-149.

Everson, M. D., & Boat, B. W. (1990). Sexualized doll play among young children: Implications for the use of anatomical dolls in sexual abuse evaluations. *Journal of the American Academy of Child and Adolescent Psychiatry, 29*(5), 736-742.

Everson, M. D., & Boat, B. W. (1994). Putting the anatomical doll controversy in perspective: An examination of the major uses and criticisms of the dolls in child sexual abuse evaluations. *Child Abuse & Neglect, 18*(2), 113-129.

Faller, K. C. (1995, November). *Computer-assisted interviewing of children who may have been sexually abused.* Paper presented at the Midwest Conference on Child Sexual Abuse and Incest, Middleton, WI.

Faller, K. (1996). Interviewing a child who may have been abused: A historical perspective and overview of controversies. *Child Maltreatment, 1*(2), 83-95.

Fenson, L., Dale, P. S., Reznick, J. S., Bates, E., Thal, D., & Pethick, S. J. (1994). Variability in early communicative development. *Monographs of the Society for Research in Child Development, 59*(5, Serial No. 242).

Fenson, L., & Ramsay, D. S. (1980). Decentration and integration of the child's play in the second year. *Child Development, 51,* 171-178.

Fivush, R. (1996, May). Work presented at a meeting of the Preschool Consultation Group, St. Paul, MN.

Fivush, R., Gray, J. T., & Fromhoff, F. A. (1987). Two-year-olds talk about the past. *Cognitive Development, 2,* 393-409.

Fivush, R., & Hamond, N. R. (1989). Time and again: Effects of repetition and retention interval on two-year-old's event recall. *Journal of Experimental Child Psychology, 47,* 259-273.

Fivush, R., & Hamond, N. R. (1990). Autobiographical memory across the preschool years: Towards reconceptualizing childhood amnesia. In R. Fivush & J. A. Hudson

(Eds.), *Knowing and remembering in young children* (pp. 223-248). New York: Cambridge University Press.

Fivush, R., & Hayden, C. (1997). Narrating and representing experience: Preschooler's developing autobiographical recounts. In P. van den Froek, P. J. Bauer, & T. Bourg (Eds.), *Developmental spans in event comprehension and representation: Bridging fictional and actual events*. Hillsdale, NJ: Lawrence Erlbaum.

Fivush, R., Hudson, J., & Nelson, K. (1984). Children's long-term memory for a novel event: An exploratory study. *Merrill-Palmer Quarterly, 30,* 303-316.

Fivush, R., Kuebli, J., & Clubb, P. A. (1992). The structure of events and event representations: A developmental analysis. *Child Development, 63,* 188-201.

Fivush, R., Pipe, M., Murachver, T., & Reese, E. (1997). Events spoken and unspoken: Implications of language and memory development for the recovered memory debate. In M. Conway (Ed.), *Recovered memories and false memories* (pp. 34-62). London: Oxford University Press.

Forensic Mental Health Associates. (1984). Anatomical Drawings. 2688 Crystall Circle, Cunedin, FL 34698.

Fraiberg, S. (1959). *The magic years*. New York: Scribner.

Freedman, J., & Combs, G. (1996). *Narrative therapy: The social construction of preferred realities*. New York: Norton.

Freud, S. (1920). Beyond the pleasure principle. In J. Strachey (Ed.), *The standard edition, Vol. 18* (pp.1-64). London: Hogarth Press.

Friedrich, W. N. (1988). Behavior problems in sexually abused children: An adaptational perspective. In G. E. Wyatt & G. J. Powell (Eds.), *Lasting effects of child sexual abuse* (pp. 171-191). Newbury Park, CA: Sage.

Friedrich, W. N. (1993). Sexual behavior in sexually abused children. *Violence Update, 3*(5), 7-11.

Friedrich, W. N. (1997). *Child Sexual Behavior Inventory*. Odessa, FL: Psychological Assessment Resources.

Friedrich, W. N., Grambsch, P., Broughton, D., Kuiper, J., & Bielke, R. L. (1991). Normative sexual behavior in children. *Pediatrics, 88,* 456-464.

Friedrich, W. N., Grambsch, P., Damon, L., Hewitt, S., Koverola, C., Lang, R., Wolfe, V., & Broughton, D. (1992). Child sexual behavior inventory: Normative and clinical comparisons. *Psychological Assessment, 4*(3), 303-311.

Garbarino, J., Guttman, E., & Seeley, J. (1986). *The psychologically battered child*. San Francisco: Jossey-Bass.

Gardner, R. A. (1987). *The parental alienation syndrome and the differentiation between fabricated and genuine child sex abuse*. Cresskill, NJ: Creative Therapeutics.

Garvey, C. (1984). *Children's talk*. Cambridge, MA: Harvard University Press.

Goldman, R., & Goldman, J. (1982). *Children's sexual thinking*. Boston: Routledge & Kegan Paul.

Goodman, G. S., & Aman, C. (1990). Children's use of anatomically detailed dolls to recount an event. *Child Development, 61,* 1859-1871.

Goodman, G. S., Aman, C., & Hirschman, J. (1987). Child sexual and physical abuse: Children's testimony. In S. Ceci, M. Toglia, & D. Ross (Eds.), *Children's eyewitness memory* (pp. 1-23). New York: Springer-Verlag.

Goodman, G. S., Bottoms, B. L., Schwartz-Kenney, B., & Rudy, L. (1991). Children's testimony about a stressful event: Improving children's reports. *Journal of Narrative and Life History, 7,* 69-99.

Goodman, G. S., & Hegelson, V. (1985). Child sexual assault: Children's memory and the law. *University of Miami Law Review, 40,* 181-208.

Goodman, G. S., Hirschman, J. E., Hepps, E., & Rudy, L. (1991). Children's memory for stressful events. *Merrill-Palmer Quarterly, 37,* 109-158.

Gordon, B., Schroeder, C., & Abrams, J. (1990). Age and social-class differences in children's knowledge of sexuality. *Journal of Clinical Child Psychology, 19,* 33-43.

Gordon, T. (1975). *P.E.T.: Parent effectiveness training.* New York: Signet.

Grossmann, K., Grossmann, K. E., Spangler, G., Suess, G., & Unzer, L. (1985). Maternal sensitivity and newborn orienting responses as related to quality of attachment in Northern Germany. In I. Bretherton & E. Waters (Eds.), *Growing points of attachment theory and research. Monographs of the Society for Research in Child Development, 50,* (1-2, Serial No. 209), pp. 233-256.

Gunnar, M. (1995, September). In B. Azar, The bond between mother and child. *APA Monitor,* p. 28.

Gunnar, M. (1997, December). *Stress and coping during infancy.* Speech presented at Zero to Three, 12th National Training Institute, Nashville,TN.

Hamond, N. R., & Fivush, R. (1991). Memories of Mickey Mouse: Young children recount their trip to Disneyworld. *Cognitive Development, 6,* 433-448.

Hart, S., & Brassard, M. (1987). A major threat to children's mental health: Psychological maltreatment. *American Psychologist, 42*(2), 160-165.

Hart, J., Gunnar, M., & Cicchetti, D. (1995). Salivary cortisol in maltreated children: Evidence of relations between neuroendocrine activity and social competence. *Development and Psychopathology, 7,* 11-26.

Hayne, H., Greco, C., Early, L. A., Greisler, P., & Rovee-Collier, C. (1986). Ontogeny of early event memory: II. Encoding and retrieval by 2- and 3-month-olds. *Infant Behavior and Development, 9,* 461-472.

Haynes-Seman, C., & D. Baumgarten. (1994). *Children speak for themselves: Using the Kempe interactional assessment to evaluate allegations of parent-child sexual abuse.* New York: Brunner/Mazel.

Hewitt, S. K. (1991). Development of expressive language and the treatment of sexual abuse. In W. N. Friedrich (Ed.), *Casebook of sexual abuse treatment* (pp. 53-69). New York: Norton.

Hewitt, S. K. (1991). Therapeutic management of preschool cases of alleged but unsubstantiated sexual abuse. *Child Welfare, 70*(1), 59-68.

Hewitt, S. K. (1994). Preverbal sexual abuse: What two children report in later years. *Child Abuse and Neglect, 18*(10), 819-824.

Hewitt, S. K. (1995, October). *Treating traumatized two-year-olds and their families.* Paper presented at the 12th Annual Association for Play Therapy International Conference, San Francisco, CA.

Hewitt, S. K., & Arrowood, A. A. (1994). Systematic touch exploration as a screening procedure for child abuse: A pilot study. *Journal of Child Sexual Abuse, 3*(2), 31-43.

Hewitt, S. K., & Friedrich, W. N. (1991). Effects of probable sexual abuse on preschool children. In M. Q. Patton (Ed.), *Family sexual abuse* (pp. 57-74). Newbury Park, CA: Sage.

Hewitt, S. K., & Friedrich, W. N. (1995). Assessment and management of abuse allegations with very young children. In T. Ney (Ed.), *True and false allegations of child sexual abuse: Assessment and case management* (pp. 125-139). New York: Brunner/Mazel.

Hewitt, S. K., Friedrich, W. N., & Allen, J. (1994, January). *Factors in assessing sexual abuse allegations in a sample of two-year-old children.* Presentation at the Conference on Child Maltreatment, San Diego, CA.

Howe, M.L., & Courage, M.L. (1993). On resolving the enigma of infantile amnesia. *Psychological Bulletin, 113*(2), 305-326.

Hudson, J. A. (1993, May 11). Early memory is linked to language skill. Minneapolis Tribune.

Hudson, J. A., & Nelson, K. (1986). Repeated encounters of a similar kind: Effects of familarity on children's autobiographical memory. *Cognitive Development, 1*, 253-271.

Hunt, J. S., Komori, L. A., Kellen, L. M., Galas, J. R., & Gleason, T. R. (1995, July). *Faulty and non-productive questioning techniques: Potential pitfalls of the child interview.* Paper presented at the Society for Applied Research in Memory and Cognition, Vancouver, BC, Canada.

Ireton, H. (1992). *Child Development Inventory.* Minneapolis, MN: Behavior Science Systems.

Jampole, L., & Weber, M. K. (1987). An assessment of the behavior of sexually abused and non-sexually abused children with anatomically correct dolls. *Child Abuse and Neglect, 11*, 187-192.

Johnson, T. C. (1997, October). *Safe and therapeutic visits for children.* Presentation at the Western Regional Symposium on Child Abuse and Sexual Assault, Eugene, OR.

Jones, D. P. H., & McGraw, J. M. (1987). Reliable and fictitious accounts of sexual abuse to children. *Journal of Interpersonal Violence, 2*(1), 27-45.

Jones, D. P. H., & McQuiston, M. (1986). *Interviewing the sexually abused child.* Denver, CO: The C. Henry Kempe National Center.

Karen, R. (1994). *On Becoming Attached.* New York: Time-Warner Books.

Kendall-Tackett, K. A., Williams, L. M., & Finkelhor, D. (1993). The impact of sexual abuse on children: A review and synthesis of recent empirical studies. *Psychological Bulletin, 113*, 164-180.

Kennedy, H. G., & Grubin, D. H. (1992). Patterns of denial in sex offenders. *Psychological Medicine, 22*, 191-196.

Kidsrights. Huckle family of four, multi-ethnic doll sets. 10100 Park Cedar Drive, Charlotte, NC 28201. 1-800-892-KIDS.

Koocher, G. P., Goodman, G. S., White, S., Friedrich, W. N., Sivan, A. B., & Reynolds, C. R. (1995). *Psychological science and the art of anatomically detailed dolls in child sexual abuse assessment* (Final report of the American Psychological Association Anatomical Doll Task Force). *Psychological Bulletin, 118*, 2.

Lamb, M., Sternberg, K. J., Esplin, P. W., Hershkowitz, I., Orbach, Y., & Hovav, M. (1997). Criterion-based content analysis: A field validation study. *Child Abuse & Neglect, 21*(3), 255-264.

Leichtman, M., & Ceci, S. (1995). The effects of stereotypes and suggestions on pre-schoolers reports. *Developmental Psychology, 31*(4), 568-578.

Levitt, C. (1993, June). Medical evaluation of the sexually abused child. *Primary Care, 20*, 543-354.

Lindblad, F., Gustafsson, P. S., Larsson, I., & Lundin, B. (1995). Preschoolers' sexual behavior at daycare centers: An epidemiological study. *Child Abuse and Neglect, 19*, 569-577.

Loevinger, J. (1976). *Ego development: Conceptions and theories.* San Francisco: Jossey-Bass.

Lyon, T. D. (1996). Assessing children's competence to take the oath: Research and recommendations. *APSAC Advisor, 9*(1), 1, 3-7.

Lyon, T. D., & Flavell, J. H. (1994). Young children's understanding of "remember" and "forget." *Child Development, 65,* 1357-1371.

MacFarlane, K., & Waterman, J. (1986). *Sexual abuse of children.* New York: Guilford.

Mahler, M., Pine, R., & Bergman, A. (1975). *The psychological birth of human infants.* New York: Basic Books.

Main, M. (1991). Metacognitive knowledge, metacognitive monitoring, and singular (coherent) vs. multiple (incoherent) models of attachment: Findings and directions for future research. In P. Marris, J. Stevenson-Hinde, & C. Parkes (Eds.), *Attachment across the life cycle.* New York: Routledge.

Main, M., Kaplan, N., & Cassidy, J. (1985). Security in infancy, childhood, and adulthood: A move to the level of representation. In I. Bretherton & E. Waters (Eds.), *Growing points of attachment theory and research. Monographs of the Society for Research in Child Development, 50 1-2, (Serial No. 209),* pp. 66-104.

Mannarino, T., & Cohen, J. (1996). The weekly behavior report: A parent-report instrument for sexually abused preschoolers. *Child Maltreatment, 1*(4), 353-360.

Marques, J. (1995, September). *How to answer the question, "Does sex offender treatment work?"* Paper presented at the International Expert Conference on Sex Offenders, Utrecht, The Netherlands.

Marshall, W. L. (1994). Treatment of denial and minimization in incarcerated sex offenders. *Behavior Research and Therapy, 32,* 559-564.

Marshall, W. L. (1996, February). *Treatment of sex offenders.* Paper presented at the Hennepin County Bench Board Meeting, Minneapolis, MN.

Marzolf, D. P., & DeLoache, J. S. (1994). Transfer in young children's understanding of spatial representations. *Child Development, 65,* 1-15.

McCune-Nicholich, L. (1981). Toward symbolic functioning: Structure of early pretend games and potential parallels with language. *Child Development, 52,* 785-797.

McGrath, R. J. (1993). Preparing psychosexual evaluations of sex offenders. *Journal of Offender Rehabilitation, 20,* 139-158.

Miller, P. J., Hoogstra, L., Mintz, J., Fung, H., & Williams, K. (1993). Troubles in the garden and how they get resolved: A young child's transformation of his favorite story. In C. A. Nelson (Ed.), *Memory and affect in development* (Vol. 26, pp. 87-114). Hillsdale, NJ: Lawrence Erlbaum.

Morgan, M. (1995). *How to interview sexual abuse victims.* Thousand Oaks, CA: Sage.

Myers, J. (1997). *A mother's nightmare—Incest.* Thousand Oaks, CA: Sage.

Myers, J. (in press). *Legal issues in child abuse and neglect practice.* Thousand Oaks, CA: Sage.

Myers, N. A., Clifton, R. K., & Clarkson, M. G. (1987). When they were very young: Almost-threes remember two years ago. *Infant Behavior and Development, 10,* 123-132.

Myers, N. A., Perris, E. E., & Speaker, C. J. (1994). Fifty months of memory: A longitudinal study in early childhood. *Memory, 2,* 383-416.

Myers, J., Saywitz, K., & Goodman, G. (1996). Psychological research on children as witnesses: Practical implications for forensic interview and courtroom testimony. *Pacific Law Journal, 28,* 1-91.

Nash, J. M. (1997, February 3). Fertile minds. *Time, 149*(5).

Nelson, K. (Ed.) (1989). *Narratives from the crib.* Cambridge, MA: Harvard University Press.

Nelson, K. (1993). Events, narratives, memory: What develops? In C. Nelson (Ed.), *Memory and affect in development: The Minnesota Symposia on Child Psychology* (Vol. 26, pp. 1-24). Hillsdale, NJ: Lawrence Erlbaum.

Newcombe, N., & Fox, N. A. (1994). Infantile amnesia: Through a glass darkly. *Child Development, 65,* 31-40.

Oates, K., & Shrimpton, S. (1991). Children's memories for stressful and non-stressful events. *Medicine, Science and the Law, 31,* 4-10.

Ohr, P. S., Fagen, J. W., Rovee-Collier, C., Hayne, H., & VanderLinde, E. (1989). Amount of training and retention by infants. *Developmental Psychobiology, 22,* 69-80.

Ornstein, P., Gordon, B., & Lazarus, D. (1992). Children's memory for a personally experienced event: Implications for testimony. *Applied Cognitive Psycholology, 6,* 49-60.

Palmer, N. R. (1988). Legal recognition of the parental alienation syndrome. *The American Journal of Family Therapy, 16*(4), 361-363.

Pancake, V. R. (1988). *Quality of attachment in infancy as a predictor of hostility and emotional distance in preschool peer relationships.* Unpublished doctoral dissertation, University of Minnesota, Minneapolis, MN.

Park, K. A., & Waters, E. (1989). Security of attachment and preschool friendships. *Child Development, 60,* 1076-1081.

Paveza, G. (1988). Risk factors in father-daughter child sexual abuse: A case control study. *Journal of Interpersonal Violence, 3,* 290-306.

Perris, E. E., Myers, N. A., & Clifton, R. K. (1990). Long-term memory for a single infancy experience. *Child Development, 61,* 1766-1807.

Perry, B., Pollard, R., Blakley, W., Baker, W. L., & Vigilante, D. (1995). Childhood trauma, the neurobiloby of adaptation, and "use-dependent" development of the brain: How "states" become "traits." *Infant Mental Health Journal, 16*(4), 271-291.

Peterson, C. (1990). The who, when and where of early narratives. *Journal of Child Language, 17,* 433-455.

Pezdek, K., & Roe, C. (1994). Memory for childhood events: How suggestible is it? *Consciousness and Cognition, 3,* 374-387.

Pezdek, K., & Roe, C. (1997). The suggestibility of children's memory for being touched: Planting, erasing, and changing memories. *Law and Human Behavior, 21*(1), 95-106.

Phipps-Yonas, S., Yonas, A., Turner, M., & Kauper, M. (1993). Sexuality in early childhood: The observations and opinions of family day-care providers. *CURA Reporter, 23*(2), 1-5.

Piaget, J. (1970). Piaget's theory. In P. H. Mussen (Ed.), *Carmichael's manual of child psychology.* New York: Wiley.

Pipe, M. E., Dean, J., Canning, J., & Murachver, T. (1996). *Telling it like it is, was and will be: The impact of talking about events on memory.* Manuscript in preparation.

Poole, D. A., & Lindsay, D. (1995). Interviewing preschoolers: Effects of nonsuggestive techniques, parental coaching, and leading questions on reports of nonexperienced events. *Journal of Experimental Child Psychology, 60*(1), 129-154.

Price, D. W. G., & Goodman, G. (1990). Visiting the wizard: Children's memory of a recurring event. *Child Development, 61,* 664-680.

Quinsey, V. L., Lalumiere, M. L., Rice, M. E., & Harris, G. T. (1995). Predicting sexual offenses. In J. C. Campbell (Ed.), *Assessing dangerousness: Violence by sexual offenders, batterers, and child abusers* (pp. 114-137). Thousand Oaks, CA: Sage.

Quinsey, V. L., Rice, M. L., & Harris, G. T. (1995). Actuarial prediction of sexual recidivism. *Journal of Interpersonal Violence, 10,* 85-105.

Random House Webster's college dictionary. (1995). New York: Random House.

Renken, B., Egeland, B., Marvinney, D., Mangelsdorf, S., & Sroufe, L. A. (1989). Early childhood antecedents of aggression and passive-withdrawal in early elementary school. *Journal of Personality, 57*(2), 257-281.

Rogers, R., & Dickey, R. (1991). Denial and minimization among sex offenders: A review of competing models of deception. *Annals of Sex Research, 4,* 49-63.

Rosen, H., & Kuehlwein, K. (Eds.) (1996). *Constructing realities: Meaning-making perspectives for psychotherapists.* San Francisco: Jossey-Bass.

Rudy, L., & Goodman, G. (1991). Effects of participation on children's reports: Implications for children's testimony. *Developmental Psychology, 27,* 527-538.

Saywitz, K. (1992). Enhancing children's memory with a cognitive interview. *The Advisor, 5*(3), 9-10.

Saywitz, K. (1994, January). *Interviewing techniques: Cognitive interviewing and how not to interview preschoolers.* Presentation at the San Diego Conference on Responding to Child Maltreatment, San Diego, CA.

Saywitz, K., & Goodman, G. (1996). Interviewing children in and out of court: Current research and practical implications. In J. Briere, L. Berliner, J. Buckley, C. Jenny, & T. Reid (Eds.), *APSAC handbook on child maltreatment* (pp. 297-318). Thousand Oaks, CA: Sage.

Saywitz, K., Goodman, G., Nicholas, G., & Moan, S. (1991). Children's memories of physical examinations that involve genital touch: Implications for reports of child sexual abuse. *Journal of Consulting and Clinical Psychology, 59*(5), 682-691.

Saywitz, K., & Lyon, T. (1997). Sensitively assessing children's testimonial competence (Final report to the National Center on Child Abuse and Neglect, Grant 90-CA-1553). Los Angeles: University of California.

Saywitz, K., & Snyder, L. (1996). Narrative elaboration: Test of a new procedure for interviewing children. *Journal of Clinical & Consulting Psychology, 64*(6), 1347-1357.

Saywitz, K., Snyder, L., & Lamphear, V. (1996). Helping children tell what happened: A follow-up study of the narrative elaboration procedure. *Child Maltreatment, 1*(3), 200-212.

Scheeringa, M. S., Zeanah, C. H., Drell, M., & Larrieu, J. A. (1995). Two approaches to the diagnosis of posttraumatic stress disorder in infancy and early childhood. *Journal of the American Academy of Child and Adolescent Psychiatry, 34*(2), 191-200.

Schirvar, J. (1998). *Psychological characteristics of children 24- to 36-months-old with sexual abuse allegations.* Unpublished doctoral dissertation, Minnesota School of Professional Psychology at Minneapolis, MN.

Schlank, A. M., & Shaw, T. (1996). Treating sexual offenders who deny their guilt: A pilot study. *Sexual Abuse: A Journal of Research and Treatment, 8,* 17-23.

Schore, A. N. (1996). The experience-dependent maturation of a regulatory system in the orbital prefrontal cortex and the origin of developmental pychopathology. *Development and Psychopathology, 8,* 59-87.

Sheingold, K., & Tenney, Y. (1982). Memory for a salient childhood event. In U. Neisser (Ed.), *Memory observed: Remembering in natural contexts* (pp. 201-212). New York: Freeman.

Sivan, A. B., Schor, D. P., Koeppl, G. K., & Noble, L. D. (1988). Interaction of normal children with anatomical dolls. *Child Abuse and Neglect, 12,* 295-304.

Snell, W. E., Belk, S. S., Papini, D. R., & Clark, S. (1989). Development and validation of the sexual self-disclosure scale. *Annals of Sex Research, 2,* 307-334.

Sorenson, T., & Snow, B. (1991). How children report. *Journal of Child Welfare, 70*(1), 3-15.

Spence, M. J., & DeCasper, A. J. (1987). Prenatal experience with low frequency maternal-voice sounds influences neonatal perception of maternal-voice samples. *Infant Behavior and Development, 10,* 133-142.

Squire, L. R. (1987). *Memory and brain.* New York: Oxford University Press.

292   ASSESSING ALLEGATIONS OF SEXUAL ABUSE

Sroufe, L. A. (1983). Infant-caregiver attachment and patterns of adaptation in pre-schoolers: The roots of maladaptation and competence. In M. Perlmutter (Ed.), *Minnesota Symposium in Child Psychology* (Vol. 16, pp. 41-43). Hillsdale, NJ: Lawrence Erlbaum.

Sroufe, L. A. (1989). Relationships, self, and individual adaptation. In A. J. Sameroff & R. N. Emde (Eds.), *Relatioship disturbances in early childhood: A developmental approach* (pp. 70-94). New York: Basic Books.

Sroufe, L. A. (1996). *Emotional development: The organization of emotional life in the early years.* New York: Cambridge University Press.

Sroufe, L. A., Cooper, R. G., & DeHart, G. B. (1992). *Child development: Its nature and course.* (2nd ed.). New York: McGraw-Hill.

Sroufe, L. A., Egeland, B. E., & Kreutzer, L. (1990). The fate of early experience following developmental change: Longitudinal approaches to individual adaptation in child-hood. *Child Development, 61,* 1363-1373.

Steller, M., & Koehnken, G. (1989). Criteria-based content analysis. In D. C. Raskin (Ed.), *Psychological methods in criminal investigation and evidence* (pp. 317-245). New York: Springer-Verlag.

Stern, D. (1985). *The interpersonal world of the infant: A view from psychoanalysis and developmental psychology.* New York: Basic Books.

Stern, P., & Walsh, W. (1995). Professional exchange: The role of child interview special-ists. *APSAC Advisor, 8*(2), 10-13.

Steward, M. (1993). Understanding children's memories of medical procedures: "He didn't touch me and it didn't hurt!" In C. A. Nelson (Ed.), *Memory and affect in development* (Vol. 26, pp. 171-226). Hillsdale, NJ: Lawrence Erlbaum.

Steward, M. S., (1992). Preliminary findings from the University of California at Davis' child memory study: Development and testing interview protocols for young chil-dren. *The Advisor, 5*(3), 11-13.

Steward, M. S., Steward, D. S., Farquhar, L., Myers, J. E. B., Reinhart, M., Welker, J., Joye, N., Driskill, J., Morgan, J. (1996). *Interviewing young children about body touch and handling. Monographs of the Society for Research in Child Development (Serial No. 248), Vol. 61,* pp. 4-5.

Stossel, J. (1995, September 8). Truth on trial: Do children lie about sexual abuse? In V. Neufelt (Executive Producer), *20/20.* New York: American Broadcasting Company.

Sugar, M. (1992). Toddler's traumatic memories. *Infant Mental Health Journal, 13*(3), 245-251.

Terr, L. (1988). What happens to early memories of trauma? A study of twenty children under age five at the time of documented traumatic events. *Journal of the American Academy of Child and Adolescent Psychiatry, 27*(1), 96-104.

Terr, L. (1991). Childhood traumas: An outline and overview. *American Journal of Psychiatry, 148,* 10-20.

Thoennes, N., & Tjaden, P. G. (1990). The extent, nature, and validity of sexual abuse allegations in custody/visitation disputes. *Child Abuse & Neglect, 14,* 151-163.

Thompson, W. C., Clarke-Stewart, K. A., & Lepore, S. J. (1997). What did the janitor do? Suggestive interviewing and the accuracy of children's accounts. *Law and Human Behavior, 21,* 405-426.

Todd, C. M., & Perlmutter, M. (1980). Reality recalled by preschool children. In M. Perlmutter (Ed.), *Children's memory. New directions for child development* (Number 10, pp. 69-85). San Francisco: Jossey-Bass.

Undeutsch, U. (1989). The development of statement reality analysis. In J. C. Yuille (Ed.), *Credibility assessment* (pp. 101-120). Dordrecht, Netherlands: Kluwer Academic.

U.S. Department of Health and Human Services, Children's Bureau. (1998). *Child maltreatment 1996: Reports from the States to the National Child Abuse and Neglect Data System.* Washington, DC: Government Printing Office.

Vandenberg, B. (1991). Is epistemology enough? An existential consideration of development. *American Psychologist, 46*(12), 1278-1286.

VanderLinde, E., Morrongiello, B. A., & Rovee-Collier, C. (1985). Determinants of retention in 8-week-old infants. *Developmental Psychology, 21*, 601-613.

Visitation Creations, P.O. Box 55, 111 Howard Street, Clarksville, MO 63336-0055/. Phone 573/242-3778. (This organization supplies information on creating visitation centers in your community.)

Vygotsky, L. S. (1978). *Mind and society.* Cambridge, MA: Harvard University Press.

Walker, A. G. (1994). *Handbook on questioning children: A linguistic perspective.* ABA Center on Children and the Law, 1800 M Street, NW, Washington, DC.

Warren, S., Huston, L., Egeland, B., & Sroufe, L. A. (1997). *Child and adolescent anxiety disorders and early attachment.* Unpublished manuscript, University of Minnesota.

Waters, E., Wippman, J., & Sroufe, L. A. (1979). Attachment, positive affect, and competence in the peer group: Two studies in construct validation. *Child Development, 50,* 821-829.

Watson, M. W., & Fischer, K. W. (1977). A developmental sequence of agent use in late infancy. *Child Development, 48,* 828-836.

Welch-Ross, M. K. (1995). Developmental changes in preschoolers' ability to distinguish memories of performed, pretended, and imagined actions. *Cognitive Development, 10,* 421-441.

Wellman, H. M., & Johnson, C. N. (1979). Understanding of mental processes: A developmental study of "remember" and "forget." *Child Development, 50,* 79-88.

White, S., & Santilli, G. (1988). A review of clinical practices and research data on anatomical dolls. *Journal of Interpersonal Violence, 3*(4), 430-442.

Winnicott, D. W. (1965). The theory of the parent-infant relationship. In D. W. Winnicott, *The maturational processes and the facilitating environment* (pp. 37-55). New York: International Universities Press. (Original work published 1960)

Wooley, J. S., & Wellman, H. M. (1993). Origin and truth: Young children's understanding of imaginary mental representations. *Child Development, 64,* 1-17.

Yuille, J. S. (1994, July). *The step-wise interview: A protocol for interviewing children.* Handout presented at the Minnesota Institute of Legal Education Conference on Responding to Allegations of Child Sexual Abuse.

Yuille, J. S. (1996, September). *Investigating allegations of child abuse: An interview protocol.* Presented at 12th Annual Midwest Conference on Child Sexual Abuse and Incest, Middleton, WI.

Yuille, J. S., Hunter, R., Joffe, R., & Zaparniuk, J. (1993). Interviewing children in sexual abuse cases. In Goodman, G. & B. Bottoms (Eds), *Child victims, child witnesses: Understanding and improving testimony.* New York: Guilford.

Zeanah, C. H., Anders, T. F., Seifer, R., & Stern, D. (1989). Implications of research on infant development for psychodynamic theory and practice. *Journal of the American Academy of Child and Adolescent Psychiatry, 28,* 657-668.

Zeanah, C. H., & Benoit, D. (1995). Clinical applications of a parent perception interview in infant mental health. *Child and Adolescent Psychiatric Clinics of North America, 4*(3), 539-554.

Zeanah, C. H., Boris, N. W., Heller, S. S., Hinshaw-Fuselier, S., Larrieu, J. A., Lewis, M., Palomino, R., Rovaris, M., & Valliere, J. (1997). Relationship assessment in infant mental health. *Infant Mental Health Journal, 18*(2), 182-197.

Zero to Three/National Center for Clinical Infant Programs. (1994). *Diagnostic Classification: 0-3. Diagnostic Classification of Mental Health and Developmental Disorders of Infancy and Early Childhood.* (Available from Zero to Three/National Center for Clinical Infant Programs, 2000 14th Street North, Suite 380, Arlington, VA 22201-2400. Phone: 703/528-4300. Fax: 703/528-6848)

Index

About the Author

Sandra K. Hewitt is a child psychologist in private practice in St. Paul, Minnesota. She has a PhD from the University of Minnesota (1981) and has worked in a variety of settings: schools, colleges, in- and outpatient mental health, Head Start, and medical settings. She helped create and direct a specialty child abuse center at Children's Health Care–St. Paul, and currently works part time on the Failure to Thrive team at Hennepin County Medical Center. Her involvement with sexually abused children spans 22 years, with an increasing focus on abuse assessment, intervention, and research with very young children—a topic she speaks about, both nationally and internationally. She has conducted some research in this area and authored articles and book chapters about preschool children and sexual abuse. Sandy and her husband have three children and live in Stillwater, Minnesota.